The Beautiful Reward

Jaclyn Palmer

ISBN: **0615976867**
ISBN-13: **978-0615976860**

DEDICATION

To my husband who planted this dream years ago, and encouraged me each step of the way. To my son; my favorite gift from God. And to Jerry and Paula for instilling in me a love for words and a love for God.

CONTENTS

ACKNOWLEDGMENTS

Much gratitude to Elizabeth Jost for her talent and time as my Editor. Much applause to Steve Miller for his creativity and design. The cover far exceeds my deepest dream. Much giggles to My Girls; to those penned in this book and to those etched on my heart … Thank you for the many giggles and weekly babbles. Much caffeine to you who are graciously curling up with me on this journey through Matthew.

1

IS MY GRANDMOTHER RIGHT?

Matthew One

"Now the birth of Jesus Christ was on this wise: When as His mother Mary was espoused to Joseph, before they came together, she was found with child of the Holy Ghost. Then Joseph..."Matthew 1:18

"Opinions are like butts. Everyone has one; no one wants to hear them." Thank you, Grandma, for such sweet, ever so girly, words of wisdom. My grandmother was a wise woman, don't get me wrong, but she was full of wise cracks and was quick to declare her favorite statements each and every time she heard some sort of nonsensical imprudence. I can just picture her sitting in her chair in the back corner of her living room listening to the radio, watching the news, listening to a TV Evangelist, waving her right hand in front of her, huffing a sigh of disgust, declaring, "It's all about Jesus. None of this other stuff matters. They should just shut up." There is something extremely comical about hearing your grandmother say shut up. It never got old!

With my grandmother in mind, I contemplate this strongly opinionated subject called (whispered in a rather hushed tone) submission, and laugh. I grew up with an opinion about this word; I witnessed many women perform duties based upon their opinion of this word and heard many men proclaim their view of this concept. Their opinions gave me mine, 'I don't get it, I don't want it, it can't be Biblical.' Then I met ... The One.

My opinion does not matter. The past or the future does not change anything. Being married or being single does not equate in this matter. It's all about Jesus. No, this book is not about marriage. Does the Apostle Paul reference submission and marriage to be hand in hand? Yes, but that is not what this book is about. What you are holding is a personal resource to meet and or fall in love with The One, Jesus Christ. We will do so, not based on our own opinions or experiences, but by looking into the book of Matthew and studying the hearts and lives of the characters seen throughout each chapter. We will be seeing Jesus for who He was as a man and who He is as a Savior.

August 7th, 1994. I was 16 years old working at a Christian camp in Schroon Lake, New York. I was sitting in the back of the chapel between two of my girlfriends. The preacher spoke of missionaries dying for their faith, he spoke of individuals living for their faith, then he spoke of personal faith; faith in ... The One. The One who willingly and sacrificially died on the cross for my sin, was buried, and rose again, offering me God's free gift of Salvation and a home eternal with His Father, my Father, my God. And lo and behold, my grandmother was right. Opinions truly don't matter...It's all about Jesus.

As we walk through this study together I ask you to keep your Bible close. I understand that the Bible can seem intimidating at times. With reference to The Message by Eugene Peterson, a book written to help clarify the Word of God, I hope to help you enjoy and understand the Bible more clearly. I, myself, am an avid King James reader. I love Old English. To me, it is beautiful and poetic. It is inspiring and authentic. It is what I read and study in my personal time with God, which is why I reference it as my main source throughout this book. Oh, and get a pen. To some, writing in a journal is as natural as breathing, for others it is as natural as me baking edible bread or making cream cheese frosting that doesn't resemble rotten cottage cheese or (hang my head in shame) baking a birthday cake without the help of a box (I guess it's smart to make sure all of your fire alarms work). Let's just say, for some, writing in a journal is as natural as me being in a kitchen.

Really? Does a house need a kitchen? For me, all it does is get dusty. Books. Books are a much better creation than an oven. For a book feeds your brain and satisfies your soul. Even Jesus says, Man shall not live by bread alone. How's that for justifying my disdain for the kitchen? Either way, This study is yours. If you like to write, write. If you don't, don't. Whichever you choose, I hope and pray this is an enjoyable journey for you. Now, with your Bible and pen, let's begin.

The book of Matthew begins with the earthly lineage of Jesus Christ. There are sixteen verses full of names begetting names. Some names we are familiar with such as Abraham, Isaac, and Jacob. Others, like Ozias, Joatham and Achaz, are not so familiar. When we get to Verse 16 however, we come across two people we know. Two people who exemplify this art of submission to a T; their submission is displayed in their individuality. These two people pave the way in submission so beautifully because of their habit in living their lives in submission to their God.

"And Jacob begat Joseph the husband of Mary, of whom was born Jesus, who is called Christ." Matthew 1:16

"Therefore the Lord himself shall give you a sign; b*ehold, a virgin shall conceive, and bear a son, and shall call* H*is name Immanuel." Isaiah 7:14*

The beauty of Mary's character is magnified greatly in Luke 1:26-56, a beautiful account of Mary's heart. It is here that we see tidbits of what a wonderful woman she was. What I love about her story is the fact that her characteristics were clearly evident, but she, herself, was not the focus. Her story was not about her, yet she lived that story with grace throughout her lifetime. She had this reputation recorded in Luke before she gained the position found in Matthew.

Take a moment to consider her reputation in Luke. Mary was a resident of Nazareth, a city known for its impurities and low reputation (vs. 26). She was a virgin with a physical purity that stemmed from the heart (vs.27).

She was noticeably consistent and faithful in her daily life (vs. 28). She was thoughtful and considerate (vs. 29), inquisitive and respectful (vs. 34), and humble and submissive to the will of God (vs. 38).

Matthew 1:25 tells us, Mary remained a virgin not in order to be deemed the Mother, nor did she do so for Joseph. Mary lived a life of purity because she wanted to please God. She was submissive daily, not because of her position, but because she loved her God. If this were not true in her life, she would have struggled with her submission to the angel Gabriel. She knew Nazareth was not "high society," yet she accepted that with grace. She did not allow her city to mold her future; she allowed God to do the molding. If she were not content in her present life, do you think she would have been able to handle the hardships that came with her future calling? Her natural submission to God applies when you consider her humility, her strength, and her open-hearted acceptance.

Content with the world in which she existed, Mary was humble, yet strong enough to speak and to accept. Mary is a picture of grace to all who behold her. To have submission, humility, strength, and acceptance so evident in your life shows to all that you have learned those values and put each into practice and embraced their purity and their power in your day to day life. For Mary, submission wasn't an opinion to have, rather a life to live out of love for her God.

Read Luke 1:26-56 and Matthew 1:16 and 18. What do you see in Mary's life that you admire? Mary was highly favored of the Lord; she was a model example from which each of us can learn. No matter where we are in life, the Holy Spirit can use her story to impact ours. Take some time to record the area in Mary's life that challenges your heart. What did you see in Mary that encourages you and that you would desire to be said of you? Secondly, what can you do to plant or grow that seed in your life?

Mary:

____

____

____

You:

____

____

____

"Mark the perfect man, and behold the upright: for the end of that man is peace." Psalm 37:37

When a man lives his life according to the Word of God, there is great strength, great conviction, and a grand responsibility of accountability to God that makes me want to stand and applaud those men who stand strong daily. It is a beautiful thing to behold. Joseph is our case in point.

The same thing could be said of Joseph that was said of Mary. He was true to his character before he obtained a position. It is evident in this chapter alone why God chose him to be the earthly father of His dear Son. Joseph was a man of integrity and devotion. He had a walk with God and was obedient to Him. He was in love with his bride and his actions let it be known. We know this about him by reading this passage:

"Then Joseph her husband, being a just man, and not willing to make her a public example, was minded to put her away privily. But while he thought on these things, behold, the angel of the Lord appeared unto him in a dream, saying, Joseph, thou son of David, fear not to take unto thee Mary thy wife: for that which is conceived in her is of the Holy Ghost." Matthew 1:19-20

As a man, he gave up his goals. That is hard to do. I love goals. I love putting little checkmarks beside my goals. I have goals that I make every year and I have goals that I make every day. Goals give us motivation, they give us drive. It can be frustrating when our goals are interrupted by someone else's goal. Joseph humbly accepted his new goals. He gave up his reputation as a hard working carpenter and traded it in for the reputation of one who 'doesn't know what he is getting himself into.' Joseph handled this new reputation with strength and pride. He gave up his right in marriage. He loved his God so dearly that he willingly loved his wife only in word until The Son of God was born. This, my friend, is a strong man. A man of control, a man of strength, a man of love. Immediate obedience to such lofty ideals does not happen unless simple obedience has already become your natural response. God knew Joseph's obedience and had entrusted him with His Son.

"Then Joseph being raised from sleep did as the angel of the Lord had bidden him, and took unto him his wife: And knew her not till she had brought forth her firstborn son: and he called His name JESUS." Matthew 1:24-25

If it were not for the love of these two individuals, Verses 24 and 25 would not be possible. It makes me wonder what would be said of us in our times of simple obedience.

Take a moment to study the heart of Joseph in Vs. 19-25. Read through his character. Just as you did with Mary, write down what you saw in Joseph that you respect. What did you see in Joseph that encourages you and that you would desire to be said of you? Note the sacrifices he willingly gave up on behalf of what

God asked of him.

Secondly, what can you do to plant or grow that seed in your life? Consider these questions of obedience in your own life, how swiftly do I obey? In those areas of 'small' obedience, how do I perform? If, like Joseph, I was woken in the night to spend time with God, would I rise from sleep immediately to do as was bidden by the Spirit to do? Are you a Joseph; an obedient child? Would God be able to entrust you with a calling that sounds too big to you, yet perfect for you in His eyes?

Joseph:

____

____

____

You:

____

____

____

We are going to notice this quality of submission in the lives of many men and women seen throughout the pages of the Bible. Mary and Joseph are the perfect example to begin with. Not because they were perfect, but because they were real. Real in their love for God.

Take a minute with your dictionary and journal the definition of submission. Along with each definition, write down its meaning to you, then conclude with an evaluation of this ‘heart submission’ presence in your life. Does your life display the qualities of heart submission and simple obedience?

Submission:

Definition:

____

____

Evidence:

____

____

Evaluation:

____

____

See, that wasn't so bad. Feel free to reward yourself with a latte, or if you're one of "those kitchen people" then eat one of your edible, unburned, homemade pastries. Before we reward ourselves, may I say one more thing, the Bible tells us to hide God's word in our heart so that our lives are not centered on the battle of sin, but rather centered on loving Him. At the end of each chapter there will be a Memory Goal. Here you will find a verse or two to sit still with. Read the verses, ponder the meaning of God's word, and challenge yourself to think about the verse throughout your day. Make God's word personal to you. You will find that when you take the time to think about a verse throughout the day then you are naturally allowing God to find His place in you, in your heart. Colossians 1:16 encourages us to "Let the word of Christ dwell in (us) richly in all wisdom." If you want His presence, if you want wisdom, let His word dwell in you. In other words, meditate on His words until it is engraved upon your heart.

Memory Goal:

"Thy word have I hid in mine heart, that I might not sin against thee." Psalm 119:11

2

DID YOU LEAVE IT BLANK?

Matthew Two

"Then Herod, when he had privily called the wise men, inquired of them diligently what time the star appeared...And when he (Joseph) arose, he took the young child and His mother, and departed..." Matthew 2:7, 14, 21

Now we know. We know the meaning of Submission, not marriage submission, not submission as we knew it. True submission is submitting to the power of another. Now knowing that this book is not a marriage book or a book about submission to others, but that it is about you and me willingly looking at God and seeing God as who He is, we can begin this journey. Are you willing?

There may be some who, upon reading the first chapter, laughed when I actually left an open space for you to "fill in the blank." But you have remember this, if you did not fill in the blank in your copy of this book…good. You officially made this book into your own personal study and I applaud you. Filling in a blank is not the desired outcome (that's just a bonus tool). If you conclude a chapter with a greater understanding of the Book of Matthew, of love, of submission, of Jesus, then you have accomplished the desired outcome.

For those who left the dictionary search with a blank and a smile, may I aid you in this personal word study? Here are the definitions of submission found in my favorite dictionary, the Strong's Concordance of the Bible. Submission means "to place under, subject to – to obey, be under obedience, put under, submit self-unto; and, surrender – submit to."

Defense, anger, confusion, and Opinions tend to surface at this word submission. Do you agree? It is a concept that seems to repel more than any sin that ought to disgust us. My question is, why? Why does submission have such a bad taste? Here is your opportunity to disregard my grandma's opinion and express yours. I have a feeling you have one running through your mind right now. This is your journal and the perfect place to express it.

Questions to ponder: If you were brought up under this mentality of submission, was it Biblical or religious? Is your opinion based on personal experience or by viewing others? Are they positive displays or negative? Today, what does the word and/or idea of submission mean to you:

____

____

____

____

____

____

I put extra lines for those of you whose answer was accompanied with an increased heart rate. I encourage you to read the definitions of submission you found and recorded in Chapter 1 and then read your present view of submission one more time before continuing. Do they coincide? Are the definitions contrary to your belief? Our goal in this study is to erase any inappropriate memories or mindsets that we may have regarding submission and see, time and again, that it is designed to be a display of love from and to God.

This chapter is a great place to begin. This chapter is full of men. Men. Manly Men. Men that will teach us something monumental regarding our study at hand. How? One, we will see Wise Men who respect authority all the while knowing whom they really serve. Two, we will see a Mean King who feels as if all submission ought to be directed to him. And Three, we will conclude with the life of a Just Man who simply … loves.

Because of the perversion of this word, many of us feel as if we are giving up our own sense of identity when we submit to another. There are people who take their views and force them on others as a fulfillment of their own power and pride. If this is your feeling regarding submission, may I say, Biblical submission is not led by fear. It is not performed out of obligation. It is not forced upon one individual to another. It is not led with an iron fist. This form of submission is not of God; it is tyranny.

King Herod is a grand example of this perversion. His was the leadership the wise men had to encounter. Their drive was solely to see the living Scripture, the Word of God in the flesh. They had lived a life of study and devotion for a single purpose, to seek and find the Christ. They believed God. They believed the Scriptures. Oh, how they longed to see the face of Christ! It is this drive that set their search apart from any others, and brought them to their knees in His presence.

"In the beginning was the Word, and the Word was with God, and the Word was God." John 1:1

"Now when Jesus was born in Bethlehem of Judaea in the days of Herod the king, behold, there came wise men from the east to Jerusalem, saying, "Where is He that is born King of the Jews: for we have seen His star in the east, and are come to worship him."

These men were devoted. They allowed nothing to stand in their way. They had studied. They had prepared. They were ready to find the King of the Jews and to bow down and worship Jesus Christ. Throughout their journey, we see the true heart of these men. They traveled a lengthy path, giving of their time and finances, all the while unabashedly proclaiming the King of Kings in their quest to locate Him. This journey they were embarking on had been a long standing dream. They reached Jerusalem knowing their dream was getting closer to becoming a reality, they had finally reached the city of Jerusalem. Surely they were getting close. They asked, they expressed, they cried out, "Where is He?" Then they were brought before Herod.

"Then Herod, when he had privily called the wise men, inquired of them diligently what time the star appeared. And he sent them to Bethlehem, and said, Go and search diligently for the young child; and when ye have found him, bring me word again, that I may come and worship him also. When they had heard the king, they departed." Matthew 2:7-9

I wish we knew the responses of these men to the king. All we know is, "When they had heard the king, they departed." That alone speaks volumes of their character and willingness to allow Herod to head up their mission. Within their hearts, they knew this was neither Herod's call nor theirs, but God's. They were submissive. Do you see that? They placed themselves willingly under the authority of another. The wise men saw Herod for who he was, a man. He was a man of great political authority and they honored him accordingly. But they saw Herod as a man, a man who wanted to take control of their quest and thereby secure his position as the king. They could have fought their position and stood their ground. Yet, through their sacrifice of humility, and continuance in submission to God, the wise men were able to do what God needed them to do, which was to proclaim the birth of Jesus Christ.

"When they saw the star, they rejoiced with exceeding great joy. And when they were come into the house, they saw the young child with Mary His mother, and fell down, and worshiped Him; and

when they had opened their treasures, they presented unto Him gifts; gold, and frankincense, and myrrh." Matthew 2:10-11

What a journey these men embarked upon! Their *quest* for the Christ child ended with a beautiful display of humble worship. They were grown men who fell on their knees before a young child, knowing this boy will one day pay for their sins on the cross, allowing them an eternity with God the Father above. The drive of these men centered on the promises of the Word and they did not let themselves, or a tyrant, get in the way. What an amazing display of submission to God. Here the wise men were so focused on God that even when Herod stepped in with all his pride, anger, and demands, the wise men continued in submission to God so much so that Herod thought he was the recipient of their obedience. All the while, God gets the glory and the Wise men get the blessing.

Herod's side of the story is slightly different. He entered the political domain at the age of 15 and was promoted to the position of king over Judaea. He resurrected the temple of Jerusalem, which allowed Herod the opportunity to appreciate himself greatly. Over time, he was perceived as mighty and powerful. His Greek name alone stated his reputation, "the image or ode of a hero." He was too busy portraying the image of what he deemed was a great king, that he lost focus on reality. The reality being, God is the one who sits upon the throne. Verse 6 says:

"...there shall come a Governor, that shall rule My people, Israel."

This prophesied governor was not Herod, nor was this prophesy a hidden mystery. When Herod feared the truth and demanded to know its validity, his scribes knew just where to look.

"When Herod the king had heard these things, he was troubled, and all Jerusalem with him. And when he had gathered all the chief priests and scribes of the people together, he demanded of them where Christ should be born." Matthew 2:3-4

In his eyes, someone was going to rise up and usurp his throne. Needless to say, this troubled Herod. Irate and fearful, he called together his chief priests and scribes and demanded an answer.

It was at this time his conversation with the wise men took place. It was not until the passing of two years that Herod realized he was not exactly as in control as he thought.

"Then Herod, when he saw that he was mocked of the wise men, was exceeding wroth, and sent forth, and slew all the children that were in Bethlehem, and in all the coasts thereof, from two years old and under, according to the time which he had diligently inquired of the wise men." Matthew 2:16

This man was in full submission to himself, his position, his reputation, and his image. This led him down a prideful, self-indulged, and shamelessly angry path. His pride got hurt and children suffered the consequence. I believe the city of Jerusalem was aware of this man's capabilities for evil. He had proven his character to them in ways that caused all Jerusalem to fear. One does not declare a nationwide heartache without previously building up to such a level of tyranny. When an ill display of submission is laid out and demanded to be followed, fear is likely to be present. Take this time to learn from Herod what not to do in your daily life, and what to watch for in your heart. His behavior is extreme, but it started small and built up through years of pride and selfishness.

Also, be aware of "those who have rule over you" (Hebrews 13:7, 17). We will be discussing this more in the chapters to come, but permit me to say, submission is a beautiful gift received from God and offered to God from us. When it is demanded, to the point of harm, it is no longer the gift designed and given to us by God. It can be twisted in the hands of man. Be wise and be protective of the innocent. Do not allow fear to harm you or hurt a precious child.

Enter Joseph. While Herod is the character we must not emulate, we see that Joseph is the portrait of the character that we are striving to attain. We saw Joseph in Matthew 1 as a devoted man to God. Matthew 2 quickly brings us to the end of his story as we know it. This makes me sad. I would love to know so much more about this man of strength and character, but then my husband comes home and I see it. When I read of Joseph and when I watch my husband I conclude this thought about men who are called to be men. This is a good thing. But when men become husbands and fathers they are given an amazing opportunity to become the physical picture of the very Love of God. All men? In my tainted eyes it is hard to say yes, for my husband is the one man who demonstrates God's Love in its purest form. Maybe that is just it. This man, as my husband, displays God's love to me as his bride. If all men - as husbands and dads - stepped up and loved with the Pure Love of the Father, then many hearts would be changed, healed, and settled. I am thankful that I don't have to search out a book on Joseph. I am blessed to live with one. However, what is a Joseph?

His drive was solely to protect his family. It is clear to see that he knew the voice of God, he was prepared to receive it, and he was comfortable obeying the call. Three different times Joseph was directed to rise, take Mary and Jesus, and go. The first account we see is in Verses 13-15 in which Herod's pride was leading him to mass destruction. His determination to remain king was leading him to slaughter the innocent. Jesus was in the age-range of Herod's murderous decree. Therefore, God had given Joseph the command to flee into Egypt and Joseph readily obeyed.

"And when they were departed, behold, the angel of the Lord appeareth to Joseph in a dream, saying, Arise, and take the young child and His mother, and flee into Egypt, and be thou there until I bring thee word: for Herod will seek the young child to destroy him. When he arose, he took the young child and His mother by night, and departed into Egypt: And was there until the death of Herod: that it might be fulfilled which was spoken of the Lord by the prophet, saying, out of Egypt have I called My son."
Matthew 2:13-15

The second command came upon the death of Herod. During this time, two men led two very different lives. Herod, filled with hatred until the time of his death, was poisoned by his own emotions, and Joseph, living in Egypt in the center of God's plan, was blessed by his obedience.

"But when Herod was dead, behold, an angel of the Lord appeareth in a dream to Joseph in Egypt, saying, Arise, and take the young child and His mother, and go into the land of Israel: for they are dead which sought the young child's life. And he arose, and took the young child and His mother, and came into the land of Israel." Matthew 2:19-21

Finally we see their arrival home. What strikes me in this passage is the fear we see in Joseph's heart. A fear we haven't seen since the time of Mary's pregnancy. Here we are, years later, and again he fears for his family. But he only fears for a moment, for God is faithful and Joseph was obedient. This is a beautiful relationship between a Father and a child.

"But when he heard that Archelaus did reign in Judaea in the room of his father Herod, he was afraid to go thither: notwithstanding, being warned of God in a dream, he turned aside into the parts of Galilee: And he came and dwelt in a city called Nazareth: that it might be fulfilled which was spoken by the prophets, He shall be called a Nazarene." Matthew 2:22-23

Other than their visit to Jerusalem when Jesus was 12 years old, Joseph is last seen here. In the first chapter, we saw the introduction of Joseph. We saw his natural love and devotion, and his swift obedience to God. In Matthew 2, we see the conclusion of the recorded story of this chosen man of God. Note how his coming and his going are both marked by obedience to the Father.

In this chapter you have studied the life and heart of three different personalities. We have seen submission to authority, submission to self, and obedience to God. Each sheds light on truths that we can learn from. As you prepare yourself to grow in the area God is laying upon your heart, consider a few thoughts about these men then record your heart below.

What drove these men to be what they had become? Who did they obey? Who did they ultimately submit to? How can we apply their testimony in our homes and workplaces this week?

The Wise Men.

____

____

____

____

Herod.

____

____

____

____

Joseph.

____

____

____

____

Memory Goal:

"But without faith it is impossible to please Him: for he that cometh to God must believe that he is, and that he is a rewarder of them that diligently seek Him." Hebrews 11:6

"The true follower of Christ will not ask, "If I embrace this truth, what will it cost me?" Rather he will say, "This is truth. God help me to walk in it, let come what may!" A. W. Tozer

3

SHARE A SMILE

Matthew Three

"Then cometh Jesus from Galilee to Jordan unto John to be baptized of him. But John forbad Him, saying, I have need to be baptized of thee, and comest thou to me? Matthew 3:13-14

So far we have seen that submission is a natural action of obedience when the focus is on Christ, and that it is a voluntary act that can be displayed with both good and evil intention. In Matthew 3 we will see the heart behind the submission. The heart is more important than the act when submitting. Rather, it is a reaction that is stemmed from the depths of one's own heart. We will see that it is humility.

Have you ever had someone come to you for help or advice in an area that you yourself needed help with? I sit here thinking back to many awkward conversations to relate with. Once, I remember attending a ladies evening Bible study. It was open discussion on one of Paul's letters. We shared our insights, learned from one another, then closed in prayer. Typical. Good. I was heading to my souped up 1990 Toyota Tercel (with no air, but had great tires) when a woman approached me with a question. A sex question. I was 20. I was not married. I wasn't engaged to be married. I had never had sex. I didn't even use the word sex. My face went red. My tongue was dry. My response was … moot. To this day, I don't know what I said or how that conversation came to an end. I'm just so very glad that it did.

I could have used John's response and said something like, 'I am the one that will need sex advice, and you are coming to me?' Regardless of what I said or did not say, this feeling of inadequacy is my closest encounter to what John had to have felt when Jesus came to him and asked to be baptized of John. You can see John's hand going up in quiet protest as he breathlessly responds, 'Jesus, I can't. I need to ask that of you, not you of me.'

What greater example of humility can we find than that which we see in the earthly life of our precious Lord and Savior Jesus Christ? Jesus didn't need to be baptized of John, He could have baptized himself. In fact, baptism is a step of obedience that connects you to Jesus. Technically Jesus is the very meaning and creator of baptism. Yet, living as man, He desired to obey as man. Who better to help Him in this area than the man called to go before Him? Secondarily, John the Baptist, an ordinary man who willingly gave his words, ministry, and life over to the furthering of the name of Jesus Christ, compounds that example. I encourage you to read Matthew 3 and note these two prime examples of humility recorded in this beautiful passage.

As you read, take some comparable notes of the parallel characteristics between Jesus, the image of sinless perfection, and John, a man of a sinful nature. Also keep in mind that they are of the same age, and they are members of the same family (Luke 1 and 2). Although their earthly fathers and upbringing differ, their Heavenly Father remains the link that ties their love and devotion together.

Feel free to record your thoughts below:

____

____

____

____

____

Jesus' profile is expounded on throughout the book of Matthew and we will delve into each characteristic trait as we approach them, but John is only mentioned in a few short chapters. Therefore, we are going to focus on him in this particular study. Before we learn from John, we need to learn about John. The very best way to know someone is to know their history. Lucky for us, John's history is bound in the pages of the Bible. We will begin in Isaiah to see the prophecy of John and will conclude in Matthew where his final testimony is displayed.

"The voice of him that crieth in the wilderness, prepare ye the way of the LORD, make straight in the desert a highway for our God." Isaiah 40:3

John's purpose was to be the forerunning mouth of Jesus. I love that John was faithful and true to his calling from the start. He didn't wait until Jesus appeared or until he knew Jesus was watching. The heart of John stirred him on while he was still young. How do I know this? Partly speculation and partly through indirect evidence. Let me explain. John died around the age of 30. He was born a few months before Jesus and died in the year 30/31 AD. A year or so before his death was the account of Jesus' baptismal. At this point, John had a crowd that followed him faithfully, he had Pharisees and Sadducees watching him (Matthew 3:7), and he had a reputation that preceded him. These things do not just happen. Anyone can gain a crowd. Do something unique and followers are rather easy to come by.

Critics on the other hand could care less who you are or what you do until you have earned yourself a stable name and proven yourself to be loved and adored, and therefore criticized.

John also had a reputation. Towns knew when he was going to arrive. They waited for his arrival and planned their schedules around his revivals. Every man knew of the camel hair wearing, locust eating, wilderness surviving, traveling preacher. He was one of a kind, and a kind many desired to be associated with. In fact, being baptized by John the Baptist was an honored and privileged opportunity (Matthew 3:4-6).

In this chapter we see the pronouncement of John's birthright. You can just imagine the built up excitement within his soul. He was a preacher of the Scriptures. Preachers tend to study earnestly in order to teach correctly. Surely he had studied and memorized Isaiah's prophesy. I can only imagine that Isaiah's prophecy had been his drive throughout his life and his motivation to press on over the years, despite the popularity and attacks.

Suddenly, as he is yet again surrounded by his followers, he sees his cousin, his Savior, his very purpose and calling walking towards him. Can you hear his words? Can you feel the built up emotion within his soul as he opens his mouth and boldly proclaims the words that have been etched in time?

"Behold, the Lamb of God which taketh away the sins of the world." John 1:29

The power of the Living Scripture is a beauty worth noting. When a heart is filled with its words, and a mouth is ready to proclaim its truth to a hungry ear, then the purpose of the Bible becomes a powerful reality. John had his calling. He had his words. All he had to do was be there and be ready. What a gift to be so lucky to have his calling spelled out for him. If only we were able to press forward, knowing someday the Lord will be there in our presence in which we too can proudly proclaim the words that have been pressed in our hearts throughout the years!

Girls, can I tell you this? We have a calling! We have a

purpose! We are children of the King! Upon calling on the name of the Lord Jesus Christ, asking for His forgiveness, and seeking after His residence in your heart and life, you were then called a Child of God. From that point you are automatically called to walk worthy of a holy calling. It is a humbling call. 2 Timothy 1:9 says,

"Who hath saved us, and called us with an holy calling, not according to our works, but according to His own purpose and grace, which was given us in Christ Jesus before the world began."

"I therefore the prisoner of the Lord, beseech you that ye walk worthy of the vocation wherewith ye are called, with all lowliness and meekness, with longsuffering, forbearing one another in love; endeavouring to keep the unity of the Spirit in the bond of peace." Ephesians 4:1-3

"Let us be glad and rejoice, and give honour to Him: for the marriage of the Lamb is come, and His wife hath made herself ready. And to her was granted that she should be arrayed in fine linen, clean and white; for the fine linen is the righteousness of saints. And he saith unto Me, write, blessed are they which are called unto the marriage supper of the Lamb..." Revelation 19:7-9

Live a life of meekness, longsuffering, and love for all who are around you. Whether that is the man in your life, your children, your family, your pastor, or the girls at church, ultimately live for God, who has given us the call and the ability to perform such a beautiful task. Endeavor to keep the path of unity and peace that was paved at the cross.

Do you think that your calling is nothing in comparison to John's? Have you ever been to a woman's fellowship or Bible study where the Spirit of peace was not present? It is awful, and catty, and heartbreaking. Prayer time is gossip hour, worship time is catch up time, and the teaching falls on "I already know this" ears. In that situation you are called! Are you going to follow the example of John the Baptist and proudly proclaim your undying affection for the Lamb of God to this group and fulfill your calling to be that one voice to turn the conversation back to Jesus? That does not mean you have to prepare a sermonette or lead a group discussion. It could be a simple statement of your desire to learn more about Jesus. Are you going to just attend church and get what you can, never truly being the woman you were chosen to be?

Humility is a great example of submission. In order to challenge ourselves in the path of humility let's hear the two messages of John the Baptist, "Repent ye: for the kingdom of heaven is at hand" (Vs. 2). The first is the message of salvation. He preaches salvation to all who are near. Salvation is a day in one's life where one repents of their sin and asks Christ for forgiveness, acknowledging Him as their Savior, and believing that He died, was buried, and rose again. Salvation is a gift from God for all mankind.

"For all have sinned and come short of the glory of God." Romans 3:23

"For the wages (payment) of sin is death; but the gift of God is eternal life through Jesus Christ our Lord." Romans 6:23

"Christ died for our sins according to the Scriptures; And that he was buried and that he rose again the third day according to the Scriptures." 1 Corinthians 15:3-4

"For whosoever shall call upon the name of the Lord, shall be saved." Romans 10:13

Salvation is simple. Have you received Jesus Christ as your Savior? This is John's message. Imagine walking your daily life without communication with God through prayer, *the* understanding of the Bible, and without God's wisdom. That is life without Salvation. What does Salvation mean to you? John says, "Repent ye: for the kingdom of heaven is at hand" (Matthew 3:2). Have you repented?

Record your story of salvation below:

____

____

____

____

____

____

John's second message is quite different. Where his first message was simple and intended for the open hearted, his second is pointed and powerfully directed to those who were hard of heart. It was for those who are determined to stand ground on their religious foundation to the point that Jesus' life was perceived as ill minded. Allow me to introduce the Pharisees to you. My Old Scofield Study Bible defines them as, "correct, moral, zealous, and self-denying, but self-righteous, and destitute of the sense of sin and need." We will see much of these men throughout the chapters to come, but it is interesting to note that their first appearance in Scripture is accompanied with an open invitation for Salvation. John's message reveals their denial:

"O generation of vipers, who hath warned you to flee from the wrath to come: Bring forth therefore fruits meet for repentance: And think not to say within yourselves, we have Abraham to our father: for I say unto you, that God is able of these stones to raise up children unto Abraham. And now also the ax is laid unto the root of the trees: therefore every tree which bringeth not forth good fruit is hewn down, and cast into the fire. I indeed baptize you with water unto repentance: but He that cometh after me is mightier than I, whose shoes I am not worthy to bear: He shall baptize you with the Holy Ghost, and with fire: Whose fan is in His hand, and He will thoroughly purge His floor, and gather His wheat into the garner; but He will burn up the chaff with unquenchable fire." Matthew 3:7-12

Yes, John had his enemies. Can you see the boldness on John's face and the anger in the eyes of the Pharisees and Sadducees? These men were the images of religion. They held the title, the status, and the positions of religious leadership. Yet, John knew more than these men would allow themselves to know. John knew Jesus. For the Pharisees to admit that Jesus Christ was the prophesied Messiah meant that religion has to be thrown away.

Jesus Christ is not a religion full of empty laws; He is God who became man so that men might have a relationship with God through Him. Jesus Christ is salvation. There are many people today who are too deep in the law of religion as the Pharisees were in the day of John the Baptist. John said to them what the Bible is crying out to us today, be mindful that your love for Christ remains of the heart, and not for the sake of man. John warns those clinging to the Old Testament and to the laws of old that everything is about to change through the blood of Christ and through His resurrection.

What is religion to you? What differs between obedience to religion and having a relationship of humility with Jesus Christ? Have you ever thought about there being a difference? Record your thoughts below:

____

____

____

____

____

____

Take this time to journal a study on humility being the backbone of submission, I encourage you to compare John's calling and devotion to your own. Secondly, review Jesus' display of humility in Verses 13-17. If you have a ministry that you are involved in, then challenge your heart to delve in with just a touch more love. If you don't have a ministry, then find one. There is forever a need for a humble servant. It can be within a marriage, at home, in a workplace, or even with a girl at church in need of a friend or a simple smile. Consider your call through salvation and make humility your ministry. Reach out and proclaim the bonds of peace. What is the definition of humility? Is it evident in your life?

What are some ways you can challenge yourself in this area of growth?

Humility.

Definition:

____

____

Evidence:

____

____

Evaluation:

____

____

____

If you are interested in more study of John, his story is found in the following passages. His life is fascinating. I left some room below for you to write any thoughts, questions, or findings you come across in your study of John the Baptist.

Matthew 4:12; 11:1, 11, 14; 17:12

Mark 1:14; 6:14; 9:11

Luke 1:17, 57; 3:20; 7:18, 27

John 1:6, 32; 3:26

Acts 1:5; 13:24; 18:24; 19:1

John the Baptist:

____

____

____

____

____

____

____

____

Memory Goal:

"Humble yourselves in the sight of the Lord, and He shall lift you up." James 4:10

"For there is one God, and one mediator between God and men, the man Christ Jesus." 1 Timothy 2:5

4

LET'S PLAY FOLLOW THE LEADER

Matthew Four

"Then was Jesus led up of the spirit into the wilderness to be tempted of the devil. And they straightaway left their nets, and followed him. And they immediately left the ship and their father, and followed Him. And there followed Him great multitudes of people..."
Matthew 4:1, 20, 22, and 25

Submission is being willing to follow the leader. We have all been there haven't we? Playing the age old game of Follow the Leader whether on the playground at school, church, or even yesterday with your children. It is a simple game with one rule, follow the person in front of the line and do whatever he or she does. Simple enough. It is not a difficult game to understand. However, playing it can present some challenges. Let's say the leader is older, taller, faster and/or stronger. Keeping up with a more advanced player can be considered difficult for someone that may have two older sisters who are way taller and faster and are forever slamming doors on their fingers. If you are anything like…that example, you might fail miserably at the game. If the leader does things that are way too strange or embarrassing, I would rather not do that either. I would stomp my foot and walk away.

Lucky for me, I am not asked to play follow the leader with someone too advanced or strange. I am asked to follow my Leader, God the Father. Jesus, Peter, Andrew, James and John were asked to follow the same leader. Each of them dropped what they were doing and began following in the way that they were led. We are going to learn a lot from the callings laid out in this chapter about how to follow. As we read, study, and pen our thoughts, I want you to keep your life's leaders in mind. Remembering all the while that they themselves are not the recipients of your submission; God is.

Obviously, our foremost leader is God above, but second to Him we have leaders all around us. Some we have chosen like husbands and politicians. Some are chosen for us like law officers and bosses. Regardless of the position, a leader is a leader, and we are to follow.

Who are your leaders? 1 Timothy 2:1-4 exhorts us to pray and give thanks, "for all men; for kings, and for all that are in authority." We should do this so, "That we may lead a quiet and peaceable life in all godliness and honesty...It's acceptable in the eyes of God...And that all men might be saved." Hebrews 13:7 and 17 tells us to remember and obey those who have rule over us. Ephesians 6:7 tells us how we ought to submit by following, "With good will doing service, **as to the Lord**, and not to men."

Take a moment to review the passages above by looking them up and marking them in your Bible, then record the names of your leaders down below. Use this list as your personal prayer list:

____

____

____

____

Jesus is our first and greatest example of submission through following. His submission is beautifully spelled out in Philippians 2:5-8:

"Let this mind be in you, which was also in Christ Jesus: Who, being in the form of God, thought it not robbery to be equal with God: But made Himself of no reputation, and took upon Him the form of a servant, and was made in the likeness of men: And being found in fashion as a man, he humbled himself, and became obedient unto death, even the death of the cross."

Jesus is submission. Submission itself is exemplified both in His Godhead and in His person. He knows no other way. Who better to model our lives after than our Savior Jesus Christ?

"Then was Jesus led up of the spirit into the wilderness to be tempted of the devil. And when He had fasted forty days and forty nights, He was afterward an hungered." Matthew 4:1-2

Jesus followed the leading of the Spirit into the wilderness for a 40 day and night fast. When the fast came to an end, temptation was waiting for Him by way of the devil. Let's take a moment to discover the meaning of temptation before we talk about the three temptations placed before Jesus. Temptation can come in two forms. One, it can be allowed by the Spirit in order to test your faith in Jesus. It is difficult and trying, but when you come through the fire there is peace and joy that cannot be defined. It is a joy brought on by Christ and Christ alone. Along with joy comes a comfort that refreshes you from the battle you just fought. This combination of joy and comfort erases the pain of your test with the victory you have just won. If this joy is a desire of your heart then allow yourself time to curl up with the book of Philippians. Learn from the Apostle Paul how to receive joy from your Father in times of hardship.

Take some time to record a particular verse on Joy and how it has affected your outlook on a present situation. James 1:2 was a verse that got me through the rollercoaster called college; that time in my life where I wanted to stand for what I believed in, but was in angst over what it was I truly believed. As temptations to walk away from God came up, I began to face them with joy. It took me awhile to figure out what I would desire to stand on in the end. The answer, I realized, was Jesus. It's funny how I have to learn this lesson time and again. Yes, there were a lot of religious things and spiritual ideas that I was tired of, but James 1:2 strengthened me in my walk. It helped me to decipher what things were done in vain (religious acts) and what was done with joy (done with Jesus). I learned then that talking with Him and reading His word was joy. In this new found joy is where I stood.

What is your verse and your experience with Joy?

____

____

____

____

____

____

"There hath no temptation taken you, but such as is common to man: but God is faithful, and will not suffer you to be tempted above that ye are able; but will with the temptation also make a way to escape, that you may be able to bear it."
1 Corinthians 10:13

Temptation is promised us in the Bible. Do not take that with defiance or defeat. Rather, take it as a compliment because temptation is evidence of the presence of the Holy Spirit in your life. The Holy Spirit is not going to test the faith of a non-believer who does not have a faith in Christ, or of a dormant child, whose faith is so hardened that it proves fruitless. There is a sad truth in many Christians today regarding the power of salvation in their present lives. It is as if the day of salvation came, but life continued without its power. We tend to tune out when Salvation is presented, forgetting that Salvation is alive and it affects our daily life. Take comfort that with temptation comes the presence and strength of the Spirit. He has faith in you, period. Walk in that. You can overcome the trial at hand. God knows He can bring you to victory. What a comfort and promise!

The second way temptation comes, is through the flesh. James tells us in Chapter 1, Verse 14:

*"But every man is tempted, when he is drawn away of his own lu*st, *and enticed."*

Peter knew this when he took his eyes off Jesus in the midst of the storm, focusing, rather, on fear. Fear is a major temptation for me. Each of us knows what temptation is strongest for our flesh. Maybe it is not a battle with an emotion as Peter. Maybe it is a physical temptation that draws and captures the desires of your flesh. Whatever your temptation may be, rest assured that this form of temptation is not of God. This form of temptation only comes by way of the world, the flesh, and the devil. Be careful not to confuse sin with the testing of the Holy Spirit.

Going back to 1 Corinthians 10:13, it states that there is no temptation that will come into your life that is not common among those around you. Whatever you are facing, there is *someone* you know that has either walked that path before you, or is following right behind you. Let's look at the three temptations brought before the man, Christ Jesus:

"And when the tempter came to Him, he said, If thou be the Son of God, command that these stones be made bread." Matthew 4:3

Jesus humbly submitted to the leading of the Holy Spirit as He entered, stayed, and fasted alone in the wilderness for 40 days and 40 nights. The Bible does not say how much time passed between the final days of His fast and the tempting of the devil. It does say, however, that afterward He hungered and the tempter came to Him. Knowing the tactics of the devil, He did not waste time.

Life is tiring. To that we can relate. Many of our days are spent with much determination to accomplish what must be done in order to go to bed in peace, all to get up the next day and do many of the same tasks all over again. Ah, the sweet life of womanhood! We know what it is like to be tired and hungry. You become "hangry" and feel yourself transform into the Incredible

Hulk loudly declaring, "You don't want to see me when I get Hangry." Rooaar! I have many friends who agree that this is simply the worst possible combination.

When we read Verse 3, we ought to be able to relate to the tempting at hand, physical hunger. After a long day of work, or even a strengthening day of fasting, how do you respond when the feelings of hunger and exhaustion take over? Do you ride the emotions of the flesh and cave to irresponsible and, at times, harmful decisions? Consider the gift the Spirit has freely given us, the gift of self-control. This gift is part of the fruit of the Spirit (Ephesians 5:22). It is the evidence of our Salvation. Unless you have gone through a 40-day fast, your level of hunger has never reached the level Christ was on and He responded with Scripture.

Spend time rereading Verses 1-4 and consider the physical desires of Christ, the weakness of His flesh, and the strength of His spirit. Compare what comes out of His mouth to what comes out of yours during those times of physical exhaustion. Christ responded with the use of memorized Scripture found in Deuteronomy 8:3. How do you rate in this area of self-control?

Self-Control:

____

____

____

____

____

"...If thou be the Son of God, cast thyself down: for it is written, He shall give His angels charge concerning thee: and in their hands they shall bear thee up, lest at any time thou dash thy foot against a stone." Matthew 4:6 (Psalm 91: 11-12)

The second common temptation thrown at Jesus was pride. The devastating power of pride is seen throughout the Bible.

Isaiah 14 gives the account of the birth of pride. If you are unfamiliar with where pride originated, I encourage you to read this chapter. Much is written about this sin in the book of Proverbs. David's son, Solomon was promised by God that his heart's desire would be answered. His heart's desire makes me think, what is pressing on my heart? What would my request be? As a mom; a good school for my son that offers academic and spiritual education with free tuition. As a wife; our love and laughter will continue indefinitely. As a woman; anything I put on, no matter the day of the month, it will look perfect and wonderful in every way. As I ponder this 'free request' my list easily grows. Both serious and humorous desires are flying through my thoughts and it is fun to think about. This is what Solomon was promised. His response covered every base in his world. His response was that of one word. His response was wisdom. With wisdom the book of Proverbs was penned. Here are a few of Solomon's words regarding this issue of pride that stemmed from his gift of sound wisdom.

"The fear of the Lord is to hate evil: pride, and arrogancy, and the evil way, and the forward mouth, do I hate." Proverbs 8:13

"Boast not thyself of tomorrow; for thou knowest not what a day may bring forth." Proverbs 27: 1

James 1:5 tells us that if we lack wisdom all we have to do is ask God for it and he will liberally give it. According to the Free Online Dictionary, wisdom is "the ability to discern or judge what is true, right, or lasting." Wisdom is from God. It is honest and beneficial. Pride is quite opposite. As we see in Isaiah 14, pride is from Lucifer. It is selfish and deceitful. Pride and wisdom should not walk together. Here, in our passage, we see the very picture of wisdom and pride up close.

Jesus was familiar with pride's history. He was there when Lucifer's heart fell privy to it. He knows Satan's story. In fact, Jesus came to die in order to pay the price for this enslaving sin. Be ever so cautious not to allow pride into your heart. Pride is a foolish act of boasting over something we ultimately have no control over. Pride is nothing more than a selfish reaction that degrades the handiwork of our Creator, taking all He has accomplished in you as your own doing. How foolish of Satan to tempt Jesus with a thing that he hates (Proverbs 8:13). I love Jesus' response to this test of pride:

"It is written again, Thou shalt not tempt the Lord thy God." Matthew 4:7 (Deuteronomy 6:16)

Jesus does not bother with Satan's foolishness, nor does He waste time proving Satan wrong. He simply shuts Satan down with the power of Scripture. We have the same power of Scripture today. Study this issue of pride and take Christ's example to heart. Don't be fooled into thinking that pride is not a temptation for you. If Satan attempts its deceit in Jesus' life, why wouldn't he attempt it in yours? Be ready; ask God daily for wisdom and memorize God's Word. It is a sure fire way to shut Satan down.

Journal below where pride came from, who created pride, and what damage was caused by pride. Then read about pride's earthly inception recorded in Genesis 1. Again, note where the temptation of pride came from, who stirred pride on, and what insurmountable damage pride brought forth for all mankind.

Pride:

____

____

____

____

____

"Again, the devil taketh Him up into an exceeding high mountain, and sheweth Him all the kingdoms of the world, and the glory of them; And saith unto Him, All these things will I give Thee, if Thou wilt fall down and worship me." Matthew 4:8-9

Lastly, we see Jesus being tempted by power. I cannot help but smile at Satan's stupidity. He is blinded so desperately by himself that he forgets who he is speaking with, Jesus Christ, the Son of God, the Creator of Heaven and earth, the sole Creator of everything and everyone, including Lucifer himself. Satan is offering power to the one who alone gives power. How foolish of this prideful creation. God declares:

"Woe unto him that striveth with his Maker!" Let the potsherd strive with the potsherds of the earth. Shall the clay say to him that fashioneth it, What makest thou? Or thy work, He hath no hands?" Isaiah 45:9

What does having power mean to you? Is it something that causes you to fall into the snares of the devil? Does Satan blind you with the temptation of power and position? Does having a name of importance and prestige mean more to you than displaying a reputation of light to a lost world? Let God reign in power in your life. Do not fight for it, for it is His to give and His to take away. Read God's response to Satan found in Matthew 4:4. Do you see a common theme in Jesus' victory in His time of temptation? Scripture. There is power in the written Words of God. Learn from the Leader and follow His simple and free plan for conquering the temptations that come; memorize Scripture.

"The way of a fool is right in his own eyes; but he that hearkeneth unto counsel is wise." Proverbs 12:15

Who are you following? According to Solomon, you are either a fool following your own heart, or you are wise, following in the ways of counsel. A fool does what he wants, he chooses for himself the path in which he takes, the attitude in which he desires to live. The fool decides his own fate, taking it as both a self-burden and a badge of self-pride. He takes his eyes off God and falls down in worship of the devil. No one would ever claim that sentence to be their heart's cry, of course, but Christian, your actions speak much louder than any empty word that proceeds out of your mouth. To put it bluntly, when you do your own thing, you become a fool bowing down at the feet of Lucifer. He desired this of Jesus. Jesus concluded:

"*Get thee hence, Satan; for it is written, Thou shalt worship the*

Lord thy God, and Him only shalt thou serve." Matthew 4:10

There are those who seek counsel, good Godly counsel, and still choose to cave into the hands of Satan. Proverbs advises each of us to hearken unto counsel. James tells us to, "be doers of the Word and not hearers only" (1:22). When opportunity, great or small, comes your way, you ought to run to counsel; seek after wisdom as to whether or not you should accept or steer clear of the situation. In addition to seeking counsel, you need to be like Jesus in His matter of timing and response. When temptation came His way it was immediately before Him. He did not have time to seek counsel or wisdom, but He had no need to do so, for He walked ever so close to God. Jesus had prepared himself for such a time as this. He had done exactly what He commands us to do; hide His Word in our hearts that we may not sin against Him (Psalm 119:11). Pray to the Father that you walk not into temptation, and that you will be delivered from evil. You see, it is truly as simple as obedience. Love God through your time and actions every day; when Satan even thinks about attempting his presence in your life, it will sound as foolish as it does when he offered world power to the Creator of the world.

Satan is a fool. God is wise. We are who we follow. To finish out this chapter, focus on the four men who followed after Jesus. See who they were as family members, workers, etc., and notice what they were willing to give up in order to follow their Master. Add yourself to your thoughts and journal your history as a follower of Jesus. When did you begin following Him by way of receiving Jesus as your Savior and what is He asking of you today? Are you following the Leader?

As a side note, each of these men took their opportunities immediately. They were ready for leadership without having to confer with others. Why do you think that is? I cannot help but think that they were like Jesus. They were prepared in their walk with the Savior.

Peter and Andrew: Verses 18-20

James and John: Verses 21-22

Memory Goal:

"It is written, Man shall not live by bread alone, but by every word that proceedeth out of the mouth of God." Matthew 4:4

"There hath no temptation taken you, but such as is common to man: but God is faithful, and will not suffer you to be tempted above that ye are able; but will with the temptation also make a way to escape, that you may be able to bear it."
1 Corinthians 10:13

CALL IT LIKE IT IS

Matthew Five

"Ye are the light of the world, A city that is set on an hill cannot be hid." Matthew 5:14

Matthew 5 is the beginning of a three chapter series on the Sermon on the Mount. Jesus' earthly ministry is on the rise. He had gathered His twelve disciples (cf. Luke 6), separated from the multitudes, and began teaching these chosen men what is expected of them, and what their calling will mean to their daily way of life. These words are intended for you as well. He is not talking to the world at this time, nor is He reaching out to the lost or backslidden. Jesus is focusing on His true followers, His friends. Take His message to heart and apply it to your thoughts and actions. The Sermon on the Mount is personal.

Jesus desires for us to love. It is by our love that men know we are His disciples. Before Jesus explains what our actions ought to be, He reaches into the heart of our motives. If you don't have love, than the nine beatitudes listed in this chapter will be impossible. Jesus had great faith and confidence in His disciples. He was sending them off with nothing more than a charge to demonstrate love from within to the unsaved world.

"And thou shalt love the Lord thy God with all thine heart, and with all thy soul, and with all thy might." Deuteronomy 6:5

When we give all of our love to God it results in a correct heart attitude. In Verses 3-12, we will see three issues of the heart that we need to develop in our life in order to fulfill our calling of submissive love, our attitude towards sin, attitude towards God, and attitude towards the world. Before beginning this heart study, pray. Get on your knees before your God, praising Him for who He is. Ask Him to, "Open Thou mine eyes, that I may behold wondrous things out of Thy law" (Psalm 119:18).

The greatest difference between Bible reading and Bible studying is that sweet moment of worship with the King of Kings.

"Blessed are the poor in spirit (humble): for theirs is the kingdom of heaven. Blessed are they that mourn (see sin as God see's it): for they shall be comforted. Blessed are the meek (power under control): for they shall inherit the earth. Blessed are they which do hunger and thirst after righteousness: for they shall be filled." Matthew 5:3-6

Our first attitude to evaluate is our attitude toward sin. That sounds like fun, right? Isn't this the last thing we want to "evaluate?" Yet, it is the first thing Jesus approaches. Are you like me, when you hear the phrase, "sin evaluation?" Isn't it easier to think of others and their sin issue, or to tune out and pretend that you didn't hear what was being said? Makes me wonder, is this quite possibly why Christ began His sermon with this note of honest sin evaluation? Without purity from sin, we cannot sustain a clean heart before God. However, when we love God from the heart, sin will be seen with different eyes. Sin is sin, call it like it is.

I spend too many days justifying my issues away that I find myself spending more time justifying than praying. Why not just pray? Why do we do this? Why do we refrain from confessing a sin that He already sees? Do we not confess to God in fear of what He might know? As if we have the ability to coddle a sin so dearly that God Above cannot see. This concept was tried and failed back in the Garden of Eden. I highly doubt it is going to work for us today. We live in the flesh therefore sin is a reality. This battle between the spirit and the flesh will never cease. However, it does not have to be a state of bondage in our life. The apostle John tells us in his epistle:

"Whosoever is born of God doth not commit sin; for his seed remaineth in him: and he cannot sin, because he is born of God."
1 John 3:9

Yes, it is easier said than done. But, if we dwell in the Holy Spirit, and if we submit wholly to Him, then when we read "Don't sin," we take that as an encouragement to press on in holiness, rather than scoffing at the idea. What is your sin? What is your attitude towards sin, the sin of the world as well as the sin in your life? Get this area in check. Consider the Biblical mindset regarding sin according to Verses 3-6, and take note of the rewards promised to those who adapt to this godly way of thinking?

Attitude toward Sin:

____

____

____

____

____

"Blessed are the merciful: for they shall obtain mercy. Blessed are the pure in heart: for they shall see God. Blessed are the peacemakers: for they shall be called the children of God."
Matthew 5:7-9

Our next evaluation is on our attitude toward God. Once we

have the right vision when it comes to sin, our attitude about God becomes clearer. God is more than the Creator of the Universe. He gave us His only begotten Son, Jesus Christ. He gave us the daily presence of the Holy Spirit. He cares for us every minute of every day. Too often we forget how much He loves us. He did not save us and then let us go. He saved us and continues to keep us. In those hours in which we feel alone and deserted it is because we have forgotten to grasp onto our Father's hand as a child with his earthly father. He is there, always.

"But God, who is rich in mercy, for His great love wherewith He loved us, Even when we were dead in sins, hath quickened us together with Christ, (by grace ye are saved)"Ephesians 2:4-5

"Let us therefore come boldly unto the throne of grace, that we may obtain mercy, and find grace to help in time of need." Hebrews 4:16

Not only does God love us, sent His Son for us, and holds us daily in His hands, but He also gave us gifts to better our lives and to impact those around us. These gifts are mercy, purity, and peace. God has provided these three attributes in our lives. It is in our hands as to what we do with them. So here's my question: Does mercy spill from you onto others? Oh my! If you answer that as my friend, Dawn, then your yes would be accompanied with a tearful eye just thinking about that soul in need of God's mercy. Then again, if you answered as Michelle, then your laughter will ring as sweet as hers. Then there's me who would look confused at that question as different situations and individuals cross my mind, some being mentally marked with a yes and others as a no. Clearly my mercy is relative. Where are you in this world of mercy? If we stop and think about the mercy He displays in our life, then it should make us wonder, who am I to stop God from sharing His mercy with another soul in need of Him?

Next to being merciful is having a heart of purity. Having a heart of purity is the spiritual root that produces our physical and sexual purity. This clean heart is what keeps our thoughts spotless and focused on Christ. In 1 Peter 1:18-19 Peter declares this purity, God's purity, as "without blemish and without spot?"

That's purity! On paper, attaining this attribute that Mary displayed in Matthew 1 is as easy as seeing sin as God sees it, and confessing our every sin to God, then allowing the Holy Spirit to fill our hearts with His purity. In reality, it's as easy as our personal will allows it to be. This is where submission to Him comes in.

Ready for the last one? Peace. How peaceable are your relationships? Why is my first response to these questions laughter? Oh my goodness, I am the "self-evaluation" queen, but still they are painful. This does not mean that you have picturesque relationships with everyone you know. That would be heavenly. We are not there yet. Human nature causes that to be impossible. What this 'peacemaker' means is that you are exemplifying peace as much as you spiritually can. For some relationships peace is a natural element, it is a natural glue that binds you to this person or group of people. For other relationships, not so much. In those cases, this is where submission comes in. With a clean heart and pure eyes, you evaluate the relationship at hand and with God's grace you demonstrate peace, period.

Mercy, purity, and peace. You've received each of these upon salvation and every day since. Are you embracing them? Sometimes we have a hard time accepting such free gifts as these due to our feelings of low self-worth. Friend, you are the very picture of God's mercy, God's purity, and God's peace. They are given for you, and they are in you, they are right there for you to embrace. If you are sitting in these gifts, are they attributes of your home? Are you making it possible for their evidence to be seen? Are you doing your part?

Give mercy, and God promises that you will receive it. Be pure, and you will see God's presence. Live in peace, and you will be seen as a child of God. Yes, we all want the fruit, but if you notice, the fruit comes after you do your part; receive the love of Jesus and smile. God wants to bless, and He wants to know that you want to be blessed. What step are you missing? What do you need to strengthen in order to receive? Self-evaluate:

Attitude toward God:

____

____

____

____

____

Lastly, we see the attitude toward the world around us:

"Blessed are they which are persecuted for righteousness' sake: for theirs is the kingdom of heaven. Blessed are ye, when men shall revile you, and persecute you, and shall say all manner of evil against you falsely, for My sake. Rejoice, and be exceeding glad: for great is your reward in heaven:" Matthew 5:10-12

This reaction from the world, of persecution and hatred, is a promise; it will happen. Your siblings, your ex-husband, your children, your friends, etc. will be watching you the moment you turn your life over to Him. They knew who you were before Jesus Christ became your Savior. Now, when they hear you say Jesus with a smile rather than out of anger, they do not know how to react. Some will consider you a hypocrite, a phony. When you turn down a drink, offered to you by those who knew you as a drunkard, you may be mocked. What does Jesus say about this? Their persecution is a sign that you are truly living for God. Jesus says you may face persecution when you choose to turn your life around, but He gives rewards for that too!

God offers the promises of faithfulness to all who endure the hardship of verbal accusations that are not true. If you can stand and testify as the Psalmist, "Thou hast proved mine heart; thou hast visited me in the night; thou hast tried me, and shalt find nothing; I am purposed that my mouth shall not transgress," (Psalm 17: 3). If you are in love with the Lord with all your heart, soul, and mind, then read over the promises above and cling to them.

Jesus then tells us what to do with the world. He gives us a plan, a goal, something to focus on, rather than focusing on the lies being presented to us. Study this plan found in Verses 13-16. Take the time to rewrite His plan as your own personal goal. Remember, the one showing anger to you is the one in dire need of the Savior's love. I know it is hard to show love when you are being attacked, but if you focus on shining, rather than recovering, it will get easier day by day. You will find a smile.

Attitude toward the World:

____

____

____

____

____

The rest of the chapter illustrates the greatest changes that occur when love for God supersedes obedience to the law. Six times we read Christ saying, "You have heard; but I say." Six times Christ stretches the Old Testament law into a practical step toward love. Christ explains why it is important to see the truth:

"Think not that I am come to destroy the law, or the prophets: I am not come to destroy, but to fulfill. For verily I say unto you, till heaven and earth pass, one jot or one tittle shall in no wise pass from the law, till all be fulfilled. Whosoever therefore shall break one of these least commandments, and shall teach men so, he shall be called the least in the kingdom of heaven: but whosoever shall do and teach them, the same shall be called great in the kingdom of heaven. For I say unto you, that except your righteousness shall exceed the righteousness of the scribes and Pharisees, ye shall in no case enter into the kingdom of heaven." Matthew 5:17-20

Religion says, obey the law. Jesus says, love the Lord. The only way your righteousness can exceed the righteousness of religion is through the acceptance of the precious blood of Christ shed for you on Calvary's tree.

Christ approaches six laws and turns them into heart issues. Murder, adultery, divorce, oaths, revenge, and love are transformed into hate, lust, responsibility, wisdom, humility, and love. Take the time to read the laws of old compared to the love of Christ, and note the differences between the two. If there is one that touches your heart, commit a parallel verse to memory to serve as a reminder to how you will submit in love to God.

Murder-Hatred: Matthew 5:21-26

"Thou shalt not kill." Exodus 20:13

____

____

____

____

Adultery-Lust: Matthew 5:27-30

"Thou shalt not commit adultery." Exodus 20:14

____

____

____

____

Divorce-Responsibility: Matthew 5:31-32

"When a man hath taken a wife ...because he hath found some uncleanness in her: then let him write her a bill of divorcement." Deuteronomy 24:1

___

___

___

___

Oaths-Wisdom: Matthew 5:33-37

"And ye shall not swear by My name falsely, neither shalt thou profane the name of thy God: I am the LORD." -Leviticus 19:12 (cf. Deuteronomy 23:23)

___

___

___

___

Revenge-Humility: Matthew 5:38-42

"And if a man cause a blemish in his neighbor; as he hath done, so shall it be done to him; Breach for breach, eye for eye, tooth for tooth;" Leviticus 24:19-20 (cf. Exodus 21:23-25; Deuteronomy 19:18- 21)

___

___

___

___

Love-Love: Matthew 5:43-48

"Thou shalt not avenge, not bear any grudge against the children of thy people, but thou shalt love thy neighbour as thyself: I am the LORD." -Leviticus 19:18

____

____

____

____

Memory Goal:

"For whosoever shall keep the whole law, and yet offend in one point, he is guilty of all." James 2:10

"For the law made nothing perfect, but the bringing in of a better hope did; by the which we draw nigh unto God." Hebrews 7:19

"For the grace of God that bringeth salvation hath appeared to all men. Teaching us that, denying ungodliness and worldly lusts, we should live soberly, righteously, and godly, in this present world; Looking for that blessed hope, and the glorious appearing of the great God and our Saviour Jesus Christ;" Titus 2:11-13

"When you read, "Be ye therefore perfect, even as your Father which is in heaven is perfect." It does not mean sinless perfection. It means full development; growth into maturity of godliness." Scofield Study Bible

I LOVE MY CLOSET

Matthew Six

"But seek ye first the kingdom of God, and His righteousness; and all these things shall be added unto you." Matthew 6:33

I love my closet. One Mother's Day, my husband surprised me with a freshly painted bedroom closet. It wasn't so much the painted closet that touched my heart, but the image of my husband purchasing and willingly painting our closet pink. Now, that is a gift! By the end of that year my closet had been transformed into a beautiful serene place for me, accented with Audrey Hepburn photos, jeweled purse hooks, beautifully girly jewelry displays, and added shoe shelves. It made even his UPS uniforms look dazzling. This is my favorite room of the house; I love my closet.

However, when I read, "when thou prayest, enter into thy closet," in Matthew 6:6 this is not where I go to pray. For me, there are too many pretty distractions. In this chapter we will see the differences between how to pray as Jesus does and how not to pray as the Pharisees did. As we explore the heart of the Christian walk, the heart of submission, I want to begin by locating your closet, your place of prayer, and set a scheduled time to meet with God in that closet.

"But thou, when thou prayest, enter into thy closet, and when thou hast shut thy door, pray to the Father which is in secret; and thy Father which seeth in secret shall reward thee openly."
Matthew 6:6

I love my closet. Not just the pink dream room described above, but my closet with God. For me, it is in my library. This room in my house is quiet, calm, and always clean. I am the only one to ever utilize this space. There are no distractions; I cannot even see my kitchen sink from this room. Girlfriends of mine meet the Lord at their kitchen table, beside their bed, in the car outside their child's school, and even in their bedroom closet. The goal is to find a location where you can clear your mind, step away from your schedule, and spend some time alone with God. Do you have a place in mind? If not, 'try on' different locations as if you are trying on a new pair of shoes. You know what they say, If the shoe fits…

Now to find a set time, a busy schedule may need a little revamping in order to prioritize. Some of us need to adapt to our change of routine. That would be me. When my schedule changes and my routine is altered I feel lost and empty. It is rather pathetic (and often mocked by those who know this sad truth), but it is my reality nonetheless. Here are a few ideas. Consider an earlier rise in the morning, or turning in earlier at night. Nap time may no longer include a nap for you, or maybe your lunch break can include both your physical and spiritual food. Altering a schedule is tiring, but trust me, you will feel more rested when you are in the arms of God. He will sustain. Jesus tells you to enter into your closet and pray; this requires a determined act. A determined act requires a plan. Write your plan down and commit your closet and schedule to God.

Closet/Time:

____

____

____

Without prayer, submission is impossible. Prayer is the heart of the Christian walk, the heart of submission. Jesus, God in the flesh, knew the importance of prayer, and fell to His knees alone in prayer throughout His earthly ministry. Jesus also knew what His disciples were going to face throughout their lives. So He uses this sermon to relay the importance of prayer to these men. He teaches them how to pray, and what to expect when they pray.

Jesus' sermon applies to us as well. We cannot grow in our submission to Him unless we first follow in His footsteps of purposed prayer. He is not speaking of the pray without ceasing mindset given to us by Paul, this is a purposeful prayer. This is a commitment set aside daily between you and God alone. This is that prayer that enables us to pray without ceasing (1 Thessalonians 5:17). Without this prayer, a constant prayer life is unattainable. God desires nothing less than you, the best form of you, humbly on your knees in awe of Him. It is this kind of prayer that separates church attenders from Christ followers. It is this relationship in prayer that grows you from the milk of the Word to the meat. It is what surrounds you with showers of blessings, rather than just sprinkles. If there is one thing you strive to glean out of this chapter, may it be a stronger prayer life.

"Therefore, when thou doest thine alms, do not sound a trumpet before thee, as the hypocrites do in the synagogues and in the streets, and when thou prayest, thou shalt not be as the hypocrites are: for they love to pray standing in the synagogues and in the corners of the streets, but when ye pray, use not vain repetitions, as the heathen do: Moreover when ye fast, be not, as the hypocrites, of a sad countenance:" Matthew 6:2, 5, 7, and 16

Remember those Pharisees sitting under the preaching of John the Baptist? They refused to believe in Jesus Christ because of their laws of obedience to God. Well, here they are again; this time sitting under the preaching of Jesus himself. These religious Pharisees had memorized the law; they studied the God of Abraham. They promoted prayer and demonstrated it abroad. Yet, Jesus references them as hypocrites and heathens. Their display of trumpets, public stances, memorized prayers, and publicized fasts were all empty in the eyes and ears of God. There was no reason for God to hear their prayers, for they were not prayed for God's providence. These displayed prayers were for the eyes and ears of men, and that is where the Pharisees rewards were found.

Jesus says, "Be not ye therefore like unto them: for your Father knoweth what things ye have need of before ye ask Him. After this manner therefore pray ye" (Matthew 6:9). He says, "This is your Father you are dealing with, and he knows better than you what you need. With a God like this loving you, you can pray very simply. Like this" (The Message). At times you might be in your prayer closet, alone with God, shut off from all distractions and thoughts, and find that your prayers seem empty, meaningless or void, feeling as if something is wrong or missing. When this happens, cling to the example of prayer given to you by your Savior. This prayer covers every need of your heart, and every emotion you may be facing.

If you are unsure of how to express your heart to God, read Verse 8. He already knows, just say it. Nothing will come as a surprise to Him. All too often, getting the words out brings relief to our soul. If you feel like you are praying to the couch rather than to God, pray Verses 9-10. Remind yourself who God is and what He did for you at Calvary; remember what He did for you yesterday. If you are feeling void of purpose or reason, Verse 10 will revive your vision. Verse 11 reminds us that He will provide our daily needs. Are you in need of forgiveness, or do you need to seek it out? Verse 12 assures us God will bring comfort to your heart if comfort is needed, He will bring conviction and boldness as well.

"And lead us not into temptation, but deliver us from evil: For thine is the kingdom, and the power, and the glory, forever. Amen." Matthew 6:13

The key difference between the empty prayer of the Pharisees and the new prayer instructed by the Lord, is the spirit of humility and understanding as to what prayer is truly about. Prayer is about your relationship with your Father, not a verbal affirmation of yourself.

To ask the Father to set a protection around you from yourself (temptations) and Satan (evil), shows that you are asking God to be your leader, your protector, your God.

Immediately after offering His example prayer, Jesus explains forgiveness. There are many things we are to pray for, however, lest we forgive, nothing else will be heard. Some have felt the feeling of release that follows the sincere act of forgiveness, others are holding on to hurt, leading them to bitterness rather than forgiveness. Forgiveness is hard. Yet, it is the one matter of prayer He reiterates. In the midst of Christ's words of prayer (vs. 9-13) and fasting (vs. 16-18), He pauses in order to place the importance of forgiving one another. It appears as if forgiveness toward others is a vital key to having an open communication with God. With this thought, what does your prayer life say about your ability to forgive? Who is in need of your forgiveness? Why should you give it? Are you willing to allow your relationship with Christ to grow by way of this needful gift called forgiveness?

Be honest with God. If needed, start fresh with Him right now. Pray through His prayer (vs. 9-13). Do not let that sin we talked about in Chapter 5 halt your conversations with Jesus. Really, is it worth it? Once you have received God's forgiveness, forgive others. Jesus powerfully warns, "But if ye forgive not men their trespasses, neither will your Father forgive your trespasses." Just as we are to pass on His mercy, purity and peace, so are we to offer His forgiveness. Take time now to be honest with God…

The Lord's Prayer/Forgiveness:

____

____

____

____

____

Treasure chests are big, beautiful boxes filled with small, delicately shiny, pieces of gold, silver, jewels, and diamonds, every girl's dream come true. How perfectly that collection of treasure would display in our pink closets of the world! Truth be told, how often do you ponder on such things as jewelry, clothing, or (take a deep breath) shoes? Some, I know, scoff at such simplicities in the world and would rather obtain a collection of more reasonable treasures found in the realm of technology, or something else their heart desires. To each their own. None of our dreams are wrong, all, however, come with a warning:

"Lay not up for yourselves treasures upon earth, where moth and rust doth corrupt, and where thieves break through and steal: But lay up for yourselves treasures in heaven, where neither moth nor rust doth corrupt, and where thieves do not break through nor steal: For where your treasure is, there will your heart be also." Matthew 6:19-21

Be mindful of the true value of what you treasure. It may have cost a pretty penny to purchase, but it is a penny that could easily be stolen, damaged, or may even become ... outdated (Gasp!). When it comes to our girly things, becoming outdated is a sad, sad thing. For my self-declared "geeky" friends, outdated treasures are yesterday's news. When these situations occur, it saddens our hearts, but we continue on with the next new thing. This is why I am waiting to upgrade my VCR. Yes, seriously, I still have a VCR.

When we go back to the beginning of this Sermon on the Mount, we read of Christ's ideals for our lives, we see what matters most to Him, love, forgiveness, and prayer. It is this treasure chest that God desires to find in our hearts. For love, God's love, cannot be taken away. Forgiveness will not cause damage; it repairs the damage. And prayer will never go out of style. People are always around us, always there for us to reach out to, show kindness to, and share God's love with. When we refrain from sharing love and forgiveness with others, it saddens God's heart.

Because of His love for others, Jesus gives us the solution for the correct treasure chest. It is said, "Eyes are the window to the soul." With Jesus Christ as our Savior, our soul is alive. Without Christ in our life, our soul is dead. If this saying is true, then our eyes ought to be reflecting only His light, allowing others to see Jesus when they look in our eyes. It allows others to see our vision and our focus. If you are saved, where is your light? Are you living in the light provided by the Hands of God, or are you making your own little sparks, giving God place as your Savior, but offering Him little room to be your God?

"The light of the body is the eye: if therefore thine eye be single, thy whole body shall be full of light. But if thine eye be evil, thy whole body shall be full of darkness. If therefore the light that is in thee be darkness, how great is that darkness!" Matthew 6:22-23

Ultimately, Jesus is earnestly telling His disciples, telling you, to open your eyes! Fully open them to see the face of Jesus Christ, His nail-printed hands, the body that bled for you. See Him with all that you are. Your heart ought to beam when you consider this Man, His love, God. Jesus points out a very hard warning of having a half-hearted vision. If you are walking the fence, the darkness in your eyes will be truly darkening to those who see it. Speaking to the Laodicean church, God says, "I know thy works, that thou art neither cold not hot: I would thou wert cold or hot. So then because thou are lukewarm, and neither cold not hot, I will spew thee out of My mouth" (Revelation 3: 15-16).

Christian, if you don't want to live for God, then don't. Be cold. If you do want to live for God, live for God. Be hot. Whatever you do, do not wallow in the shadows of lukewarm apathy. The soul that desires nothing of the light, yet cringes from the darkness, residing in the middle of a spiritual disconnect, is a soul hiding under a bush, a dim candle for no one to see. Hell's mouth, however, is open wide.

"No man can serve two masters; for either they will hate the one, and love the other; or else he will hold to the one, and despise the other. Ye cannot serve God and mammon." Matthew 6:24

What is in your treasure chest? What do you desire to see there? Does it compare with what God sees? Secondly, be honest about your temperature. Does God see you as hot, cold, or lukewarm?

Record your thoughts below:

____

____

____

____

____

____

____

"Therefore I say unto you, take no thought for your life, what ye shall eat, or what ye shall drink; nor yet for your body, what ye shall put on. Is not the life more than meat, and the body than raiment? Take therefore no thought for the morrow: for the morrow shall take thought for the things of itself. Sufficient unto the day is the evil thereof." Matthew 6:25, 34

How great is our God! Jeremiah says of Him, "His ways are not our ways. His thoughts are not our thoughts." Yet, when He hears our prayers, He hears our requests simply. Although we may express them as big prayers and small prayers, He doesn't. We saw in the previous chapter that what we consider small, hatred and lust, are comparatively the same as what we consider big, murder and adultery. Just the same, the wants and needs of our hearts are comparably the same in God's eye. God looks at your needs and desires as a way to shower down blessings on you. Open your hands wide when you pray, for when you pray, believing, you will receive. This is a promise. Jesus tells His disciples, who were recently out of work, that in order to follow Him, think of this:

"If God so clothe the grass of the field, which today is, and tomorrow is cast into the oven, shall He not much more clothe you, o ye of little faith? Therefore take no thought, saying, what shall we eat? Or, what shall we drink? Or, wherewithal shall we be clothed?" Matthew 6:30-31

These men were having the same heart issue we women struggle with today. God settled their minds with the same words He leaves for us, "your heavenly Father knoweth that ye have need of all these things. But seek ye first the kingdom of God, and His righteousness; and all these things shall be added unto you" (Matthew 6:32-33).

Food, drink, clothes, what are those to you? Even the most practical of women have to admit that they are everything to us. Come on, without food we would be hungry, without drink we would be dead, and without clothes we, well we would be celebrating our birthday one too many times. These three things are important to all mankind. They are a necessity. That being said, because they are everything we need to live, they are everything to God. You are everything to God. He created the plants; He provides for them. He created you; how much more will He provide for you? Too many hours are wasted in panic and worry. Worry is a sin. It is a lack of trust in the Father. We do not know what tomorrow holds, God does. We are not promised tomorrow, why waste today worrying over something completely out of your hands? God created today. He created you. He knows what He is doing. Trust Him, and take no thought.

In this chapter, we took a step back from submission in order to root our heart of submission in the power of prayer. Which matter of prayer needs to be brought to God and laid before Him with pure trust in His power to provide? Read Matthew 6:25-34 again, commit God's commands and promises to heart.

Take No Thought...

____

____

____

____

____

Memory Goal:

"But seek ye first the kingdom of God, and His righteousness; and all these things shall be added unto you." Matthew 6:33

"Whereas ye know not what shall be on the morrow. For what is your life: It is even a vapor, that appeareth for a little time, and then vanisheth away." James 4:14

7

DRIVING IN REVERSE

Matthew Seven

"Ask, and it shall be given you; seek, and ye shall find; knock, and it shall be opened unto you." Matthew 7:7

Submission without its root in prayer is an impossibility. In other words, attempting to do something you don't know how to do, without asking how to do it, is um … stupid. For example, we could say that one might venture to move her husband's 1999 blue, stick-shift, Ford Ranger out of the driveway in order to get her 1999 yellow Ford Mustang out of the garage. Let's say she was slightly unsure as to how to maneuver the afore mentioned truck in any gear except reverse and therefore found herself driving backward down the driveway and around the entire neighborhood in order to park along the house. Just trust me on this, it could have happened. For the most part I am good at asking for help. But every once in a while…well, I don't want to talk about it anymore…

Throughout this three-chapter sermon, it is evident that the birth of submission in your life, is found in the prayer of salvation. As you grow in the Word, so does your natural ability to submit to the words of Jesus Christ. In turn, submission to those around you becomes a final outcome. In His conclusion, Christ offers some final words of warning and advice: do not judge, pray to your Father, be kind, and be wise. Moreover, be saved and live your salvation.

Jesus knows mankind, does He not? He laced together your reality with His power of prayer so beautifully, that if you took the smallest advantage of His presence, life would truly be ideal. Our problem, however, is our devotion to our flesh. We spend time dwelling on the reality around us like the laws (Matthew 5:21-48), our spiritual reputation (Matthew 6:1-7), and our treasures and cares (Matthew 6:19-34). Instead we should dwell on the simplicities found in Jesus' statements concerning prayer.

The heart of Christ's message takes on a deeper meaning when you read it for yourself. What I mean is, that you should take His message personal. You, a child of God, are being spoken to by Jesus Christ your Savior. Read what He has for you today:

"Judge not, that ye be not judged, for with what judgment ye judge, ye shall be judged." Matthew 7:1-2

In a parallel passage, Luke writes, "Judge not, and ye shall not be judged: condemn not, and ye shall not be condemned: forgive, and ye shall be forgiven" (6:37). Sin is sin. Judging is as grave a sin as the sin you are judging. There is none better than you; there is none worse than you, nor are the sins, convictions, or lack of convictions in others of any value to you. Jesus teaches this lesson to Peter in the end of the book of John. Peter, who was caught up in knowing what will differ between he and John, is told by Christ, "If I will that he tarry till I come, what is that to thee? Follow thou Me" (John 21:22). What another person does or does not do is none of your concern. Their walk with God is between them and God, likewise your walk with God is between you and God.

"For instance, a person who has been around for a while might well be convinced that he can eat anything on the table, while another, with a different background, might assume he should only be a vegetarian and eat accordingly. But since both are guests at Christ's table, wouldn't it be terribly rude if they fell to criticizing what the other ate or didn't eat? God, after all, invited them both to the table. Do you have any business crossing people off the guest list or interfering with God's welcome? If there are corrections to be made or manners to be learned, God can handle that without your help." Romans 14:2-4 (The Message)

"Who art thou that judgest another man's servant: to his own master he standeth or falleth. Yea, he shall be holden up; for God is able to make him stand. But why dost thou judge thy brother: or why dost thou set at nought thy brother: for we shall all stand before the judgment seat of Christ. Let us not therefore judge one another anymore: but judge this rather, that no man put a stumbling block or an occasion to fall in his brother's way." Romans 14:4,10,14

I encourage you to read Romans 14 in full before pressing on to Christ's next teaching on prayer. Romans 14 sheds a bright light on the importance of confidently living your convictions. Our walk and our convictions differ one from another. Who are we to say which is right and which is wrong? We are not God; judging is not our job. When we judge, we compare one flesh to another's. This is what Jesus does not want His children to do. Paul says, "Be found faithful. ... yea, I judge not mine own self. ...but he that judgeth me is the Lord" (1 Corinthians 4:2-4). Let's choose to be as Paul, and let God be the judge.

Who/What do you find yourself judging? Secondly, what is God trying to judge in you in order to draw you closer to Him? Could it be this very area of judging?

____

____

____

____

____

"Ask, and it shall be given you; seek, and ye shall find; knock, and it shall be opened unto you: For every one that asketh receiveth; and he that seeketh findeth; and to him that knocketh it shall be opened." Matthew 7:7-8

What should we be asking for, seeking after, and knocking on? This lesson on prayer is not a prayer of salvation, for God is talking to His followers. It is not the daily prayer of needs, forgiveness, and protection. We have already dedicated our time in prayer regarding these matters. This leaves you with the next step, to know who you are in your position in the Lord.

You are a princess to the King of Kings. God Almighty is your Heavenly Father. Consider this truth, a good father desires little more than to fulfill their child's needs. To be able to provide for a child a well-balanced meal or that new Darth Vader mask is a rewarding feeling. If you, in your flesh, desire to tend to your child, how much more does God, in His sovereignty, desire to care for you?

The question here is not, will God provide? He promises He will throughout His Scriptures. The question is, will you let God provide? Do you see God as your Father? Do you see yourself as His daughter? I sit in awe each time I hear of a 'daddy's little girl.' As a little girl who grew up without her daddy, this concept is fascinating to me. However, any girl who identifies as a daddy's little girl can testify of her father's love for her. When a problem arises, or a need is present, she easily throws her arms around her daddy's neck and tells him the matter on her heart, without fear, anxiety, irritation, anger, or complacency in her conversation with her father. She is simply a girl asking her daddy as she always has. I love the picture of that bond. I dare to say, I envy that reality.

Whether you can relate to the 'daddy's little girl' or feel a hundred miles away from that position, the truth of God's word places you there in your relationship with God the Father. This is the reality I know. The reality I was able to embrace as a little girl. This Father/daughter relationship formed me into the woman I am today.

"For ye have not received the spirit of bondage again to fear; but ye have received the Spirit of adoption, whereby we cry, Abba, Father." Romans 8:15

Through the sweet blood of Jesus, you have been adopted by God the Father, giving you the family right to boldly approach God, calling Him, Abba, Father, Daddy.

"Let us therefore come boldly unto the throne of grace, that we may obtain mercy, and find grace to help in time of need." Hebrews 4:16

Secondly, your position in the Lord gives you a relationship with the Holy Spirit. This relationship is so vital to your daily life, yet too often overlooked. You may pray to God for your needs and thank Jesus for your salvation, but do you utilize the power of the Holy Spirit?

"And I will pray the Father, and He shall give you another Comforter, that He may abide with you forever; even the Spirit of truth; whom the world cannot receive, because it seeth Him not, neither knoweth Him: but ye know Him; for He dwelleth with you, and shall be in you." John 14:16-17

The Holy Spirit is your force for life. He is your truth, your guidance, your wisdom, and He provides the comfort you need to be sustained. I feel like I ought to have a comparison here with the word 'Force' and this film called Star Wars. My husband has every Star Wars figure from his childhood. My son has a profound adulation for those figures. My editor holds a deep fanhood for this epic phenomenon. However, I'm sad to say, I grew up with two older sisters in Barbie world. There was no force. Nothing black. No lightsabers. Simply love, pink, and convertible cars. Having said all that, the Holy Spirit is your force. Period. If you have a comparison using Star Wars, by all means, share with your lightsaber jedis in order to grow your relationship with the Holy

Spirit. Oh, and if you can fashion a useful comparison between the Holy Spirit and Barbie....I'm all ears! For now, the Holy Spirit is your force for life. How?

"But the fruit of the Spirit is love, joy, peace, long-suffering, gentleness, goodness, faith, meekness, temperance: against such there is no law." Galatians 5:22-23

As you walk in the Spirit, His fruit begins to pour out of you. The Spirit enables you to become something new, someone full of sweet fruit, with a heart ready to submit to God's leading. In Matthew 7, we see the Holy Spirit desires to lead us down the road less traveled, with kindness towards others and with open eyes towards hypocrisy.

First, we see the proof of the Holy Spirit in Verse 12, "Therefore all things whatsoever ye would that men should do to you, do ye even so to them: for this is the law and the prophets." The Golden Rule, do unto others as you would have them do unto you, is a lot easier said than done, unless you are filled with the Spirit. The ease of kindness is a sure sign of a Christian who is filled with the Holy Spirit. If this is an area you struggle with, the solution is found in your salvation. The Spirit is there, get your flesh out of the way, and let the Spirit reign. That is submission!

Next, we have the road less traveled, "Enter ye in at the strait gate: for wide is the gate, and broad is the way, that leadeth to destruction, and many there be which go in thereat: Because strait is the gate, and narrow is the way, which leadeth unto life, and few there be that find it" (vs. 13-14). The two roads found in Matthew 7:13-14 are depicted beautifully in Psalm 1:1-6. In both passages, we see the two roads offered to all; one is straight and narrow, traveled by those who seek council and live it and those who take advantage of the presence of the Holy Spirit. The other is broad and wide, full of those who deny Jesus Christ as the way of salvation.

Lastly, we see the need for open eyes. "Beware of false prophets, which come to you in sheep's clothing, but inwardly they are ravening wolves. Ye shall know them by their fruits" (Matthew

6:15-16). Do you see the importance of displayed fruit? Fruit does not achieve your own salvation, but it shows salvation to those around you.

Follow this thought with me. You get saved. Immediately, the Holy Spirit takes up residence in your life. Along with the Spirit, comes His fruit. You naturally display this fruit, until your flesh demands its old position as boss. At this point, you battle within as to who is going to take charge of your heart, your dead self or the living Spirit. Whom we choose has no effect on your name written in the Lamb's Book of Life; your salvation is eternally secured (John 10:27-30). However, this choice, as to who will reign, is the only visual others have of the changing power of the Holy Spirit in your life.

"Abide in Me, and I in you. As the branch cannot bear fruit of itself, except it abide in the vine; no more can ye, except ye abide in Me." John 15:4

The Spirit will never leave you nor forsake you, but if you continually quench the Spirit you can cause His fruit to decay, leaving a sour display of the love of God. By your fruit you are known. All of mankind has fruit, each life will produce something. Your fruit should differ from the fruit of the unsaved. Christ even says, your fruit should differ from the fruit of religion, for the fruit of religion is the fruit of hypocrisy. Christ says, "It will be hewn down, and cast into the fire" (Matthew 7:15-23). He is clear on this point, a life will produce the matter of the heart.

There are some, however, that will attempt a life of hypocrisy. Many will be led astray by their practiced sincerity and charisma. Open your eyes to the character of the speaker, hold their message in the light of the Bible, then determine the sincerity and truth of the message. The Spirit promises wisdom for all who seek it (James 1:5). Seek it, lest you be led astray by foolish speaking.

In conclusion, we return to a thought presented in Chapter Three, how evident is your salvation in your life today? Through salvation, God is our Father, the Spirit is our guide, and Jesus is our Savior. The final question in this chapter is, are you using these simple truths found in God's word to build your house, or are you using them to pass judgment onto others, to present yourself holier than you really are? These truths are tools that ought to be used to build up your life in Christ. When the rains and storms of life beat upon you, what will stand? This chapter encourages us to discover and admit who we are, not who we say we are, or who we try to be, but how God sees us. Evaluate yourself through God's eyes. You are His daughter! Are you living from the heart? I challenge you to confront your relationship with God, the Holy Spirit, and Jesus Christ.

Record your thoughts below:

____

____

____

____

____

____

____

Memory Goal:

"Let us therefore come boldly unto the throne of grace, that we may obtain mercy, and find grace to help in time of need." Hebrews 4:16

The promise that stands with the decision to be wise is far greater than the shame that comes with the choice of foolishness.

8

WERE YOU SPEAKING TO ME?

Matthew Eight

"But the men marveled, saying, what manner of man is this, that even the winds and the sea obey Him!" Matthew 8:7

Submission is something expected from all of God's creation. Here in this chapter, we see a perfect picture of the swift demonstration of submission shown by a variety of God's creations. Men, water, and animals all obey the voice of Jesus Christ. This is a great lesson on submission for us! We are the one creation to whom a free will has been given, yet we are the one creation who defies the idea of creator/creation submission. Pride and selfishness find their way into our hearts, causing disobedience to the voice of our Creator. Strive to learn from the examples of swift submission to a clear command heard from the very voice of God.

How acquainted are you with the voice of your Savior? The Old Testament depicts God's voice as a loud noise for all to hear, yet as a voice intended for His child to hold dear. In the New Testament, we hear His voice through the recorded words of Jesus Christ. As Christians, as His sheep, our hearts know when we are hearing the voice of God as we read His Word. To hear you must spend time in conversation in prayer, heed to the words of our authority, and ultimately walk in the Spirit.

"And, behold, the glory of the God of Israel came from the way of the east: and His voice was like a noise of many waters: and the earth shined with his glory." Ezekiel 43:2

"And, behold, the Lord passed by, and a great and strong wind rent the mountains, and brake in pieces the rocks before the Lord; but the Lord was not in the wind: and after the wind an earthquake; but the Lord was not in the earthquake: And after the earthquake a fire; but the Lord was not in the fire: and after the fire a still small voice." 1 Kings 19:11-12

"My sheep hear My voice, and I know them, and they follow Me." John 10:27

The voice of Jesus is heard through the pages of Matthew. When you read His words, hear them. In this chapter we see the power of His voice as it heals, convicts, and calms. We see the healing of the dreadful disease of leprosy (vs.1-4), the distant healing of a gentile (vs. 5-13), and the sweet healing of a common concern, fever (vs. 14-18). There are no limitations to the power of His voice. His voice still sounds today; His power still reigns today. Whether you are facing a dreadful disease, a distant relation is suffering, or laid up on the couch with your tissue box, Jesus' voice heals. Remember, you may feel as if your prayer is too big to give to God or too small to bother God, but in God's ears, your prayers are His opportunity to share His love with you all over again.

Not only do we see Jesus' voice heal, we see its convicting power over the faithfulness demonstrated in our lives. If we compare the conversation recorded in Verses 19-22 with the callings and responses of the 12 disciples in John 1:35-42 and Matthew 9:9, we understand what Christ is saying and what He wants us to hear. There is no procrastination, no turning back; God's kingdom cannot be put off.

There were two brothers, one expressed to his father how he would love to help in the fields, the other straightforwardly declared, no. When the day came, the eager son never showed up for his declared commitment, yet the son, who verbally denied his father's request, presented himself to his father. Your words are nothing when your actions prove them to be false; your actions demonstrate your heart more than your words ever will (Matthew 21: 28-32).

Next we see the power of Jesus' voice over the storm, and the comfort surrounding the individual that, encumbered by the waves, is held in the arms of God. This picture of the calming voice of God over the tempestuous sea, is beautifully scripted in Psalm 107:

"They that go down to the sea in ships, that do business in great waters; These see the works of the Lord, and His wonders in the deep. For He commandeth, and raiseth the stormy wind, which lifteth up the waves thereof. They mount up to the heaven, they go down again to the depths: their soul is melted because of trouble. They reel to and fro, and stagger like a drunken man, and are at their wits' end. They cry unto the Lord in their trouble, and He bringeth them out of their distresses. He maketh the storm a calm, so that the waves thereof are still. Then are they glad because they be quiet; so He bringeth them unto their desired haven. Oh that men would praise the Lord for His goodness, and for His wonderful works to the children of men! Psalm 107:23-31

Poetry is a beautiful thing. Any time words are used to express love within one's heart I eat them up. I love it. It is so unique and so personal. This psalmist focused his verbal adoration as a sailor in the midst of the sea. May I challenge you? Don't roll your eyes my non-poet friend! Ability or not, we have words, we have a heart, and we love Jesus, through that simple combination I challenge you to write a personal adoration to Jesus for his voice in your life. It can be a line, a letter, a sonnet, or something crazy like a limerick. Whatever it is, say thank you to Jesus for being your Jesus.

____

____

____

____

Finally, we see Jesus' power over Satan. I saw a drawing years ago that I will never forget. While in college, I looked around my classroom of some 500 students to find the cause of the giggles growing in the room. The laughter grew even more as each of us realized it wasn't a troublemaker causing the interruption this time, rather a drawing produced by the instructor himself on the overhead projector. I cannot recall which class period I was in, or what the test was even about, but I can clearly remember the drawing. One line cascaded down the left side of the overhead, with a second line, as a wave, ran left to right across the screen, with random curly cues bobbing, if you will, in the water. Without making a sound, the instructor slowly added one little pig tail at a time; eventually, the 'water line' was full of little pig tails. This elementary drawing of drowning pigs was quite humorous for a room full of adolescent Bible students, and an image sketched into my memory each time I read the account in Verses 28-34:

"They landed in the country of the Gadarenes and were met by two madmen, victims of demons, coming out of the cemetery. The men had terrorized the region for so long that no one considered it safe to walk down that stretch of road anymore. Seeing Jesus, the madmen screamed out, "What business do you have giving us a hard time? You're the Son of God: You weren't supposed to show up here yet!" Off in the distance a herd of pigs was browsing and rooting. The evil spirits begged Jesus, "If you kick us out of these men, let us live in the pigs."

Jesus said, "Go ahead, but get out of here!" Crazed, the pigs stampeded over a cliff into the sea and drowned."
Matthew 8:28-32 (The Message)

Living in the mountainside among the gravestones, without the necessities of life, food, shelter, or clothing, lived a soul without love, without care. Yet, this soul, surrounded by fear within and without, hopeless, and with no control, looks up and sees Jesus.

"But when he saw Jesus afar off, he ran and worshipped Him,"
Mark 5:6

How is it that a soul in such depravity recognizes Jesus Christ as the only way of freedom from its imprisonment? How is it that the demons recognize Jesus Christ as the final authority over their existence? The answer to the unexplainable power of Jesus is none other than the name of Jesus.

Is your cry for freedom through the name of Jesus comparable to that of a dying soul? Are the demons submitting to his authority more readily than you? These are just a few questions for us to ponder as we continue on this quest to read His word in order to hear His voice.

The Voice of God:

____

____

____

____

____

____

Beginning in this chapter, I want to encourage you to challenge yourself in the area of personal Bible study. Whether you expound on each topic, or focus on one that is particularly needful for you, purpose to stretch yourself. Take your time going through this book; do not place a timeline on your study. Rather, read the Scriptures and meditate on one little jewel at a time. Journal these jewels to help you remember and embrace them even more. And have fun! Studying God's Scripture is amazing, wonderful, and fulfilling. Take advantage of the Bible. It is a precious gift God has given to you.

Study Options:

The similarities among the submissive:

Matthew 8:2, 5-9, 26b, 29-32

____

____

____

____

____

____

Christ's response to the faithful:

Matthew 8:3-4, 7 and 13

____

____

____

____

The actions of the healed:

Matthew 8:4, 15

Responses of the viewers:

Matthew 8:16, 27, 33

Christ's statement to the fearful:

Matthew 8:26 and 32

____

____

____

____

____

____

____

Memory Goal:

"Oh that men would praise the Lord for His goodness, and for His wonderful works to the children of men!" Psalm 107:31

"Study to shew thyself approved unto God, a workman that needeth not to be ashamed, rightly dividing the word of truth." 2 Timothy 2:15

*"We go from a "great tempest" (*vs. *24) to a "great calm" (*vs. *26) because of a great Savior!" Warren W. Wiersbe*

9

AUGUST 15, 2001

Matthew Nine

"Then touched he their eyes, saying, according to your faith be it unto you." Matthew 9:29

"How is my faith? Do I believe in the power of Jesus enough to see Him take care of and provide for my needs?"

- My first journal entry; 2001

I pondered this thought in August of 2001. Six months later I began facing the start of a battle with Multiple Sclerosis. Within months I lost the use of my right arm, making Chinese a rather difficult meal to consume. I purchased a gray cane from a local corner store, sweetly nicknamed, Candy, by my present first grade class, and eventually stepped down from my one-year teaching career due to an inability to walk or drive.

It was July 14, 2004, three years later, when my husband and I listened in awe as my neurologist quietly stated,

"You always tell me you are praying people; this is the only explanation I can give." He went on to inform us that the three lesions on my brain, and the one on my spine, were gone. Gone. We were told this was an impossibility, a medical mystery. To this we smiled, for we knew, "With God all things are possible."

Today as I reread the start of my journal journey, I can see the difference Christ made in me through my season of hardship. I see the power He demonstrated in my life through His hand of healing, and I stand proudly, yet humble, as I answer my original question of faith and say, "Yes, I believe in the power of Jesus." I ask you now, how is your faith? Do you believe in the power of Jesus enough to see Him take care of and provide for your needs? Can you testify of His providence in your life due to your faith or do you sit back, determined the stories of healing found in the Bible are nothing more than good stories? Some say, it is not my faith, but God's sovereignty, that heals. I believe this fully, yet I also see the words of Christ spoken to those whose faith abounds. God's hand of healing begins with the Spiritual healing found in Salvation. Notice each time Jesus heals a physical need, the faith of one is recognized and received by Jesus Christ. Prayer works; faith heals.

"The effectual fervent prayer of a righteous man availeth much."
James 5:16

What was/is your story? Where was/is your faith?

____

____

____

____

____

____

There is power in faith. Prayer takes faith; faith leads to prayer. This is a beautiful cycle that comes free with the gift of Salvation. If you are not utilizing this power, may the faith found in Matthew 9 light your fire and encourage you to follow in the submission of His healing. Before delving into your personal study, focus on the words, actions, and heart seen in those who have this faith in Christ. You will see the faith of a friend, the faith of a father, the faith of an ill-laden woman, the faith of the physically blind, and the faith of the scattered.

"And, behold, they brought to Him a man sick of the palsy, lying on a bed; and Jesus seeing their faith said unto the sick of the palsy; Son, be of good cheer; thy sins be forgiven thee. And he arose, and departed to his house." Matthew 9:2, 7 (Mark 2: 3-12; Luke 5: 18-26)

The faith of a friend is so vital for every human heart; that is the message of this passage. True friendship goes both ways and often switches roles. It switches from crying the tears to being the shoulder that is cried upon, and back again. Think about that friend whom you carried through their dark time, whether a physical illness in which you prayed for healing, a spiritual battle where you presented needed Scripture, or an emotional sadness when all you could do was sit there in silent support. Whatever you did for that friend in their darkest hour is a natural response of a friend.

These four men were friends. By their faith in the power of Jesus, these men unified their efforts to get their unsaved, paraplegic friend to the Savior at all costs. By their faith, this man was forgiven of his sins. The faith of another did not save this man, rather the demonstrated faith of friends led him to his personal faith in Jesus Christ. Then, to prove to the unbelieving Pharisees, Jesus fully healed this man from a lifelong plague, restoring his every muscle so he could rise and walk. How beautiful is the hand of God? There was no need for physical therapy, no rising in probable pain. Just an ordinary miracle of God requested and believed by faith.

"Arise, take up thy bed, and go unto thine house. And he arose, and departed to his house." Matthew 9:6-7

To offer my shoulder for a friend to cry on is a rewarding position for me. I feel honored to help a friend through their tears and frustrations. I love to bring a smile or laughter to the brokenhearted, for it brings a smile to my own heart. To touch a friend's life is one of life's favored achievements. On the other hand, to be the friend with the tears, allowing another to carry them for me, is a difficult challenge. I tend to hide my prayer requests in the safety of my marriage, and hinder the strengthening among friends.

I thought nothing of this until a few close friends expressed their hearts, "You are always there for us, but you go through your hardships alone. It makes us feel sad and helpless."

To be a faith friend requires both positions; presenting your friend to Jesus, and being presented to Jesus. Prayer saves; prayer heals. There is power in the prayers of a faith-bound friend. This I am in the process of learning; I'm testing it out, for it is a new goal stirred on by the words of my faith-bound friends. Have I mastered this? No! It's like ordering pizza. I won't do it. What if Mr. Domino's man doesn't like my picky order? What if he tells me no? Then what would I do? I'll tell you. I would hang up frazzled and sit with a bowl of Mini Wheats. Pizza ordering is frightening. My chest is tightening just at the thought. Regardless of my fearful denial of a large pizza, light cheese and pineapple on the whole thing, green peppers and onions on one half, and pepperoni and ham on the other, I'm not asking my friends to accommodate my ridiculously picky pizza order, I'm asking them to present me to Jesus.

Can you do what I am going to make myself do right now? Contact your faith friend with a prayer request. If you don't have a request pressed on your heart, then take this time to let your friend know that you are praying for their request at this very moment. Are you proud of me? I am practicing what I am preaching. I am sending out a text message to my circle of faith friends asking them to pray with me on behalf of a test result that I am waiting on.

Funny, the first response I received was from Elizabeth, the very friend that asked me to learn this lesson years ago, promising to pray and thanking me for sharing this prayer with her. Faith friends are so vital. Wherever you are in the friendship (praying or being prayed for), don't take it lightly. Your responsibility is the privilege of going to Jesus.

"Behold, there came a certain ruler, and worshipped Him, saying, My daughter is even now dead: but come and lay thy hand upon her, and she shall live....he went in, and took her by the hand, and the maid arose." Matthew 9:18-26 (Mark 5: 22-43; Luke 8:41-56)

Jairus' daughter was 12 years old and lying on her death bed. It brought Jairus to his knees, helpless and empty, having no other solution but to run and fall down in worship at the Master's feet. There is little information about this man. We know he was a man of money. We know he had a position as ruler in the synagogue, and we know he had an only daughter, ill to the point of death. We may not know his story, but we do know his outcome. This father's faith is a picture of God's desire to heal at the pouring out of one's request.

"And, behold, a woman, which was diseased with an issue of blood twelve years, came behind Him, and touched the hem of His garment: For she said within herself, if I may but touch His garment, I shall be whole. And when He saw her, He said, Daughter, be of good comfort; thy faith hath made thee whole. And the woman was made whole from that hour." Matthew 9:20-22 (Mark 5:22-43; Luke 8:41-56)

This woman fought a disease for twelve years, she sought out doctors far and wide and expended her finances for their many services, all to no avail. When she heard of Jesus Christ, she went to Him, believing He would be her answer. By touching the hem of His garment, the healing power of Jesus ran through her body, and immediately, she felt her body had been healed from her terrible disease. This woman's heart is a picture of God's desire to heal with just the action of faith.

"And when Jesus departed thence, two blind men followed Him,

crying, and saying, Thou Son of David, have mercy on us. And when He was come into the house, the blind men came to Him: and Jesus saith unto them, Believe ye that I am able to do this? They said unto Him, Yea, Lord. Then He touched their eyes, saying, According to your faith be it unto you." Matthew 9:27-29

We have seen the faith of a friend help another, the faith of a father heal his child, and the faith of an individual bring healing upon herself. Here, we see a physical example of our spiritual state. If I may say, a spiritual state can be seen in both the saved and the unsaved. The unsaved display blind faith on the day of salvation, the saved grow their faith in the circumstances of life.

"Blessed are they that have not seen, and yet have believed." John 20:29

I wonder if Jesus thought of the faith found in these men, and the many others who didn't see the face of the Savior, yet cried out for His mercy when He spoke with His disciple Thomas a few years later. You see, Thomas, a disciple who knew the teaching of Jesus, refused to believe that Christ rose from the grave until he saw Christ with his own eyes. When Jesus shows himself to Thomas, it is then that Jesus corrects him of his dependence on physical eyesight and says, "Blessed are they, Thomas, that have not seen, and yet have believed."

Study Options:

The words of Jesus:

Matthew 9:2, 4-6, 9, 12-13, 15-17, 22, 24, 28-30, 37-38

____

____

____

____

____

The questions of the Pharisees:

Matthew 9:3, 10-17, 34

The responses of the healed:

Matthew 9:7, 9, 22, 25, 30-31, 33

The heart of Christ:

Matthew 9:35-38

Memory Goal:

"Confess your faults one to another, and pray one for another, that ye may be healed. The effectual fervent prayer of a righteous man availeth much." James 5:16

"So then faith cometh by hearing, and hearing by the Word of God." Romans 10:17

God may have you wait, but He will show Himself faithful.

Believe.

GIRL TIME

Matthew Ten

"The disciple is not above the master, nor the servant above his lord. It is enough for the disciple that he be as his master, and the servant as his lord." Matthew 10: 24-25

The final example of faith displayed in Chapter Nine is the faith of the scattered. As word began to spread of the miraculous healing performed by Christ Jesus, more people flocked to Christ, desiring even more healing. Jesus, in the midst of touching and saving lives, looked at the scattered crowd and verbally poured out the thoughts of His heart, "The harvest truly is plenteous, but the labourers are few; Pray ye therefore the Lord of the harvest, that He will send forth labourers into His harvest" (Matthew 9:37-38).

There was a world around Him searching for an answer. He was and is the answer. We are surrounded by this same crowd; we have the answer. The Lord is seeking after those willing to share His story to the scattered in need of a Savior. It is with this precious heart of our Savior in which the commission is laid out for His disciples. Matthew 10:1-4 paraphrases the calling of the disciples, and lists the names of the twelve whom are called. Verses 5-23 are the specific instructions intended solely for these twelve men called of God. Verses 24-42 are for those alive in the church age. Today is the era of the church age, therefore take special heed of this passage, for it is written for you.

"And when He had called unto Him His twelve disciples, He gave them power against unclean spirits, to cast them out, and to heal all manner of sickness and all manner of disease." Matthew 10:1

First, we see the disciples, the chosen twelve, Simon, Andrew, James, John, Philip, Bartholomew, Thomas the doubter, Matthew the publican, James, Thaddaeus (James), Simon the Canaanite, and Judas Iscariot the betrayer. Each man was specifically asked of Jesus to, "Follow Me." Each man responded with immediate obedience and turned away from their present lives of work, homes, and schedules. These men were called to exemplify the life of submission. They were handed the power of God, by God.

The Bible says, "For unto whomsoever much is given, of him shall be much required" (Luke 12:48). Take the time now to read through the detailed requirements laid out for the Twelve, and note what Jesus instructs them. Jesus says to stay among the Jews (vs. 5-6), preach John's message (vs. 7; 3:2; 4:17), perform my miracles (vs. 8), take nothing with you (vs. 9-10), stay where you are welcome, and depart from where you are not (vs. 11-13). Oh, and by the way, whatever happens, do not get offended (vs. 14). These are very direct instructions clearly designed for a specific calling. These men were enlisted for training, a training suitable for what the Lord had planned for them.

Following this categorized list of obedience, Christ ventures on with a warning to lead up to a deep strengthening of their faith and divine purpose that is found in Him alone. Here, they are forewarned of their soon to come reputation (vs. 16), and of the receptive response of men (vs. 17-23). Yet, they are reminded, in the midst of their situations to come, for it is not them being persecuted, but Christ. Therefore, Jesus instructed them not to rely upon themselves, but to have full dependence on God.

"The disciple is not above the master, nor the servant above his lord. It is enough for the disciple that he be as his master, and the servant as his lord." Matthew 10:24-25

Our call is much the same to swallow. With salvation comes our call to witness where we work, where we live, where we shop, and where we play. We are called to be a light to the darkened world around us. For me, the specifics of my 'darkened world' around me will differ from each of you. But that is what makes God's plan so beautiful. I am the light God needs at the private Christian school I sub for. I am the light my neighbor's in 'Sin City' need to see. I am the light that needs to shine at the malls around this dark city (it's true! People go to the mall to find that "perfect piece"...what's more perfect than Jesus?). I am the light needed each time I get together with my girlfriends whether it's our night out for sushi or staying in for games. The truth is, my light affects people wherever I am. Not because I am who I am, but because God is who He is. This is my call to shine. What's yours?

Work:____

Live:____

Shop:____

Play: ____

These twelve men were adults perfectly settled in their lives. Each was busy with specific obligations, goals, and reputations. Some were loved in the world they lived in, others weren't. Regardless of who they were in the eyes of others, Jesus looked within and saw their hearts. He knew their strengths and He knew their weaknesses. He knew their reputations and He asked them to be His faithful and true witnesses. You are no different. You have your strengths and weaknesses. You have a reputation, whether good or not. He has asked you to be His light, and unless you claim your position as the disciple to the Master and as a servant to the Lord, unless you embrace your need to submit to Him and Him alone, you cannot fulfill this task at hand.

This simplistic message, to me, is the heart of Matthew 10. It defines the position of the called to the caller, and the attitude of obvious submission that must follow. Sometimes submission is hard to swallow. I understand. I encourage you, the next time you find yourself battling with this issue of submission, think about who you are ultimately submitting too. Overlook the person at hand, and see the face of Jesus Christ.

Before you study out the duration of this chapter, I encourage you to write your heart's thoughts regarding this matter of submitting to your Savior no matter what. Think about the 'who' asking you to do the 'what.' Then think about the Savior asking you to be a light to the world by way of simple obedience, submission. You are able, for you are saved. The question is, are you willing?

____

____

____

____

____

Study Options:

His house, your position:

Matthew 10:24-25

____

____

____

____

His heart, your boldness:

Matthew 10:26-32

His calling, your honor:

Matthew 10:33-39

His leading, your habit:

Matthew 10:40-42

Memory Goal:

"The disciple is not above the master, nor the servant above his lord." Matthew 10:24

11

MEET MY FRIEND LINETTE

Matthew Eleven

"Come unto Me, all ye that labour and are heavy laden, and I will give you rest. Take my yoke upon you, and learn of me; for I am meek and lowly in heart: and ye shall find rest unto your souls."
Matthew 11:28-29

If you were asked to name someone you know that would be defined as a "teachable" individual, who would that be?

____

Why? What about him/her displays this characteristic?

____

____

____

For me, spiritually speaking, it would be Peter. He was so open to the instructions that Jesus gave him and he rapidly obeyed. Socially speaking? I think of my friend Becky. You know that friend that asks you a question or advice and then looks deeply in your eyes in order to attain every syllabic answer you have to offer? That would be Becky. But more than her, I think of Linette. Let me tell you about Linette. She is a wife of 52 years, she is a mother to 3 adult children, a grandmother, and a great-grandma too. She is a Sunday School teacher (has been since the 50s), she sings in the choir (and smiles while doing so). She is the first to sign up to help in the church office, to visit a friend who is ill, or to pray faithfully for the request at hand. She is a spiritual superwoman. I had the opportunity this past week to sit with her during our weekly ladies Bible study. The study was on Peter. Linette taught my son about Peter. She taught hundreds of children about Peter. And there she sat with her notebook open, pen in hand, writing notes about Peter that she was hearing from our speaker. To me, that is a teachable spirit. How easy it would be for my dear friend to check out because "she knows Peter." But she doesn't. She sits and she listens and she eats every word that she can consume in order to draw that much closer to her God.

In this chapter, submission is seen in the life and testimony of John the Baptist whose life exemplified his teachable spirit. We will also see the collapse of cities who failed to display this humble character trait. The lesson of this chapter is that there is an absence of the Holy Spirit when pride and apathy reign in place of the humble, teachable spirit. May we learn from the hardened hearts of the cities at hand the dangers that are faced when a teachable spirit becomes hardened with pride.

Your personal study in Matthew 11 will cover Jesus' words on John the Baptist, breaking down his reputation, calling, and purpose. Jesus' heart regarding this man is a beautiful picture of the honor that comes with a life sold out for the single purpose of fulfilling its call wholeheartedly for the Father. John the Baptist lived a life to be followed.

Take time at the end of this study to search out the submission and the teachable spirit John portrayed, even from his final prison cell.

"Ye are the light of the world. A city that is set on a hill cannot be hid. Neither do men light a candle, and put it under a bushel, but on a candlestick; and it giveth light unto all that are in the house. Let your light so shine before men, that they may see your good works, and glorify your Father which is in heaven."
Matthew 5:13-16

For now, I want to take you back to your thoughts from Matthew 5. You remember Matthew 5, our beloved "self-evaluation" of sin, mercy, purity, and peace. How are you doing in those areas by the way? Just a little accountability (with a smile) for you. For those who may have blocked it out, we studied the importance of a life led by the light of God's Word, and we created a plan to stand in the midst of a dark world. Here in Chapter 11, we will see the outcome of a light that doesn't shine. It is a light that is placed under that bushel mentioned in Matthew 5:15, rather than displayed on a candlestick. This example is followed by a changing point in Christ's message; no longer will He preach, "Repent, for the kingdom of God is at hand" to a nation as John the Baptist. Now He will proclaim, "Come unto Me," to the individual.

So here we go. Matthew 11 is a little deep and is certainly open for a much deeper study. However, this is a book on submission, therefore, we are going to search for its application by way of the teachable spirit. Any deeper study you may desire will be available in the end of this chapter and/or on your own. How's that for leaving you high and dry?

"Woe, unto thee, Chorazin! Woe unto thee, Bethsaida! For if the mighty works, which were done in you, had been done in Tyre and Sidon, they would have repented long ago in sackcloth and ashes. And thou, Capernaum, which art exalted unto heaven, shalt be brought down to hell: for if the mighty works, which have been done in thee, had been done in Sodom, it would have remained until this day." Matthew 11:21, 23

Chorazin, Bethsaida, Tyre, Sidon, Capernaum, and Sodom are six cities specifically spoken to by Jesus. Some had their doom prophesied and, for some, their destruction was already fulfilled due to the darkness within their city walls. Three of these cities were full of evil, some got a second chance. Some were founded within the nations of Israel as cities of light. Yet, when we read the pronouncement of Christ, the destruction upon the cities of light is worse than the outcome of the cities born of evil. Why?

"Ye are the light of the world. A city that is set on an hill cannot be hid" (Matthew 5:14). They tried to hide their light. In turn, hiding their light under the bushel brought shame upon the name of Jesus Christ.

When we look at the three cities of light; Chorazin, Bethsaida, and Capernaum, what they heard, what they experienced, it makes me wonder what happened to these cities?

Where did they go wrong? Why not shine?

Each of these cities witnessed the power of Jesus Christ in the flesh. Chorazin is only mentioned here in Verse 21. It is located near Bethsaida, but the history of this city is unrecorded within the Scriptures. However, "Woe unto you, Chorazin!" is a terrible and heartbreaking one-time reference for anyone to receive as their reputation.

Bethsaida was the nation that produced Philip, Peter, and Andrew (Mark 6: 45; John 1:44; 12:21). It saw its blind healed (Mark 8: 22), and witnessed 5,000 men fed by two small fish and five barley loaves (Luke 9:10-17). Capernaum presently was sitting under the very voice of Jesus as He spoke of their future doom. Capernaum was the city where Jesus worked the most. He dwelt in this city (Matthew 4:13). He preached to their hearts (Matthew 4:17). He healed their sick (Matthew 8:5; 17: 24), and He taught them with His parables (Matthew 13:18, 24). Christ had a heart for these cities;. These cities, however, lost their heart for Him. These three cities are often referred to as the Evangelical Triangle. They were visited frequently by Jesus in the flesh, but they took little notice of His miracles, bringing on their doom with their decision to harden their hearts.

"But I say unto you, It shall be more tolerable for Tyre and Sidon at the day of judgment, than for you. But I say unto you, That is shall be more tolerable for the land of Sodom in the day of judgment, than for you." Matthew 11:22, 24

The next three cities were quite different than the first three. Tyre is first seen when given to the tribe of Asher as a strong city (Joshua 19:29). It became a beautiful and rich city (Ezekiel 27), yet the king had the same heart found in Lucifer (Ezekiel 28:2; Isaiah 14:12-14). The result of their pride is recorded in Ezekiel 26. The city of Sidon is named after Sidon, the son of Noah, of Ham, of Canaan (Genesis 10:15). It was a neighboring city of Tyre, also given to the tribe of Asher (Joshua 19: 28). Sidon's king, Hiram, was a close friend of king David, and pronounced peace and friendship when David's son, Solomon, was anointed king (1 Kings 5:6). That was a strong friendship and a rooted peace treaty that carried through until the time of the Apostle Paul. This city was last mentioned regarding Paul's visit there receiving encouragement among friends (Acts 27:3). This cities demise appears to be its bonded friendship with their neighboring city, Tyre.

Sodom, known by many as a city associated with a pillar of salt (Genesis 19), is frequently referenced for its iniquity, destruction, and overt warnings from God Almighty. With over a dozen passages of evil descriptions and heart wrenching conclusions, this city is a study all on its own. I will offer the first description written of the people of the city, and the final mention of its reputation, providing a further study below for your personal time.

"But the men of Sodom were wicked and sinners before the Lord exceedingly." Genesis 13:13

In short, Christ's blood reaches out to everyone, no matter where they are. The reputation of Sodom is spread throughout the pages of the Bible. However, the blood of our Savior offers Sodom eternal life even in the last days.

"And their (the 2 witnesses) dead bodies shall lie in the street of the great city (Jerusalem), which spiritually is called Sodom and Egypt, where also our Lord was crucified." Revelation 11:8

We see the fall of three cities due to their apathy toward the Savior and the fall of three others due to their connection with pride and wickedness. Throughout the Old Testament, and throughout history, we see the rise and fall of great cities, people reaping the consequences of the sin of their nation. This is where the message of Jesus Christ takes on a new meaning.

"Come unto Me, all ye who labour and are heavy laden, and I will give you rest. Take My yoke upon you, and learn of Me; for I am meek and lowly in heart: and ye shall find rest unto your souls. For My yoke is easy, and My burden is light." Matthew 11:28-30

With Christ comes newness of life. With Christ comes wisdom and knowledge. With Christ comes an expected end. There is no confusion in the way of Christ, no regulations, no rules, no religion. Christ's offer here is a new concept for the believers at this time. The Pharisees had misconstrued the whole purpose of the Synagogue, and ultimately the Old Testament, by creating nonsensical obligations in order to prove one's level of righteousness. Jesus says enough. Come unto Me and I will give you rest from these heavy burdens of religion. My yoke is easy; My burden is light.

The Old Testament demonstrates national destruction or providential guidance as a national whole. Through Jesus, the New Testament proclaims individual punishment or spiritual encouragement based on one's personal desire to know Him. If you are tired and heavy laden due to the laws of religion, Jesus bids you to Himself to offer you rest and peace. He desires to be your door, your water of life, your daily bread, your comfort, your strength, your promised peace, your all in all, beginning on the day of salvation and continuing each day that follows.

If Jesus' words of an easy yoke are a comfort and desire of yours, then determine today to let go of the coattails of your nation, your religion, and even your family. Understand that your relationship with Christ doesn't rest on any of these. It is personal. It's individual. Where you are in your walk with Jesus Christ is solely up to you as an individual. It is the communion between your spirit and the Holy Spirit that will enable you to grow closer to God day by day. Are you willing to rid your life from the ideals of religion, and learn to embrace a free life, full of His love, found solely in His promised rest? Stepping away from religion does not mean you are stepping away from God, quite the opposite. Freeing yourself from the mandates of religion allows you to draw closer to God through Jesus Christ and through the Holy Spirit. Submission is made easy through obedience; obedience is made easy through the humility of a teachable spirit. According to Christ, submission can be seen through simply resting in Him. How precious is our Father!

Study Options:

Take some time this week to study the three cities of the Evangelical Triangle, and the three cities of evil, see their history, reputation, and demise. Record your thoughts, findings, and personal decisions below.

"A wise man learns from the mistakes of others; a fool by his own." -Latin Proverb

Jesus' teaching of John the Baptist is extraordinary. I encourage you to read through His words regarding John's reputation and record your thoughts of him/personal desires for yourself in each of these areas. Enjoy your study.

Physical Matthew 11:7-8

____

____

____

Spiritual Matthew 11:9-10

____

____

____

Reputable Matthew 11:11-12

____

____

____

Prophetical Matthew 11:13-15

____

____

____

Social Matthew 11:16-19

___

___

___

When John sent his disciples to inquire about Jesus' identity, Jesus responded, and comforted John's heart, through the use of memorized Scripture.

Christ's Use of Scripture

Matthew 11:4-6 (Cf. Isaiah 35: 4-6); 10 (Cf. Isaiah 40: 3; Malachi 3: 1); 13-15 (Cf. Malachi 4: 5)

___

___

___

___

___

___

We ought to grow in wisdom and mature in spiritual knowledge, but as we strive to glean more of His Word, we need to remain in love with the simple truths of the Word we once fell in love with. Increased wisdom from Above leads to humility; growing wise in one's own eyes leads to pride.

Jesus' Prayer

Matthew 11:25-26 (Cf. 1 Corinthians 1: 27-28)

___

___

____

____

____

____

Memory Goal:

"But of Him are ye in Christ Jesus, who of God is made unto us wisdom, and righteousness, and sanctification, and redemption: That, according as it is written, He that glorieth, let him glory in the Lord."1 Corinthians 1:30-31

Wisdom from Above leads to humility; wisdom in one's own eyes leads to pride.

12

RELAX…YOU CAN BE YOURSELF

Matthew Twelve

"For whosoever shall do the will of My Father which is in heaven, the same is My brother, and sister, and mother." Matthew 12:50

Families tend to understand the importance of personal involvement by way of verbal communication and physical participation. My husband never touches the laundry; I never dare approach the litter box. I do the dishes; he takes out the garbage. I do the shopping; he fills the gas tank. When we each do our share, our love abounds for one another day by day. Although the tasks at hand are minute, the willingness to participate leaves a great impression of love within our home.

In the family of God, there is a similar understanding as to the importance of communication and personal involvement. As His child, we are to talk to Him daily with words of thankfulness, openness, asking receiving, and with words of apology. We are to hear His words for us daily and sit with readiness of heart to hear what He sweetly wrote out for us. We are to love Him, to simply love our Father. Is that not what the heart of a child does?

Aside from verbal communication, we also have the opportunity to follow Him by way of physical participation, whether it's the simple act of obedience of baptism or attending church, or on a larger scale by heeding to the cry of the lost on the mission field. Whatever it is you need to do for God as your Father, may it be done with your whole heart and with full acceptance of your position within the family of the Father.

As a member of your family, God becomes your God and your Father. Your relationship with God becomes personal, no longer universal. Therefore, fear God out of respect for who He is, but do not be afraid of Him as your Father. Choose to live for God out of your love for Him, all the while, be prepared to receive His mercy when you fail to live up to your own expectations.

Too often we jump into a reputation that is lived out, not for God, but for ourselves and for the eyes of others. That is not how we are to live a life of love for God; that is the life of a Pharisee. A Pharisee lived according to a checklist in which they expected perfection from themselves and to all they held to its accountability. Condemnation poured out to anyone who fell short of this checklist. I am so thankful Christ did not write out a verbatim list of demands for every person to live up to. Instead, He gave us the Holy Spirit who communes with God on our behalf, to lead us where God wants us to go as an individual.

Your position in the family of God is the position of a child living in obedience and love towards your Father and to His children. If you get your heart in the same place as your position, then you have excelled in His wisdom. This equality between one's heart and one's position is the message Christ is emanating. Let your submission shine by way of a flexible heart in place of an inflexible ritual.

"But if ye had known what this meaneth, I will have mercy, and not sacrifice, ye would not have condemned the guiltless."
Matthew 12:7

Defending his disciples and attempting to open the hearts of the religious leaders, Jesus states, "I will have mercy, and not sacrifice." In other words, I would rather see a flexible heart over an inflexible routine. Once again, Jesus is going to use Scripture as His battleground. Listen to His Bible lesson. After he had claimed to have disobeyed God, Saul, the king of Israel, ordered a sacrifice as a burnt offering unto God. But God said, "Behold, to obey is better than sacrifice, and to hearken than the fat of rams" (1 Samuel 15:22; cf. 1 Samuel 14-15). God did not want His sacrifice without the heart of sacrifice. Seventeen years later, King Saul was attempting to kill the future king, David. While fleeing from the presence of Saul to save his own life, this is what happens according to 1 Samuel:

"Then came David to Nob to Ahimelech the priest: And David said unto Ahimelech the priest, the king hath commanded me a business, and hath said unto me, let no man know anything of the business whereabout I send thee, and what I have commanded thee: and I have appointed my servants to such and such a place. Now therefore what is under thine hand? Give me five loaves of bread in mine hand, or what there is present. And the priest answered David, and said, There is no common bread under mine hand, but there is hallowed bread; if the young men have kept themselves at least from women. And David answered the priest, and said unto him, of a truth women have been kept from us about these three days, since I came out, and the vessels of the young men are holy, and the bread is in a manner common, yea, though it were sanctified this day in the vessel. So the priest gave him hallowed bread." 1 Samuel 21:1-6

Saul disobeyed God in order to offer up a sacrifice; David disobeyed God in order to eat the bread of sacrifice. Saul was wrong; David was wrong. The difference between the two accounts is found within their hearts. Saul disobeyed God in self-assurance, in the name of religious ritual, whereas David disobeyed in fear of man, yet depended on God's mercy in time of need. God looked down and saw the heart of each man. God looked down and judged the matter in His eyes. God is the judge, a judge both of justice and mercy. What He does in the lives of others, what is that to thee? God has mercy. Do you? Define the word below, and evaluate your display of mercy.

Definition of Mercy:

____

____

Experience of God's Mercy:

____

____

____

Display of Your Mercy:

____

____

____

"At that time Jesus went on the Sabbath day through the corn; and His disciples were hungered, and began to pluck the ears of corn, and to eat. But when the Pharisees saw it, they said unto him, Behold, thy disciples do that which is not lawful to do upon the Sabbath day." Matthew 12:1-2

Here we see the disciples walking through corn fields, plucking corn, and eating with unwashed hands on the Sabbath (Luke 6:1). I can't help but pause here and say this, I have only been in a corn field one time and it was to pose for a picture in my pink stilettos. My father in law was with us when we pulled over for this fabulous "City girl in a corn field" photo. In his eyes this was a disgrace to all that was country. I don't remember what day of the week it was, but I was wearing pink stilettos, consider that being one in the same as breaking the law of the Sabbath.

The Pharisees were there the day the disciples were in the

corn field. In their eyes this was a high felony according to the laws of the Pharisees. The Pharisees were judging Jesus and His men for disobeying the law of God. It's ironic that Jesus warned against this very thing in Matthew 7:1-6. In the cases of both the disciples and David, the Sabbath was shamed and laws were disobeyed. Jesus used these parallel stories to reinforce God's new message (Matthew 11:28-30) that Jesus Christ, not the law, is the Lord of the Sabbath, and to set apart the difference between the Old Testament law of obligation and the present mercy of the Father.

"And he said unto them, The Sabbath was made for man, and not man for the Sabbath;" Mark 2: 27-28

The Sabbath began on the seventh day of creation (Genesis 2:2-3) and was created to be a day of rest for man and beast (Exodus 20:8-11; Numbers 15:32-36). Over time, the laws of the Sabbath began to abound, turning the Sabbath into a day of displayed righteousness for the eyes of others, rather than what it was intended to be, a day of rest. Today, to the Christian, the Sabbath is not a day to be observed out of obligation to the law, but it is to be respected as a reminder of the present rest into which we enter when we, spiritually, also ceased from our own works and trusted Christ (Hebrews 4:10). The Sabbath is our day to refocus on Christ. Many people have their opinions of the Sabbath. What's yours? I encourage you to compare your personal thoughts to what the Bible says about the Sabbath, the Old Testament Sabbath under the law versus the New Testament Sabbath set free through mercy.

Old Testament Sabbath:

Genesis 2:2-3; Exodus 20:8-11; 31: 13-17; 35:2-3; Numbers 15:32-36; 28:9, 25

____

____

____

____

New Testament Sabbath:

Cf. Matthew 12:1-14; Colossians 2:14-17 (16); Hebrews 4:1-11 (4, 9-11)

____

____

____

____

____

Study Options:

Blasphemy spilled forth out of the hearts of men when Jesus cast out a devil on the Sabbath. Jesus, knowing their thoughts, rebuked them with a powerful warning. It is here we see the unpardonable sin, the very sin Jesus Christ died for, the sin of unbelief in Him and in His Power. Here, the Pharisees are confusing the power of the Holy Spirit for the power of Satan. Satan first demonstrated this sin of misplaced power when he determined in his heart to be greater than God. (Isaiah 14:12-17) Because of this sin in his heart, God created and cast Satan into Hell. Thus the unpardonable sin of unbelief in God Almighty was birthed by Satan and punished by God Almighty. This is why the "Father sent the Son to be the Savior of the world" (1 John 4:14). He made it as simple as placing your trust in the Power of God for salvation (Romans 1:16). We should keep our hearts so pure in the light of Jesus Christ that we do not lose our vision of where the true power comes from.

The Holy Spirit; the unpardonable sin.

Matthew 12:22-32 (24/31)

____

____

Ponder this thought. The Holy Spirit dwells in your heart, therefore, you have the fruit of the Spirit within. Yet, out of the abundance of your heart, your mouth speaks. The question is, what are you saying? Evaluate your words and compare them to the fruit of the Spirit.

The Holy Spirit, the fruit of your words:

Matthew 12:33-37, Galatians 5:22-23

Is it enough to alter the appearance of the outside without refilling the inside with something else? According to this passage, when one attempts to change without the help of the Holy Spirit, it appears that you can invite evil to take residence all the more.

The Holy Spirit, the power to change:

Matthew 12:43-45

____

____

____

____

____

____

Memory Goal:

"Wherewith shall I come before the Lord, and bow myself before the high God? Shall I come before Him with burnt offerings, with calves of a year old? Will the Lord be pleased with thousands of rams, or with ten thousands of rivers of oil? Shall I give my firstborn for my transgression, the fruit of my body for the sin of my soul? He hath shewed thee, O man, what is good; and what doth the Lord require of thee, but to do justly, and to love mercy, and to walk humbly with thy God." Micah 6:6-8

Submit your heart to the Love of the Father over the Old Testament law of God.

13

YOUR PART IS IMPORTANT

Matthew Thirteen

"Who hath ears to hear, let him hear. But blessed are your eyes, for they see: and your ears, for they hear." Matthew 13:9, 16

When I was in Junior High, my church youth group attended an Awana Jubilee, a full Saturday filled with activities, games, food, fun, and boys. It was a fabulous day full of embarrassing memories. One such memory involves a skit competition based on the Parable of the Sowers. I was given the position of the seed that sprung up, "because they had no deepness of earth." I vividly recall springing up from a sitting position while proclaiming, with great excitement, "Boing!" My memory fails me on whether or not we won, but based on my performance alone I believe we should have won, this is truly all that matters.

However humorous this memory is, the reality of Christ's message in this passage is rather serious. So serious, in fact, that He blesses those who see its truth and hears the understanding that lies within its meaning. With that being said, it seems only appropriate that the question that remains is, what are we to hear?

When God created man He was intuitive in His thoughtfulness regarding our needs and abilities. He created us with perfect proportions, eyes to see and ears to hear, along with a charge and a blessing to use them wisely. May we take the time to open our ears to the depths of the Parable of the Sower, and receive the blessing of spiritual wisdom from God.

"Behold, a sower went forth to sow; And when he sowed, some seeds fell by the way side, and the fowls came and devoured them up: Some fell upon stony places, where they had not much earth: and forthwith they sprung up, because they had no deepness of earth: And when the sun was up, they were scorched; and because they had no root, they withered away. And some fell among thorns; and the thorns sprung up, and choked them: But other fell into good ground, and brought forth fruit, some an hundredfold, some sixtyfold, some thirtyfold. Who hath ears to hear, let him hear." Matthew 13:3-9

From the beginning of time, God has instructed mankind to listen to His commands. Adam and Eve were commanded not to eat the fruit off the tree of the knowledge of good and evil (Genesis 2:16-17), yet they chose not to obey (Genesis 3: 1-7). The knowledge of evil is a heart-wrenching battle that causes unnecessary spiritual warfare. When thoughts are focused on Christ, there is no room for evil, yet when evil is permitted inside, the battle of good and evil begins. This is why God set this boundary of separation from the beginning. This is what Christ is desiring for us to see and hear in this passage, to identify with the purpose of submitting to His boundary.

As we walk our way through the stories of the Old Testament we see this ongoing cycle in the lives of the men and women set out to be our examples. God sets a boundary, then man purposes in his heart what he is going to do about it. Each of these examples are representing one of the four seeds found in the above passage.

As you study each seed, identify its outcome with either a

personal testimony in your life or a Biblical character, then record your thoughts below each seed. Naturally, before you begin, pray for God's leading in your life through His Word.

"Some seeds fell by the way side, and the fowls came and devoured them up:" Matthew 13:4

The life of Queen Jezebel is an explicit example of this first seed. Having access to the truth of God's life by way of the nation of Israel, she defied the very existence of God and set out to prove her authority over His. The life of this queen ended as a fulfilled prophesy recorded in 1 Kings 21:23, "In the portion of Jezreel shall dogs eat the flesh of Jezebel" (2 Kings 9:36). There are many today that will be blinded to the blood of Christ like Jezebel. This seed represents those that are lead astray from the power of the Cross. These are not the bad, they are the lost. Ravenous birds are not the prophesied outcome for such souls, but the reality of an eternity separated from God in Hell is the darker end for them.

Verse 19: Reach out to this seed. (Matthew 3:2)

___

___

___

___

___

___

___

"Some fell upon stony places, where they had not much earth: and forthwith they sprung up, because they had no deepness of earth: And when the sun was up, they were scorched; and because they had no root, they withered away." Matthew 13:5-6

This second seed is the common story of many who have fallen away due to an eager participation in God's ministry, yet having little growth, they wither away. This seed is the one that hits home the hardest for me. These are the 'seeds' we serve with side by side. These are those that have tasted the sweet goodness of the Lord, yet slowly began to dry out due to a lack of 'moisture' (Luke 8:6). These are the ones where bitterness, pride, and hardness of heart often reign the strongest. These are the seeds that bring tears to our eyes. This is the seed we need to guard our life against by thirsting always after the Word of God, daily deepening our roots in Him.

"For it is impossible for those who were once enlightened, and have tasted of the heavenly gift, and were made partakers of the Holy Ghost, And have tasted the good word of God, and the powers of the world to come, If they shall fall away, to renew them again unto repentance; seeing they crucify to themselves the Son of God afresh, and put him to an open shame." Hebrews 6:4-6

Verse 21: Guard against this seed. (Hebrews 10:34)

____

____

____

____

____

____

____

"And some fell among thorns; and the thorns sprung up, and choked them:" Matthew 13:7

I think of Abraham and Lot facing a conflict as their families were growing and becoming at odds with each other. Two lands were before them, one lush and beautiful, bordered the city of Sodom, the other, barren and distant from any surrounding influences. Abraham offered the first choice to Lot. Lot chose the lush land for himself and Abraham graciously accepted the humble land that remained. The end of the story is as expected, Lot and his family pitched their tent toward the city, slowly filled their lives with the evil so seductively offered them, and made little room for the fruit of the Spirit to work. Lot and his family became enamored with the cares of that city, and the deceitfulness of riches choked the Spirit so that no fruit remained. Their story is recorded in Genesis 13:5-13 and Genesis 19.

Verse 22: Pray for this seed:

____

____

____

____

____

____

"But other fell into good ground, and brought forth fruit, some an hundredfold, some sixtyfold, some thirtyfold." Matthew 13:8

This good seed is you. This seed is the one determined to hold fast to the concept of submission, the one that strives with, as Luke says, "an honest and good heart, having heard the word, keep it, and bring forth fruit with patience" (Luke 8:15). This is not the one who portrays a perfect life, rather the one who lives with a short account with God. This is the child of God who learns as David did, and acknowledges their life in the flesh, but are confident in their Father. It is the seed who confesses their sin shamefacedly before their King, and accepts His great forgiveness. Let the below verse be the cry of your heart, and may you reap a field ripe with the fruit of your faithfulness.

"I acknowledged my sin unto thee, and mine iniquity have I not hid. I said, I will confess my transgressions unto the LORD; and thou forgavest the iniquity of my sin. Selah." Psalm 32:5

Verse 23: Plant this seed:

____

____

____

____

____

____

Congratulations, you just studied out a promised blessing, now be prepared to receive the showers of Heaven. Christ explains to His disciples in Verses 11-17 why He speaks in parables. He compares the differences of the eyes and the ears, basing them solely on the heart. Some, He says, hear not with their heart, but with their inflexibility of spiritual rituals, whereas the disciples have a fresh heart of submissive flexibility.

The Parable of the Sower is only the first of seven mysteries Christ reveals regarding the kingdom of Heaven. Press on in your personal study with open eyes to the written Word of God, and with open ears to the meaning you are to grasp.

Study Options:

Second mystery, tares among the wheat:

Matthew 13:24-30, 36-43

____

____

____

Third mystery, grain of mustard seed: Matthew 13:31- 32

Fourth mystery, leaven: Matthew 13:33-35

Fifth mystery, hidden treasure: Matthew 13:44

Sixth mystery, the pearl: Matthew 13:45-46

Seventh mystery, drag-net: Matthew 13:47-52

Memory Goal:

"I acknowledged my sin unto thee, and mine iniquity have I not hid. I said, I will confess my transgressions unto the LORD; and thou forgavest the iniquity of my sin. Selah." Psalm 32:5

14

AM I THE ONLY ONE?

Matthew Fourteen

"Then they that were in the ship came and worshipped Him, saying, of a truth thou art the Son of God." Matthew 14:33

Let's start this study with a personal evaluation. Don't sigh! This is an easy one. Consider your average day and take note of what your eyes focus on throughout the day, TV and computer, magazines, books, and the various people you encounter. Next figure out where these "sights" take your thoughts.

Christ says, "Blessed are your eyes, for they see, and your ears, for they hear." We expounded on the importance of our ears being tuned in to the message of our Savior in the previous chapter. This chapter, we are going to look at the few, but precious, words of Jesus, and connect them to the "sights" that He himself is made aware of. Five different times we hear the voice of Christ responding to what the disciples are focusing on.

"And Jesus went forth, and saw a great multitude, and was moved with compassion toward them, and He healed their sick." Matthew 14:13

Have you ever wanted to think only about yourself? Have you ever thought so desperately about your situation that no one else seemed to exist? I want to be transparent enough to answer yes on both accounts. I pray I never forget the phone call I received in 2002. An old college roommate of mine called in physical need. It had been awhile since we had spoken due to the speed of life. She called me for encouragement regarding her arm. To this day I'm not sure what her situation was, all I remember thinking was sorrow for myself as I sat in my wheelchair wondering why we weren't discussing my problem instead of hers. Oh, I hang my head at this hard memory. Am I the only one to have these selfish thoughts?

Jesus Christ just heard that His cousin, His forerunner, had been beheaded by King Herod. "When Jesus heard of it, He departed thence by ship into a desert place apart" (Matthew 14:12). Jesus was mourning the death of His dear friend. Jesus desired alone time with His Father. Then He turned around. Jesus took His eyes off His own sorrow and turned His vision onto the multitude seeking Him for healing.

Through Christ's example, I have made it my personal goal to turn my sorrows into prayer reminders. There are those that God brings to my heart each time I face various situations. This allows me to see others and pray for their sorrows, rather than sulking in my personal selfishness. Whose needs should you set your eyes on?

Open your eyes as Christ did, and find your strength in helping others. Record the needs you need to look at below.

____

____

____

____

____

"And when it was evening, His disciples came to Him, saying, This is a desert place, and the time is now past; send the multitude away, that they may go into the villages, and buy victuals." Matthew 14:15

"They need not depart; give ye them to eat." Matthew 14:16

Next we see the disciples' view of necessities, and Christ's view of opportunity. Hours have passed since Jesus' quest of solitude turned into compassionate ministry. The disciples looked around at the situation, the setting sun, dinner time, the desert place, and no food. With this observation, the men approach Christ with the obvious, and present to Him their plan. Have you ever observed your situation, and ventured to "open God's eyes" to the obvious? Have you ever written up your plan and expected God to concur? I wonder if God fed these five thousand men to teach us a lesson on the difference between what we see and His ability. What was your plan and how did God reign over it?

____

____

____

____

____

"And they say unto Him, we have here but five loaves, and two fishes." Matthew 14:17

"He said, bring them hither to Me." Matthew 14:18

"And He commanded the multitude to sit down on the grass, and took the five loaves, and the two fishes, and looking up to heaven, He blessed, and brake, and gave the loaves to His disciples, and disciples to the multitude." Matthew 14:19

These men focused on the 5,000 men, women and children, and the small lunch of a willing lad (John 6:9-11). Christ saw this same equation. The difference of their view is found in their heart. The disciples looked out with their eyes and tried to grasp what they saw from a practical standpoint, whereas Christ saw the same view, but set His eyes up to heaven, seeking the power of the Father.

What is your plan today based on your viewpoint? Write it out and look at it as Christ did, as an opportunity to see God's Hand of power.

____

____

____

____

____

____

____

"And when the disciples saw Him walking on the sea, they were troubled, saying, It is a spirit; and they cried out for fear." Matthew 14:26

"But straightway Jesus spake unto them, saying, be of good cheer; it is I; be not afraid." Matthew 14:27

Here you are, eyes changed from seeing the obvious to seeing the opportune Hand of God. You are surrounded by the evidence of His miraculous work in the situation that astounded you before, then you move on. Time passes, and again you are presented with another situation. Do you look at the obvious? Or do you remember who your God is? How quickly do you forget what God can do? For the disciples it had only been a couple of hours when their next situation arose. This is when faith versus fear is most evident, when you are in the midst of the storm. Do you see Jesus? If you are holding fast to your Faith in Him, then the face of Jesus is very evident in your life. If you are gasping for breath, gripping for life itself, then fear has overshadowed your faith in Christ. The disciples were in the midst of the storm. What did they see? They saw the storm. If only their hearts stayed on Christ, then their eyes would have seen Jesus, rather than the spirit of fear. How quickly they forgot what He just did and what He can do!

Though Peter was fearful, that fear settled when he heard the voice of Jesus (vs. 27) and with that renewed faith he beckoned the Lord to "bid me come unto thee on the water." Peter felt the faith that conquers fear, and wanted more. Jesus says, "Come."

"But when he saw the wind boisterous, he was afraid; and beginning to sink, he cried, saying, Lord, save me." Matthew 14:30

"And immediately Jesus stretched forth His hand, and caught him, and said unto him, O thou of little faith, wherefore didst thou doubt?" Matthew 14:31

If Peter had submitted his eyes to the love of His Savior, then his emotion of fear would not have intervened with his faith. When we submit our vision to God, we are willingly submitting the very essence of our natural emotion for His use.

Let's add to that opening self-evaluation. Now you can sigh. What are your eyes set on? When you look at your own life what is the first thing you see?

____

____

Where does that sight take your thoughts?

____

____

What emotion does that take on?

____

____

Throughout my life these blanks would have seen many different responses. At times my answers would center around physical images of myself ranging from baby weight that really had nothing to do with being pregnant but everything to do with my excused over indulgence of French fries, to physical images of myself walking with a cane. These times produced both faith and fear depending on my focus. At other times, I would have written about my spiritual walk, times where my dependence on Jesus was so beautiful, so real, and times where I was seeking God's forgiveness for taking His presence for granted. Then there are those times when there is a specific situation or individual that just seems to stand so strong in front of me that I couldn't seem to look past it. At those times I would have needed a lot more space to write on then what is given above. If this is your present state, then I gave you more lines. This is your book, your space. Write out your battle between faith in Jesus and fear of your storm. Sometimes when we see our focus on paper it opens our eyes and sets them straight.

____

____

____

____

____

Study Options:

You began a study on John the Baptist back in Chapter 3 and continued it in Chapter 11. Take some time to conclude your study on the testimony of His life as an encouragement for your personal accountability to stay faithful to your King.

The Testimony of John the Baptist:

Matthew 14:1-13; Mark 6:14-29; Luke 9:7-9 (Cf. Matthew 3)

____

____

____

____

____

____

____

"What man is he that feareth the Lord? Him shall he teach in the way that he shall choose. His soul shall dwell at ease; and his seed shall inherit the earth. The secret of the Lord is with them that fear Him; and he will shew them His covenant. Mine eyes are ever toward the Lord; for he shall pluck my feet out of the net." Psalm 25:12-15

"When thou saidst, Seek ye My face; my heart said unto Thee, Thy face, Lord, will I seek." Psalm 26:8

What is the definition of Faith? Where does faith come from? What is the greatest hindrance to growing faith? When you lack faith what should you do? When the storm is encumbering, how do you focus your eyes on Christ?

Word study on Faith:

____

____

____

____

____

____

____

Memory Goal:

"Open thou mine eyes, that I may behold wondrous things out of thy law." Psalm 119:18

Keep your eyes transfixed on Christ, for He is there in the midst.

15

DIRTY HANDS

Matthew Fifteen

"Why do thy disciples transgress the tradition of the elders: for they wash not their hands when they eat bread." Matthew 15:2

I have a son. In the world of dirty hands, need I say more? However, as a toddler, my sweet little son hated getting his hands dirty. On the playground, he climbed the stairs with the backs of his hands (honestly, I did not teach him this) When finger painting, he used a paint brush. The one time he experienced sap, forget about it, the day was over. That summer my father-in-law lovingly informed me that this was my fault and that I keep him "too clean."

I thought about it and the next time we took our little walk to the park, I took a deep breath, grabbed my sweet-smelling, clean, pudgy little boy's hands and taught him (and me) how to climb a dirty, germ-infested metal staircase with (gasp) forward facing hands. Throughout that summer we learned how to play with all things dirt. He got it. Except for finger-paint, he still won't finger-paint or spread glue with his fingertip.

When I read about the disciples whether out in the corn field or sitting with bread eating with their dirty man hands, it makes my mom-side come out wanting to send them to the bathroom with soap and water. But their dirty-hand eating habit isn't the problem here. Eating habits are never the problem. It's the heart. In this case, the heart of the Pharisees, and that is what Jesus corrects in this chapter:

"Do not ye yet understand, that whatsoever entereth in at the mouth goeth into the belly, and is cast out into the draught? (hysterical...go on) But those things which proceed out of the mouth come forth from the heart; and they defile the man.

For out of the heart proceed evil thoughts, murders, adulteries, fornications, thefts, false witness, blasphemies: These are the things which defile a man: but to eat with unwashen hands defileth not a man." Matthew 15:17-20

In the last few chapters we studied the connection our ears and eyes have to a heart of submission. In this chapter, we will continue down this path of the heart in relation to our words. Our hearts are what produce our words. If our hearts are submitted to Christ, our words will be spoken with grace. If not, the fruit of our words will not match the truth of our hearts, and our lives will be as the examples of pretense stated below in James 3:8-12. In this study, I ask you to evaluate your words. Evaluate what you say on a daily basis to those around you, your spouse, your children, your friends. This chapter will open our eyes to the necessity to submit our words to God.

Think back: what are some of the last things you said to your:

Spouse: ____

Child: ____

Friend: ____

Sibling: ____

Person who just cut you off: ____________________________

"But the tongue can no man tame; it is an unruly evil, full of deadly poison. Therewith bless we God, even the Father; and therewith curse we men, which are made after the similitude of God. Out of the same mouth proceedeth blessing and cursing. My brethren, these things ought not so to be. Doth a fountain send forth at the same place sweet water and bitter? Can the fig tree, my brethren, bear olive berries? Either a vine, figs? So can no fountain both yield salt water and fresh." James 3:8-12

"A spring doesn't gush fresh water one day and brackish the next, does it? Apple trees don't bear strawberries, do they? Raspberry bushes don't bear apples do they? You're not going to dip into a polluted mud hole and get a cup of clear, cool water, are you?" James 3:10-12 (The Message)

Jesus' response to foolishness is formed by the very Scriptures He inspires. 2 Timothy 3:16 says, "All scripture is given by inspiration of God, and is profitable for doctrine, for reproof, for correction, for instruction in righteousness: That the man of God may be perfect." Christ inspired this scripture because He knew of its affect. We see Him converse with Satan in Matthew 4, His words full of doctrine. We will see Him rebuke Peter in Chapter 17 with straightforward reproof. Here, we will see Christ correct the foolishness of the Pharisees as they question the ill behaviors of His followers. Eating with unwashed hands! Imagine the disgrace. Did we not just see this same Pharisaical approach happen in the corn fields?

Before we see the correction of the Pharisees, review your study on judging, and of the contrary reality of the mote and the beam in Chapter 7. These two defiant sins, I believe, are the heart issue of the non-submissive. Be sure to "cleanse your hands and purify your hearts" (James 4:8) of these self-righteous diseases.

Regarding Matthew 7:1-6, whose mote are you condemning while neglecting your own beam? Jesus says, "Stop." Stop living your life for Me just to prove to others that you are living for Me. Instead, give Me your heart, and watch Me live through you.

"Then came the Scribes and Pharisees, which were of Jerusalem, saying, why do thy disciples transgress the tradition of the elders? For they wash not their hands when they eat bread."
Matthew 15:1-2

The Pharisees' determination to outwit the Savior exposed their thoughts as foolishness. Jesus handles their presumptuous ways with public reproof. Yes, the disciples took a bite of bread, dishonoring the Jewish tradition, but their hearts were pure in the eyes of Jesus Christ. These men knew they were right with God; Jesus knew they were right with Him. The Pharisees truly had nothing to do with this luncheon. Yet, they open their mouths and cast forth judgment on the mote they beheld.

Forgive me for being sexist here, but women have a lot in common with these Pharisees, do we not? We are constantly judging others by their trivial actions. Things others do, things they don't do, ways they differ from you, all become an obsession for women. Why?

Jesus turns the open condemnation to where it belongs, to the beam. He says, *"Why do ye also transgress the commandment of God by your tradition? For God commanded, saying, Honour thy father and mother: and, He that curseth father or mother, let him die the death. But ye say"* (Matthew 15:3-4).

The Pharisees' beam is the shame they bring upon the law of God by altering the very definition of the Law in order to appease their own hearts. You see, the Pharisees were so tedious in their ways of obedience that their actions overshadowed the dangers of transgression in their thoughts. God expected obedience from the child to the parent, and He blessed the faithfulness within a child's heart.

"Honour thy father and thy mother: that thy days may be long upon the land which the Lord they God giveth thee."
Exodus 20:12

God is very clear in this command, a child should not reach the point where he doesn't honor his parents. A parent is always a parent, a child always a child. It is true that the relationship between a child and a parent will alter through the facets of life, but the respect and honor should always be present. This is the law of God. The religious rulers, however, made an exception to the Law of God. In other words, they changed one of the Ten Commandments in order to pacify their conviction.

"But ye say, whosoever shall say to his father or his mother, It is a gift, by whatsoever thou mightest be profited by me; And honour not his father or his mother, he shall be free. Thus have you made the commandment of God of none effect by your tradition." Matthew 15:5 (cf Mark 7: 11)

According to the Pharisees, if you explain to your parents that your financial obligation to them is going to be spent on behalf of God, then you are free from the commandment of God. It is easy for us to see the foolishness of this substitution. But are we guilty of the same offense? Do we substitute what rightly belongs to our parents with a self-actualizing sacrifice to God? Mark 7:11 uses the word Corban in place of the word gift mentioned in Matthew. The meaning is the same, a financial obligation. As a child, we have the obligation to honor our parents through a financial gift. We are to provide for our parents in a way a parent ought to provide for the child. Your gift doesn't need to be a form of a payback if they were imperfect parents, nor a form of praise if they were ideal, but an obligation of honor. Whatever God has lain on your heart to give to your parents, give it. Whether financial, physical, or emotional, do your part in providing for the needs of your parents.

Do not use your commitment to God as an excuse to rid yourself of their existence. God would rather have your obedience over a sacrifice. Honor your mother. Honor your father. There should be no excuses or substitutions. To honor your parents could be as simple as honoring their name and memory. My mother taught me something when, as a young child, my father passed away. Although he made some faulty decisions, my mother talked only of the positive, teaching me that he was still my father and through my words I could honor his name. This lesson carried me into my adult years. Physical separation from parents can be difficult, but I have learned that their memory can be honored through our words of respect. If you are in a situation where you cannot offer a tangible gift to your parents, then with your words, honor their name. However, if you are capable of obeying God to the fullest, then obey as a child of God, not as a Pharisee. Take the time now to remember who your parents are/were. Honor them with your words below, then pray for a way you can enact Exodus 20:12 and receive the blessing promised by God.

What can you do to truly honor them today?

____

____

____

____

____

____

____

"Do not ye yet understand, that whatsoever entereth in at the mouth goeth into the belly, and is cast out into the draught? But those things which proceed out of the mouth come forth from the heart; and they defile the man, For out of the heart proceed..." Matthew 15:17-19

Jesus concludes this lesson with an opportunity to instruct the disciples in righteousness (1 Timothy 3:16). It is here He teaches the connection between the heart and the thoughts of man. Christ says, do not place your concentration on futile consumption that, in the end, is cast out of the body. Instead, take thought of your words, for your words provide the best representation of your heart. According to Jeremiah 17:9, "Our hearts are desperately wicked." Yet, with Christ in our hearts, they are washed pure through His sanctification. Therefore, through His power, we then have the ability to control the evil that our hearts naturally conjure up. Paul gives us a solution in 2 Corinthians 10:5-6:

"Casting down imaginations, and every high thing that exalteth itself against the knowledge of God, and bringing into captivity every thought to the obedience of Christ; And having in a readiness to revenge all disobedience, when your obedience if fulfilled."

Paul tells us to take our every thought captive. The thoughts that carry us away from obedience need to be treated as prisoners who had set out to destroy us. That is the outcome that is predicted for runaway thoughts. We have all experienced this struggle in one degree or another. We have all seen choices made out of character, whether by a friend or yourself, when those choices were made by the heart over the Word of God.

Being in the family of the Father, you need to take advantage of the presence of the Holy Spirit in your heart. Take time daily to pray for God's protection from evil and for self-control over the thoughts and desires of your heart. Next time you find yourself accusing a fellow sister of their "unwashed hands," stop and pray for yourself instead. Turn those moments of criticism into an opportunity for self-evaluation.

"These are the things which defile a man: but to eat with unwashed hands defileth not a man." Matthew 15:20

Verse 20 records Christ's final words regarding this topic of the heart. Read His words and review Verses 1-20. Next, pen your thoughts on the "unwashed hands" of others in comparison to your thought-life. Where are your thoughts? Are they blinded by the carnal facets of life, or are they set on the eternal desires of your Father? (Cf. vs. 12-14; Colossians 3:20)

Thoughts of your heart:

____

____

Take this passage as a personal charge for your life. Be warned of the dangers of seeking after a life in the service of man. Man is not the way of salvation. Man is not the answer to a sanctified life. When you focus on living for each rule given by man or religion, you take away the very purpose of the Holy Spirit. No longer will you seek to please your God, but you will live for the appearance of a spiritual image. The Bible is very clear on how to protect yourself from this trap of living blindly versus living for God. Jeremiah 33:3 states, "Call unto Me, and I will answer thee, and shew thee great and mighty things, which thou knowest not."

Study Options:

His unlimited grace:

Matthew 15:21-28

His unlimited healing:

Matthew 15:29-31

His unlimited providence:

Matthew 15:32-39

Memory Goal:

"This people draweth nigh unto Me with their mouth, and honoureth Me with their lips; but their heart is far from Me." Matthew 15:8

"Wherefore the Lord said, forasmuch as this people draw near Me with their mouth, and with their lips do honour Me, but have removed their heart far from Me, and their fear toward Me is taught by the precept of men:" Isaiah 29:13

"O Lord, open Thou my lips, and my mouth shall shew forth Thy praise." Psalm 51:12

Do not be led astray by the blind. Rather lead the blind to the Savior through the power of words.

16

DON'T SEND ME A RECIPE

Matthew Sixteen

"Do ye not yet understand, neither remember the five loaves of the five thousand, and how many baskets ye took up?" Matthew 16:9

Leaven. In my world, this is quite the unreferenced word. When I was a small girl my mother used to bake her own bread. Whether it is was to define herself as a matronly icon, or to provide an inexpensive option in a time where money was scarce, I can remember the smell of bread lingering in the small house the four of us girls occupied. Shortly after getting married, I deemed it necessary to save a few bucks on account of my sick leave and decided to run to the grocery store and purchase a hard to locate, barely visible package of smelly powdery substance called yeast. I then went by to my little apartment and proceeded to bake my own bread.

That was the hardest loaf of bread I have ever experienced!

No, I did not try it. I threw it away! I took my stab at portraying the Little Red Hen's philosophy in life: mixing, kneading, baking, and declaring loudly, "I will!" All to learn that little Golden Book was produced for reading enjoyment, not for modeling my life after.

Today, I have a great disdain for the grocery store. I have a greater disdain for those awful yellow packets of yeast that do nothing more than bring forth a small loaf of bread not much softer than a stone. I have since inhabited my rightful place in the barnyard with the other animals defiantly declaring, "Not I." I smile as I drive around the corner to a beautiful chic bread store and hold my head high as I walk out a few minutes later with a fresh hot loaf of asiago pesto bread to serve with my weekly angel hair spaghetti dinner.

Leaven. In my world, this word belongs only in the dictionary. In God's world, however, leaven is referenced throughout both the Old and New Testaments, each time in conjunction with a Spiritual lesson. In this particular case, it is a lesson brought on by the Pharisees, taught by the Lord Jesus, and understood by the disciples. What is this lesson, and how does it apply to our quest? This is our question. What is our answer?

Let's begin in the Old Testament. God strictly forbids leaven from being part of the Passover and in meat offerings. Leaven was a representation of an additive to God's protection and law. He was protection. He was the law. Therefore, there was no reason to offer Him anything more than the meat offering requested in the pages of Leviticus. For further study, delve into Exodus 12:15; 13:7 and Leviticus 2:11; 6:17, 10:12. Pen your findings and your thoughts below:

____

____

____

____

As we enter into the New Testament and more so into the age of Grace, we find leaven referenced five different times as a reminder of the depths of added religion to the gift that God so graciously bestowed upon us by way of His Son. Matthew, Mark, and Luke each rehearse a conversation that Christ has with His disciples, brought on by the foolish prodding of the Pharisees. And Paul speaks passionately to the church at Corinth. The people of Corinth have become blind by focusing so heavily on the law, so much so that it was beginning to overpower the grace of God (1 Corinthians 5). Again, in Galatians 5, Paul writes a letter to a church regarding the danger of allowing the law of old into the church age of Grace. In this particular encounter Paul states, "If you are circumcised, what is that to thee? And if you are not circumcised, what is that to thee?" Whatever your spiritual history or personal convictions, it is nothing he says, "but faith which worketh by love."

You can feel the sadness in his heart as he asks his friends, "Ye did run well; who did hinder you that ye should not obey the truth?" (Galatians 5:7) He enforces the fact that this drive back to religion is not given by the Holy Spirit. Rather, it is of either the devil, or of one's own self-focused determination to do the Christian life in place of living with Christ. "A little leaven," he warns, "leaveneth the whole lump." (Galatians 5:9) As Eugene Peterson writes, "It only takes a minute amount of yeast, you know, to permeate an entire loaf of bread." (The Message; Galatians 5:9)

Paul received this inspiration for the churches just as Christ got His inspiration for the disciples; God inspired this truth. In our passage today, Jesus expresses the importance of remaining submissive to grace over obedience to the law. He says the law was good when the law was needed, but now grace is great, for that alone is needful.

So I ask again, what is this lesson we are to glean from this insignificant word, leaven? For me, I don't use it to bake in my kitchen; it is way too difficult and time-consuming. As I think about it now, spiritually, returning to the ways of "leaven" in my walk with my Savior would prove too difficult and time-consuming just the same. Personally, I would rather love my God through my heart then strive to master higher expectations that prove my actions to be puffed up and fermented.

How is leaven working for you? If you have mastered it in the kitchen, feel free to send me a soft loaf of bread! Fair warning to those of you who are determining right now to send me your "fail proof" bread making recipe, it will find its way on my fridge as a prayer reminder for you, but will never be read or attempted. Ask my sweet friend Julie whose quinoa recipe has been staring at me for a few years now.

Spiritually speaking, is your life seasoned so greatly with leaven that your heart is feeling hardened toward the Holy Spirit? Is obedience to man's opinion weighing you down? If yes, this is your assignment (not given as a law mind you...but as a friend who is growing in this freedom): read the book of Galatians. It is a powerful book to read and study in this area of deciphering what is law and what is the Holy Spirit. Look at your life and ask, what am I doing out of obligation to religion that is weighing me down, and what am I doing through the power of the Holy Spirit that brings me closer to my God?

"Stand fast therefore in the liberty wherewith Christ hath made us free, and be not entangled again with the yoke of bondage. A little leaven leaveneth the whole lump." Galatians 5:1, 9

The Leavened Lesson of Religious Law:

____

____

____

____

____

____

The Learned Lesson of God's Love:

____

____

____

____

____

____

The importance of a submissive heart continues strongly in the duration of this chapter. What I love about the rest of this chapter is the reward presented in Verses 24-26. Take the time to read the divine words of this passage.

"Then Said Jesus unto His disciples, If any man will come after Me, let him deny himself and take up his cross, and follow Me. For whosoever will save his life shall lose it; and whoever will lose his life for My sake shall find it. For what is a man profited, if he shall gain the whole world, and lose his own soul? Or what shall a man give in exchange for his soul? For the Son of man shall come in the glory of this Father with his angels; and then he shall reward every man according to his works." Matthew 16:24-26

What we do, we do not for reward's sake. A reward is promised to those who do things with a pure heart. This reward is not a tangible prize to boast about, but a reward specifically designed and paid for you from God Himself. This reward is life itself. Not life as is commonly lived by the society in which we are embraced, but a newness of life that comes with peace. John 14:27 says:

"Peace I leave with you, My peace I give unto you; not as the world giveth, give I unto you. Let not your heart be troubled, neither let it be afraid."

If you have chosen to believe in Jesus, I want to challenge you to study Verse 24 as it applies to where you are at this very moment. Each of us is in a different place in our walks with God. We are individual children, broken and pieced together again through the precious blood of the Lord Jesus Christ. Be confident as to where you are in Him. Not content, but confident that you are who God desires you to be, and He will work in your heart to grow you when His timing is right. Again, challenge yourself to discover exactly who you are in Him today.

Be careful not to get God's perception construed with your image at church or even in the ministry, for they are simply outlets for you to demonstrate His goodness.

Rather, make your decisions based on this; look at your heart, examine your motives, your actions, your desires, and your walk with Christ.

You in Christ:

____

____

____

____

____

____

Although we are each our own, we all have one thing in common. We have each chosen to come after Jesus Christ by way of Faith in Him. This is the foundation of your relationship with Him. If this is where you are, then embrace the newness of His presence in you. Get to know Jesus as your Lord, your Savior, and your everything. Study the four gospels (Matthew, Mark, Luke, and John) and note the sweet story of His physical life. Personally take John 14 as His prayer for you. Make His life, death, and resurrection your focus of study and spend time alone in prayer with your new King. What is Christ to you? Express your favor and love to Him below.

Your Love for Christ:

____

____

____

____

____

____

If and when you are ready for His love to move you to action, then deny yourself. This does not mean to gather the personal spiritual denials exemplified by others around you, determining to implement them into your own life. My friend, this concept is nothing short of leaven. Keep this step between you and the Savior. Pray that God would open your eyes and prepare your heart for the alteration that may be requested of you, whether it is the start of a new habit or the removal of something present in your life. Whatever the case may be, be willing to accept from the Spirit the answer in which you asked of Him and deny yourself.

Your Denial for Christ:

____

____

____

____

____

____

We need to purpose to press forward by taking up our cross in order to take the final step in following Him. I get bothered when someone is sick, or poor, or tired and they gloomily say, "Oh well, it's my cross." A physical situation is not a cross to bear in this sense; being sick or tired is purely a physical situation. It's life in a broken world. When Jesus says, "take up his cross, and follow Me," He is not referencing your situation, or an opposition of your flesh, but the controlling of your attitudes and your decisions, and determining to stand surefooted in the way you wholeheartedly decide to go.

Look at the path He is leading us down. First, it is rising and taking a step of belief, then we follow with the next step of self-denial. Lastly, now that you have made this dedication, pick up your decisions and personal convictions and keep on going. Record your determination below:

Your Determination in Christ:

____

____

____

____

____

____

____

Why? Why pursue the intensity of a cross carrier? Can it be simply because you are so greatly in love your God? The drive should start and stop right there, but the truth is that sometimes our flesh gets in the way and we need a little motivation. This is true in physical relationships as it is with the Lord. This, I believe, is why we have Verse 27, "For the Son of man shall come in the glory of his Father with his angels; and then He shall reward every man according to his works."

We have a reward coming our way. I love rewards. Rewards make me smile, they give me drive, motivation, selfish ambition, whatever you want to call it. When I know I am going to receive something, I pursue it that much more. It's my mindset of,

"I don't want this cookie as greatly as I want that little black dress." Yet, all too often I cave for that stupid little cookie and have to wait yet another weekend before I can wear that beautiful little dress.

Peter knew what his reward was at this time; he was going to become the foundation of the New Testament church (vs. 18). The disciples received a reward of insight, yet they knew not how to handle its weight (vs. 21-22). In the next chapter, a few of Jesus' men are going to witness the very transfiguration of Jesus himself, again the reward being too heavy for their comprehension. What is our reward? Are there any rewards we receive daily? Are there rewards awaiting us in the Kingdom to come?

The simple answer is, yes. My question for you is what are they? What is God graciously giving you? Bear in mind, sometimes you desire a particular "reward," might it be a bit too heavy for you right now? Answer these questions below:

____

____

____

____

____

____

____

Memory Goal:

"But the fruit of the Spirit is love, joy, peace, longsuffering, gentleness, goodness, faith, Meekness, temperance: against such there is no law." Galatians 5: 22-23

"There is therefore now no condemnation to them which are in Christ Jesus, who walk not after the flesh, but after the Spirit." 1 Corinthians 8:1

17

CAN YOU KEEP A SECRET?

Matthew Seventeen

"And Jesus said unto them, Because of your unbelief: for verily I say unto you, If ye have faith as a grain of mustard seed, ye shall say unto this mountain, Remove hence to yonder place; and it shall remove; and nothing shall be impossible unto you. Howbeit this kind goeth not out but by prayer and fasting." Matthew 17:19-20

The illustration of submission in this chapter is threefold; submission to unbelievable restraint, submission to faith, and submission to taxes. Restraint and faith seem to be a lost art for many, and we would like to see taxes become a lost art. This, however, is not a chapter on how to override the government, so let's let that dream roll right back to the secret chambers of our hearts and turn our focus yet again on what we can do to grow in simple submission.

Peter, James, and John are on a mountain top, a once in a lifetime experience, and are told to not speak a word until, "The

Son of man be risen again from the dead" (vs. 9). Meanwhile, Jesus' other disciples are down in the valley without the faith to move a mountain (vs. 20). As for taxes, well, they will come in the end. Don't they always? For now, let's see the importance of submissive restraint in this chapter.

Submission in the area of practicing restraint is a simple phrase to read, but how difficult is it to live? To live it out means that we have discovered the balance between having restraint without losing touch with reality. This is a tough balance for one to find. I love the magazine In Style, it is a monthly smile that appears in my mailbox, and its pages graze my every fleshly desire (and builds new desires I didn't even know I had). Its pages are dog-eared and circled, its articles are read and reread, yet when I step back and view it through the eyes of my husband I can't help but laugh. There is no restraint or reality in much of these magazines. They can be beautiful and inspiring, yes. They can be dream-worthy, of course, but a reality, not so much. For me to achieve the "beautiful reality" in those pages would require restraint that I am not willing to put forth, such as … not eating.

Think about this area of restraint as you read the short account of Jesus' transfiguration, note the reaction of the disciples. Peter, James, and John witnessed the physical person of Jesus Christ transform into the image of the Son of God himself before their very eyes. These three men fell speechless at the feet of Jesus as they saw His face shine like the sun. They just witnessed the most miraculous event up until this point in history.

"And (He) was transfigured before them: and His face did shine as the sun, and His raiment was white as the light." Matthew 17:2

Before them, they saw the persons of Moses and Elijah and they were talking to Jesus. With their ears they heard the very voice of God Almighty proclaim, "This is My beloved Son, in whom I am well pleased; hear ye Him" (vs. 5). In fear, these men fell on their faces at this sound and the proclamation. They heard the voice of God. These men were trying to wrap their heads around what they just saw and what they just heard. I would imagine they were striving to remember every moment, every thought, every feeling, all to hear Jesus' final words on this matter, "Tell the vision to no man, until the Son of man be risen again from the dead" (vs. 9).

Tell the vision to no man, not even the other men? How do you keep such a miraculous secret? How do you restrain from being "that person?" You know that person, the one that starts a sentence with, "Well, I'm not supposed to tell you this." Or maybe you are that person. Isn't it easy to justify the free speech theory? Or to proclaim that you are just too excited that you simply cannot keep it to yourself? Sometimes, it's these people that wonder why they are not trusted with your heart. Jesus tried these three men with the secrecy of His future death and they passed that test. Jesus knew He could trust these men with this vision as well. These men are a great example of restraint. Reading what they had to keep to themselves reminds me of Mary and all that she purposed to ponder in her heart when Jesus was born (Luke 2:19). Restraint is a great quality to possess. If you feel you are lacking in this area, it is as easy as asking the Lord for His help in your practicing and purposing to keep matters to yourself.

How are you in this area of restraint? Are you counted trustworthy by the Lord and by the loved ones in your life?

____

____

____

____

____

____

____

"Create in me a clean heart, O God; and renew a right spirit within me. Cast me not away from thy presence; and take not thy holy spirit from me. Restore unto me the joy of thy salvation; and uphold me with thy free spirit." Psalm 51:10-12

Many of us know David's story. We are familiar with his physical strength as a shepherd boy, his spiritual faith as he stoned Goliath, and with his faithfulness in leadership as the king of Israel. We are also familiar with his sin, his sin that demonstrated his lack of restraint. Through this sin, he committed adultery, he tore apart the marriage between Bathsheba and Uriah, he had Uriah killed in battle, and he lost his sweet baby boy to death. It is at this low point in his life that David pens Psalm 51. Look at how David ends his cry, "uphold me with thy free spirit." The meaning of David's words is explained beautifully in 2 Corinthians 3:15-17, in which Paul is explaining to the Corinthian Church how to change their mindset from the days of the law (prior to Christ's resurrection) to how to live daily in His grace. Imagine how that would feel. The law contains some 600 commands that were to be obeyed rigorously. If they were not, the Pharisees would be there to let you know. Now, a few decades after Christ resurrected from the dead, Paul found himself accompanied by New Testament believers still living under the weight of the law.

"But even unto this day, when Moses is read, the veil (the law) is upon their heart. Nevertheless when it (the heart) shall turn to the Lord, the veil shall be taken away. Now the Lord is that Spirit; and where the Spirit of the Lord is, there is liberty."
2 Corinthians 3:15-17

Liberty. I love this word, this idea. Through the blood of Jesus Christ as the final sacrifice for all laws and requirements, we are now free from all the heaviness of obligations and rituals. We are now nothing more than children to the Father above. In order to achieve liberty, we need to demonstrate forgiveness for others to witness.

Paul's words in Verse 18, coupled with David's plea of forgiveness in Psalm 51 reveals God's glory in Matthew 17. This is beautiful. Follow this thought. Sin is awful. It is powerful; it is always looming and always within reach. Often times we fall captive to sin's close proximity. But then the blood! The blood that forgives, that cleanses, restores, and upholds is ever present and in the heart's reach for all who believe in Jesus Christ. That is Liberty.

Amazing as it is, Jesus' blood gives us even more than love, forgiveness, and liberty. It alone gives us a new image, a transformation of flesh into glory that occurs as naturally as one who beholds his face in a mirror. This transfiguration process that takes place within is the same in which Jesus experienced in Matthew 17.

Does this alone not prove that in the eyes of the Father we are his daughters, the joint heirs of His son, Jesus Christ (Romans 8:17)? Let's take a moment to compare our transfiguration described in 2 Corinthians 3:18 with the transfiguration of Jesus Christ found in Matthew 17:2.

"But we all, with open face beholding as in a glass the glory of the Lord, are changed into the same image from glory to glory, even as by the Spirit of the Lord." 2 Corinthians 3:18

"And was transfigured before them: and His face did shine as the sun, and His raiment was white as the light." Matthew 17:2

Our face beholds the glory of the Lord, and is changed from glory to glory by the power of the Holy Spirit. Jesus Christ's face shone as brightly as the sun. The word glory appears throughout the pages of both the Old and the New Testament. When speaking of God's glory in the Old Testament, it is noted as copiousness or abundance. When the New Testament references our glory, it is stated as a 'truthful appearance' of God's glory according to the Strong's Concordance. You see, the blood of Jesus provides us with a state only available for His Children; that is the state of His very appearance. David sees this in the midst of his prayer and he receives God's instant forgiveness. David is filled yet again with His glory, and presses on in love with his Father.

In Verse 15, the color of David's prayer changes from dark to light. You can even feel the comfort of forgiveness he receives inside, just after expressing his sin to God and receiving His forgiveness. He begins then to pray, rather than cry out. He says, "O Lord, open thou my lips; and my mouth shall shew forth thy praise. For thou desirest not sacrifice; else would I give it." Oh, to be able to physically perform a deed that would demonstrate to our God how truly sorry we are for our weak flesh. But David understood the heart of God. God does not want a sacrifice. Jesus Christ is our sacrifice. What God wants is your heart, pure and simple. Look at Verse 17, "The sacrifices of God are a broken spirit: a broken and a contrite heart, O God, thou wilt not despise."

God wants you to say sorry and mean it. That is what He desires, and with that, comes true forgiveness without even a look of scorn returned to you from His precious eyes.

Is your prayer a cry of forgiveness or is your heart resolute with your Father? Express below your prayer for forgiveness, your need of help in this area of restraint (whether physical as David or verbal as the disciples), or your praise to the Father for his never ceasing love and forgiveness.

____

____

____

____

____

____

"And when they were come to the multitude, there came to Him a certain man, kneeling down to Him, and saying, Lord, have mercy on my son: for he is lunatic, and sore vexed: for ofttimes he falleth into the fire, and oft into the water. And I brought him to thy disciples, and they could not cure him." Matthew 17:14-16

Next we see the area of submission of faith. Can you feel the pain of this father? Here he is with his poor son, standing before Jesus Christ, proclaiming His deity, while pleading for an end to this battle. The disciples had to turn him away, for the matter was too big for them. Now, here sits the father at the mercy of the Son, seeking nothing more than the healing of his little boy. Immediately, Jesus rebuked the devil and the child was cured in that very hour.

If we were the disciples, I believe we would have the same question on our hearts as they did that day, "Why could not we cast him out?"(vs. 19) I deeply believe His response to us would be the same as it was to His dear men, "Because of your unbelief" (vs. 20). As Christians we are part of the New Testament church, the body of Christ. As such we are to carry one another's burdens. Yet, heartache continues to fester within this precious realm of God's people, weighing down the silent cries of many hearts around us. Why? First of all, Satan is real and he is ready to seek and destroy all who draw nigh to God. In doing this, he plants the thought within us that we are in this period of despair alone, no one is there to care. We must struggle with this sadness alone, for no one would understand. Friend, I proclaim this truth right now; you are feeling this way when you are believing a brilliant lie from the devil. You are never alone.

Secondly, we don't fight enough. Let me lay out a common scenario. Two girlfriends are talking. In the midst of the conversation one shares a burden to the other, she replies with emotion and comforting words, and they continue on and eventually depart. The burdened soul heads home, still with her burden. The comforter heads home with a sadness for her friend, says a prayer, and continues on in her day. Like I said, this is a common occurrence and a beautiful part of friendship. However, what would happen if the friend took the burden with her, praying about it on her way home, and praying again when she gets home? Waking in the night, she finds herself once again in prayer over this matter that is too big for her friend to carry alone. She continues to pray come morning, not in agony or despair, but in faith and fervency.

Consider now the beauty that would blossom from this situation if the friend determined to fast over the issue? Prayer is powerful. It is binding, strong and steadfast. But fasting is a league all in its own. Fasting is prayer at its deepest. It is fervent, mighty, and guaranteed.

"For verily I say unto you, If ye have faith as a grain of mustard seed, ye shall say unto this mountain, Remove hence to yonder place; and it shall remove; and nothing shall be impossible unto you. Howbeit this kind goeth not out but by prayer and fasting." Matthew 17:20-21

All too often we hear the message and feel the comfort of Verse 20. We feel encouraged to display the barest amount of faith required and believe our mountain will be moved, but we disregard the action required in Verse 21. It is this action of prayer and fasting that builds up our minute faith to the size of a mustard seed that enables us to move that mountain. You cannot have relocation if you do not have deliberation. Without the actions of prayer and fasting, mountains are going to remain large and feared in the lives of many Christians.

Fasting has become such an oddity today. This ought to be the first solution we run to when a trial, temptation, or burden comes our way. Strive to attain this mustard seed. Once you do, offer it to a friend. Next time one comes to you with a tearful plea, sweetly offer to fast with them and fight together. The reward is indescribable and otherwise unattainable.

I can testify time and again the mountains that have been moved by way of a fast. I can run. For some, it's easy, but for me there was a time when I couldn't even walk, and when I could it was with the use of a cane or walker. My MS had taken its toll on both of my legs. I was 23 and unable to run. Today, I run.

I can testify of a strong temptation that was breaking a girlfriend's life in two. A year I fasted regularly as she battled with a contemplative sin. Today, she is strong and sure on her foundation again.

I can testify of the cutest little angel who was born premature; doctors knew he had no hope. He survived. They knew he would have a complicated life ahead of him, no sitting, no walking, hard of hearing, and would have mental complications. Today he is the most energetic, healthy, bubbly little boy who has my heart wrapped around his little finger. Why? Because women fasted! Prayer and fasting are powerful!

Take time right now to consider a need on your heart, or in the life of someone you love, whether it is a failing marriage, a hurting child, or a battle with sin. Then ponder what might happen if you selflessly fasted. How might that help?

____

____

____

____

____

____

____

For many, fasting is sacrificing a meal or a set amount of time in order to pray for the matter on your heart. For some, fasting can include much more than food. Consider the laying aside of something that occupies your mind in order to fast like social networking, television, music, books, or hobbies. Seek the Lord for His guidance and help as to how you can begin and/or press on in this mountain-moving prayer life available for all who do it. What is it that you can fast from today and for what? I encourage you to set a date and begin today.

____

____

____

As for the final thought in this chapter, submission to taxes, let me simply say, through faith in Jesus we are a child of the King. We are no longer under the law, but under grace. That being said, Jesus points his children to areas of social obedience, particularly in the area of paying taxes. The religious sect, the Herodians, approach Peter with a question in hopes of framing Jesus as guilty to the law of the Roman government. They simply asked, "Does not your master pay tribute (taxes)?" (Matthew 17:24) Peter, quickly defended His Savior with a retorted "Yes," then he hurried to his Master.

"Simon, what do you think? When a king levies taxes, who pays – his children or his subjects?" He answered, "His subjects." Jesus said, "then the children get off free, right? But so we don't upset them needlessly, go down to the lake, cast a hook, and pull in the first fish that bites. Open its mouth and you'll find a coin. Take it and give it to the tax men. It will be enough for both of us."
Matthew 17:25-27 (The Message)

Ultimately, Jesus is saying, No, you are no longer under the law. However it is our duty to respect the government and do what is right. Have faith in Me, and pay your taxes. Taxes become a questioning topic again in Matthew 22. Feel free to use this space for your thoughts on the matter. For further study you can reference Luke 2 regarding Caesar Augustus' declaration of taxes, the Herodian's interrogation in Matthew 22: 15-22, and Romans chapter 13 as it pertains to obedience to governmental authorities.

____

____

____

Memory Goal:

"Restore unto me the joy of thy salvation; and uphold me with thy free spirit." Psalm 51:12

"But we all, with open face beholding as in a glass the glory of the Lord, are changed into the same image from glory to glory, even as by the Spirit of the Lord." 2 Corinthians 3:18

"Render therefore to all their dues: tribute to whom tribute is due; custom to whom custom; fear to whom fear; honour to whom honour." Romans 13:7

18

FROM A CHILD'S PERSPECTIVE

Matthew Eighteen

"At the same time came the disciples unto Jesus, saying, Who is the greatest in the kingdom of heaven? And Jesus called a little child unto Him, and set him in the midst of them." Matthew 18:1-2

Submission. Here we see it in its purest light, the light of innocence found in a child. We as adults need to realize the purity found in such a degree of submission that is found in the heart of a child. Picture the sweet boy in our story today, sitting in the background quietly listening in to the teachings of this man everyone is talking about. He sees the men that surround him and wonders what it would be like to be one of these men. How his eyes must have grown wide as he hears the voice of Jesus calling him to come. With purity of submission, he excitedly approaches the Master and feels himself weightless as Jesus lifts him up and places him upon His knee. The joy he must of felt at being in the midst of what he was presently daydreaming about. Yet, confusion grows inside as he hears what Jesus is telling these men,

"Verily I say unto you, except ye be converted, and become as little children, ye shall not enter into the kingdom of heaven."
Matthew 18:3

What a compliment given by the Savior! Although his shoulders may have squared just a little bit, I doubt the boy struggled with issues of pride and self-esteem. Child-like, he sat on the knee of his Savior surrounded by bewildered and humbled men. The lesson laid out by way of an innocent child is that the opposite of submission is pride. I ask you, is pride an issue? Jesus saw pride in His disciples after all this time with Him. Yes, they sacrificed it all to follow Him, but there was still evidence in them of the "pride of life." Knowing the hearts of His followers, Jesus wisely takes this opportunity to open their eyes to three specific areas of submission; being an example, accepting discipline, and offering forgiveness. I believe these are the same three areas of submission we struggle with today. They supersede the action of submitting ourselves one to another and takes submission a whole degree deeper. Prepare yourself in prayer for growth in these three areas of submission.

These areas step further within us than a physical guideline or a personal standard. It is the emptying and freeing of ourselves in areas we have held onto out of desperation, guilt, shame, or insecurity. If this study seems to be ineffective for you, feel free to enjoy the read and ponder a thought or two on your way. However, if the idea of setting an example, deepening personal discipline, or seeking and receiving forgiveness is pressing on your heart then I encourage you to take your time, read the passages of the Word of God, pray, record your thoughts, and pursue excellence. Take a deep breath, here we go.

First, we see submission by way of example in Verses 1-10. Submit your day and your power to protecting the innocence of precious children, and look to them as an example of faith and trust. It amazes me each time I curl up on my couch and watch my two guys interacting with one another. To me, it is the most amazing concept. It is as if they are of the same mind. They think exactly the same. They play exactly the same. Their jokes, songs, and humor are spot on with each other. The only difference is that one is 6'2" and the other *4'1*". Despite the size difference, my son is the replica of his father. What I love to see more than their play is the trust in their relationship. My little guy will do the craziest spins, jumps, and attacks knowing that nothing can harm him because Dad is there.

"But whoso shall offend one of these little ones which believe in Me, it were better for him that a millstone were hanged about his neck, and that he were drowned in the depth of the sea"
Matthew 18:6

Jesus encourages adults to look at the faith of a small child and learn from him. Faith does not require explanation. It requires faith. In this same breath, Jesus gives a powerful visual and promise to any adult that purposes to bring harm to a child. He explains the importance of their protection. In essence, He says, if your hand hurts a child then cut it off for your own good. If your foot harms a child then cut it off for your safety. If your eye (your focus) is painful for a child, then pluck out your eye in order to protect the innocence of a child and to secure your own safety. If you fail to do these things it would be better for you to be thrust down to the depths of the sea. Do you understand the depth of God's words here? Ultimately, a child's innocence is far greater than your own right to life.

This passage is a comfort to me and always has been. As a child, I rested in God's arms knowing that He was there comforting me, and that there is a millstone awaiting the neck of a particular individual. For years, I anxiously waited for the millstone to weigh that heap of flesh down to the depths of the sea. It was a prayer of mine. But the visible millstone and loud splash never came. Now I see, one's millstone may not always come by way of death. It may be the continual heartache and emptiness that resides in their existence. This millstone saddens me, for the weight of one man's millstone causes sorrow and confusion in the hearts of other innocent people. Without giving way to details, I will explain it this way, I am a childhood statistic. However, I am a statistic that knew the arms of God and the promise of His protection. Today, I am safe and happy, protected daily in my Father's embrace, for I am that child whose angels beheld the face of God (Matthew 18:10). And I can visibly see the effects of the millstone that hangs around the life of this individual.

Similar stories sit deep in the hearts of countless women today. Verbal abuse, physical abuse, sexual abuse, neglect, and abandonment are the shadows that lie behind the faces of many. Although we stand as adults today, we struggle with the pain of yesterday. If this is a relatable truth for you, I am so sorry for your hurt. I am truly sorry.

Take this time to reread Jesus' promise of protection once again, and take it personally, for it is a promise for you. We cannot time when the millstone will be placed and suffering brought to an end. What we can do, is rest in His comfort that we are protected.

On the other end, if you are the one who battles with self-control, please take Jesus' words to heart. The next time you feel yourself losing control, stop and look into the eyes of that child and see them as God's precious little child and walk away. Do not harm a child, period.

In what areas do you need to grow in to become as a little child? Is your faith weakened due to the harsh realities of adulthood? Are you hurting today because of yesterday's pain? Are you the source of a child's pain? Wherever you find yourself in this passage take this time now to record your status, your pain, God's promise, and your determination to submit this area of your life to God.

Submission of a child:

____

____

____

____

Secondly, we see Jesus' words regarding discipline in Verses 15-19. He begins with the simplest form of interpersonal communication, "Moreover if thy brother shall trespass against thee, go and tell him his fault between thee and him alone; if he shall hear thee, thou hast gained thy brother" (vs. 15). How quick are you in taking a trespass to your brother? According to Jesus, we are to do it immediately and privately. Do you see how personal this communication is to be? This is a conversation that is to take place between two individuals who know one another through salvation. If someone you know hurts you, offends you, (in our world of women, let's say, gossips) or sins against you in any way, you have the responsibility to put on your big girl panties and approach them about it, privately. Privately means, without talking to others about it, nor having this conversation in ear shot of others. May I add this point, if you are the one who caused the offence and/or sin, then be brave enough to take responsibility and apologize for the hurt (knowingly or unknowingly) that you caused. This ability of honest communication is what separates us from Jr. High. Talk, listen, forgive, and move on.

All too often when a trespass or offense is committed, and it is not cared for properly, then sooner or later heartache or hardness of heart is going to take place in their lives. Do not allow a relationship to come to this point. Communication oftentimes heals offenses. We are commanded not to judge, but we are also commanded to love. Finding this balance between judging and loving is discovered only through a prayerful heart. Do not be on a constant look out for sin that you can correct in the lives of others. Rather, love those around you so that if a situation arises you can freely and naturally approach the individual with a loving and honest spirit.

There are those that do not take kindly to being approached or corrected. If this is the case, Jesus, as always, has a solution. If the issue persists, your option is to bring one or two noteworthy friends along with you and together reach out to the person at hand. Speak openly, honestly, and sincerely in an attempt to uplift them and encourage them in the Lord. You will find in some situations that pride will seep into hearts that refuse to repent or take ownership of their transgression. When this happens, and this sin is affecting the body of Christ, then it becomes a church offense and therefore needs to become a church acknowledgement. Keep in mind, this situation is only applicable when one person's sin is hurting or weakening the spiritual growth of the church.

In order to master this idea of open communication, it takes a determined heart of love and honesty. It takes a person that is not easily offended, one that does not take small matters personal, but is sensitive to the Spirit. Is there a situation that is pressing on your heart as you study these words of Christ? If so, what is your position in this situation? Are you the one that needs to lovingly approach another? Do you need to bring it to a few others in order to reach out to an individual? Are you the one who needs to take ownership of your actions or words and apologize for the sake of the unity within the body of Christ? Write your situation, position, and action below.

Submission to discipline:

____

____

____

____

____

____

____

"Then came Peter to him, and said, Lord, how oft shall my brother sin against me, and I forgive him? Till seven times?" Matthew 18:21

Lastly, we see submission in the area of forgiveness. These matters keep getting better and better don't they? We see the human nature of Peter in Verses 20-35. I wonder what situation in his life stirred on his question of forgiveness. After hearing all that Christ spoke of in the previous passage regarding setting an example and confronting a hurting brother, something or someone came pressing on the heart of Peter. It came not with compassion, but with a feeling you and I know all too well, that feeling of frustration. There comes a time when we are at our wits end with an individual. If you have never felt that about anyone than praise the Lord for the peace that passes within, but if you are familiar with Peter's question, as I am, then this teaching is for you.

"Jesus saith unto him, I say not unto thee, Until seven times: but, Until seventy times seven." Matthew 18:22

Jesus answers Peter simply; you must forgive. Who is it that you are denying forgiveness? Pray for that person today and purpose to approach the issue in order to free yourself from bitterness. Forgiveness is only in your hands. Without the details as stated before, I can express to you the pain that comes when there is neglect, abuse, and denial of love. I know these feelings deeply and have faced them from a young age until a few short years ago. Young or old, heartache is indescribable. For those who relate, I am truly sorry, once again, for your pain. My heart breaks even while writing this, for the tears that are shed due to the cruelty of another's selfish behavior. Christian, wrong was committed in your life. But God has given you a new name, and a new song, and a new day. Live in it. For your future's sake, you must choose to embrace what God has given you out of love, more than embracing what was previously thrown at you in evil. Why hold onto the dirty when newness of life was displayed freely on the precious Cross of Calvary? God is so good. Jesus knows and desires nothing less than your freedom from pain. That is the heart of this scripture. Forgive, forgive, forgive and you will be free from those haunting tears, from the bondage of past words, and free from any and all bitterness that has barricaded your prayers.

Remember this also, that forgiveness brings forth wisdom. There are those that I have forgiven, yet I cannot erase the truth of the situation. That does not mean that I am holding on to the hurt, but that I am protecting myself and the innocence of a new generation from continued pain. I will not continue in a blind relationship with anyone that could endanger my child. I will pray for them. But, for me, that is where it must wisely come to an end. And with that determination, a smile easily crosses my face as I sit in the joy of my today without the hurt of my yesterday.

Free yourself of bitterness. How? Honestly, it is a choice. Next time you battle with your thoughts, remind yourself that you have already forgiven this person, regardless if they sought for it or not. Remind yourself that it is over. Believe me, forgiveness is that freeing.

I encourage you to memorize the words of Paul in order to conquer and win the power of your thoughts. That will be the hardest part that follows forgiveness, but it is an exercise that you will see the effects of greatly. I would not ask you to do something that I have not already done. I am living proof that captivity of thoughts is a must in order to succeed. And oh, this success is so sweet.

"Casting down imaginations, and every high thing that exalteth itself against the knowledge of God, and bringing into captivity every thought to the obedience of Christ; and having in a readiness to revenge all disobedience, when your obedience is fulfilled."
2 Corinthians 10:5

There is world of evaluation in this one chapter alone. Do not rush through this. Face these three key points on your knees in prayer, seek the help of your Heavenly Father, and challenge yourself to do what is needful for you. Protect the purity of children at all costs. Be a friend through times of discipline. And forgive "until seventy times seven" (Matthew 18:22), not for another's sake, but for your own.

"So likewise shall My heavenly Father do also unto you, if ye from your hearts forgive not everyone his brother their trespasses." Matthew 18:35

These final lines are for you. Fill them with the thoughts of your mind and the feelings of your heart. Purpose to release the anguish you may be storing. What have you been holding onto that the Lord has allowed for you to let go of? Let go. Replace your yesterday with His daily joy and peace.

____

____

____

____

____

____

____

Memory Goal:

"Casting down imaginations, and every high thing that exalteth itself against the knowledge of God, and bringing into captivity every thought to the obedience of Christ; and having in a readiness to revenge all disobedience, when your obedience is fulfilled." 2 Corinthians 10:5

19

GIVE IT ONE MORE TRY

Matthew Nineteen

"At the same time came the disciples unto Jesus, saying, Who is the greatest in the kingdom of heaven? And Jesus called a little child unto Him, and set him in the midst of them." Matthew 18:1-2

After Chapter 18, this verse seems extremely fitting, does it not? Is the idea of childlike faith or forgiveness a concept too big to grasp? Have you ever looked at a new concept and simply known it was impossible. I do this quite frequently, especially in the world of fitness. For Christmas this past year my husband and son surprised me with a brand new, beautiful, retro-inspired beach cruiser. It had a basket and a bell and everything girlie. I loved to look at it.

A few days before Christmas I turned 34. To some that sounds young, to others it sounds old. To me, it was extremely depressing and it had been at least 20 years since I had ridden a bicycle other than a stationary spin bike. Needless to say, when I got on the bike for the first time I kept the kickstand down and smiled big in order to pose for a picture on my new ride. Oh my, the idea that I was going to kick up the kickstand, and ride with the wind in my hair, was rather intimidating and seemed a tad impossible. However, I only fell one time.

For Christmas a few years back, my husband gave me a small box that weighed four pounds. When he handed it to me all wrapped, I excitedly grabbed it and my arms dropped to my lap. I opened the present and found two, 2-pound weights inside. I loved them. I could not lift them above shoulder height, but I loved them. They were, to me, this very verse come true. At the time, it was impossible for me to lift weights, yet they encouraged me to press on and to overcome the harm Multiple Sclerosis had run through my body. My husband knew my health was improving; he knew my lesions were gone; he knew I could do it. He knew that God had already done the impossible, and he believed that this would be possible with Him as well.

Sometimes, we see things that appear to be impossible, but when we purpose to attempt them we see that, albeit challenging, it truly is possible. When it comes to our walk with God, some things will seem impossible and no matter how hard we purpose to attempt what we know we ought to do for God, it remains impossible. This is what Jesus is talking about in this passage. With man it is impossible.

Within Matthew 19 we see two elements of life that prove this verse of impossibility, that of marriage and divorce and the limitations of a man's self-imposed spiritual determination. Let's check them out in the light of submission.

"And I will betroth thee unto me forever; yea, I will betroth thee unto me in righteousness, and in judgment, and in lovingkindness, and in mercies. I will even betroth thee unto me in faithfulness: and thou shalt know the Lord." Hosea 2:19-20

Marriage is beautiful in the eyes of God. It was created in the beginning with Adam and Eve. It was God's forever plan throughout the pages of the Old Testament, the age of the New Testament, and even today. There is grave beauty in this design. I love these verses from Hosea when it comes to God's view on marriage. Talking to the nation of Israel, His chosen people, He sets a guideline for what His love entails: righteousness, judgment, lovingkindness, mercies, faithfulness, and knowledge.

There are many verses in the New Testament that expound this commitment of love and faithfulness that a man ought to demonstrate to his bride and vice versa. God bases His love for Israel solely on His love for them. I dare say that we ought to base our love for our spouse on His love for us. Consider that marriage in which both the bride and groom love one another in the way God loves the bride and the groom. Do you see peace and civility, love and forgiveness, faithfulness and promise? Do you see submission by the one who is loved and love from the one who is submitted to? This is the plan for marriage. God demonstrated this in the Old Testament, Christ demonstrated this on the cross in the New Testament, and we are to demonstrate this in our marriages today.

Before we probe into the pharisaical debate on the permanency of marriage versus Moses' law of divorce, can we talk a little about the beauty of marriage? I understand that some are not married, some are divorced, and many are scarred from their experiences of a faulty view of marriage. May we set aside our tainted view of marriage, and see the actual beauty that ought to be established in God's plan of marriage?

In order to relay God's love for Israel to our spouse in this realm of marriage, we ought to know His ways. The Message words Hosea 2:19-20 this way, "And then I will marry you true and proper, in love and tenderness. Yes, I'll marry you and neither leave you nor let you go. You'll know Me, God, for who I really am." So who is He really? Ah, time for a word study. Does your heart smile at the thought of a word study as mine does? Please say yes, for that puts a smile on my face. Quite literally, I am smiling at my laptop at the thought of your excitement. For those of you who are looking at my words quizzically, may I say, a word study is an opportunity to understand the meaning of a word and its purpose of use. In this case we are going to look at 7 different words and expound on them. You are still looking at me quizzically… smile, this is fun.

In the back of your Bible you should find a concordance. Begin by looking up the word at hand and find another scripture that contains the same word. Write down that reference and note its connection. Another tool (my favorite) is the Strong's Concordance. It weighs 500 pounds and contains every word and scripture offered us in the Bible. If you do not have a copy laying around your house it is available online. This is used much the same way as your Bible's concordance but to a richer degree due to the definitions of each word in its Hebrew or Greek origin. Webster's Dictionary is always a fabulous resource as well.

Since we are focusing on God's love in order to strengthen our marriage (or set the foundation for a future marriage) we are going to focus on the words found in Hosea 2. Beside each key word I have included a definition from The New Strong's Concordance. I encourage you to expound on these definitions with what you discover in your own word study, and jot down a thought or memory in which you have experienced God's love in your life, or even examine your perception of marriage and substitute it with God's reality. Grow yourself in His manner of love today.

***For Ever:** the vanishing point; general time out of mind; without end*

____

____

____

____

Righteousness: doing what is right in a moral or legal manner

Judgment: a favorable sentence; a participant's right or privilege

Lovingkindness: kindness; goodness

Mercy: compassion; cherishing as in a baby or a maiden

Faithfulness: firmness; fidelity; security

Knowledge: ascertain by seeing

God's love isn't only expressed in the Old Testament, it is also written for His church throughout the New Testament. We know that the church is identified as the Body of Christ (1 Corinthians 12), and that the body of Christ is made up of individuals, and that those individuals are those who have received Him as their Savior. When we read Matthew Chapters 26-28 we can take His sufferings, His death, and His resurrection as a personal act of love demonstrated by Jesus Christ as a pure gift just for you. We will be getting deeper into those three chapters very quickly, however, I encourage you to take some time right now to remember the feelings Jesus felt in human form along with His physical sufferings, remembering all the while that you were on His heart, on His mind. What did Jesus do out of love for you? Furthermore, based on 1 Corinthians 12, who are you because of His love?

Consider this your own little mini study. Take your time to read this passage, and rely on the Holy Spirit to open your heart and direct your thoughts to the area you need in your life right now. Enjoy this study. I know it is not a word study, but it is even better; it's a heart study.

____

____

____

____

____

____

____

Lastly, we see man's love for his bride, and with this we find ourselves back in Matthew 19, back in the conversation between the Pharisees and Jesus. The conversation goes as follows, "Is it lawful for a man to put away his wife for every cause?" (vs. 3) Again, the Pharisees are setting out to see Jesus stumble upon their ingenious testing of the Scripture pointing out Moses' law written in Deuteronomy 24:1-4 in which Moses commands a writing of divorcement. Smug, the Pharisees knew they had Him trapped.

The closer we get to the purpose of Christ's human existence, the worse the Pharisees are going to become. Bear with me as I strangle them with my words throughout these chapters. Lessons in submission are found right there with them, that is, lessons in what not to do. Humbly submit to the Lord in order that pride will not seep in and boast your religious status to an unscriptural level.

"Have ye not read, that He which made them at the beginning made them male and female, And said, For this cause shall a man leave father and mother, and shall cleave to his wife: and they

twain shall be one flesh? Wherefore they are no more twain, but one flesh. What therefore God hath joined together, let not man put asunder." Matthew 19:4-6

How quickly Jesus turns their eyes to the truth. Whether or not they look is another story, but their eyes are directed to truth nonetheless. Jesus pointedly asks, "Have you not read the Bible?" I love when "religious hypocrites" are so busy proving a matter wrong that they neglect to look into the Word of God to find the answer. The answer is always in the Word of God. I have issues with the Pharisees. Let us, as women, not be likened unto this catty crowd. Promise me that you will abstain from behaving in their likeness. Try this pledge: "I (state your name), will not behave myself in the manner of these Pharisees; parading myself in a self-righteous manner before God or to His children."

Jesus takes them back to the beginning of time. Genesis 1:27 declares God's handiwork in the sculpting of Adam and the power found in His infinite breath of life. Genesis 3:23 states Adam's declaration of excitement when he wakes and finds Eve the woman created for his completion. Then in Genesis 3:24 we find the verse that Jesus rehearses to the Pharisees in Matthew 19:5, "Therefore shall a man leave his father and his mother, and shall cleave unto his wife; and they shall be one flesh."

More than half way through our study in Matthew we finally see a submission reference to marriage. It is beautiful to see that submission does not merely lie in the hands of the wife, but that it's the perfect will of God for each of His children as a natural behavior regardless of person or situation. In this case it starts with the husband.

I believe it is fair to say that through this study we can come to realize that submission is often the purest answer to the problem, simply because of the fact that it is the complete opposite of pride.

In the heart of my newlywed year I penned in my journal, "Marriage presents both you and your spouse to the Lord as one flesh. Paul commands us in Ephesians 5:21-33 all that is required of us as husband and wife, both submitting one to another, the wife submitting more than the husband, for the husband is the leader and example. Husbands are to love their wives so that he may present her perfect in the eyes of the Lord. A husband who sacrifices and loves his wife is a husband who is greatly loved of his wife. A wife who submits herself to her own husband is a wife well loved by her husband."

Again, if your experience of marriage was tainted by an example from childhood or from a personal experience, do not allow that to hinder the picture God has of His design. Sin and/or selfishness stains beauty, but God's beauty is always available to those who seek it. Paul lays out God's design in Ephesians 5. This is a great reference study to all who desire growth or encouragement for marriage, but it is Jesus' words of His Father's plan that sets an amazing foundation for all to build upon regardless of the past.

Here is the foundation and therefore your homework. Matthew 19:5-6 can be broken down into 5 actions or phrases. For each one I want your evaluation of it; who is responsible for the action, who is the phrase directed to, what is the meaning of the phrase, and what is a Biblical reference you can use to support the action or phrase?

A man shall leave father and mother:

____

____

____

____

____

He shall cleave to his wife:

They twain shall be one flesh:

They are no more twain, but one flesh:

God joined together, let not man put asunder:

The Pharisees disputed marriage yet the more in relation to Moses' law. I love how Jesus makes the love of a law a personal offense on behalf of the Pharisees, implying that they are no better than their complaining forefathers. "Moses because of the hardness of your hearts suffered you to put away your wives: but from the beginning it was not so" (vs.8). Jesus completes this fruitless conversation with the hardhearted with the conclusion to this matter of marriage and divorce. To sum up Verse 9, "Moses provided for divorce as a concession to your hardheartedness, but it is not part of God's original plan. I'm holding you to the original plan, and holding you liable for adultery if you divorce your faithful wife and then marry someone else. I make an exception in cases where the spouse has committed adultery" (Matthew 19:9 The Message).

According to Jesus, there is a red flag for scriptural divorce, adultery. I believe when God originally said, "Let not man put asunder," He was saying, keep your eyes fixed on your spouse and your spouse alone. If your eyes do not wander, neither will your body. If adultery and/or divorce have been a personal heartache for you, take rest in God's words. Adultery is wrong; it is sin. Forgive the offender as discussed in the previous chapter. I encourage you in this manner, divorce is not the sin. If you were left by your spouse and therefore entered the world of divorce, you are not the guilty; rather you are free from the law of marriage to that person and therefore free to seek marriage as portrayed in God's original plan. Seek forgiveness from God and from your spouse if you were the one who committed adultery against your spouse and children. The Lord will forgive. Accept His forgiveness and press on in your walk with the Lord. There will be consequences, but there are consequences to every sin. Do not allow that to hinder you from growing, rather use the consequences as a reminder of where you have been and where you are now. Allow it to be a reminder of God's loving and forgiving grace.

Do you have a story, a thought, a prayer, or confusion on this matter of marriage, remarriage, and divorce? If so, record your words below and talk to God about it. If your heart is not settled, then turn to a friend who will pray with you and talk your feelings through, or discuss your story with your pastor or counselor for sake of freeing your heart from any guilt or shame you may be holding onto.

____

____

____

____

____

____

____

Just as Jesus gives caution to those who enter into marriage insubordinately, and therefore strive to achieve this union of matrimony in the flesh and without the power of the Holy Spirit, so Jesus says, "those who strive to enter into heaven by their own strength, and not through the blood of Jesus, will face a spiritual impossibility."

Look at this story of the rich young ruler beginning in Verse 16. This man approaches Jesus and asks a common question, "What good thing shall I do, that I may have eternal life." If we stop at this man's question and remember that God knows the very heart of every man, then the rest of the passage makes perfect sense. It's when we focus on the response of Christ and generalize His words to all mankind that confusion may arise, as was the situation with the disciples.

Jesus responds to this man with a recorded list of the Ten Commandments; do no murder; thou shalt not commit adultery; thou shalt not steal; thou shalt not bear false witness; honour thy father and thy mother; and thou shalt love thy neighbor as thyself. The man replies, I have kept all of these from my youth, what more could I be missing? Jesus retorts, "If thou wilt be perfect, go and sell that thou hast, and give to the poor." Sorrow overwhelmed this man, and he walked away for he had great possessions.

Jesus turns to His disciples and states, how hard it is for a rich man to enter into heaven! The confusion of the disciples spills out of their mouths as they question the Savior, "Who then could be saved?" To which, Jesus speaks these most popular words, "With men this is impossible; but with God all things are possible" (vs.26).

I have heard this message preached many times in a way where this conversation is generalized to mankind, but in truth it is a conversation between one individual heart of man and the Lord Jesus Christ. You see, many of us have asked what we need to do in order to get saved. We are each told to believe on the Lord Jesus Christ and we will be saved (Acts 16:31). With that we open our hearts and ask Jesus to be our Saviour and our God, making our salvation possible through Him.

There are those, much like this man in our story, that approach the Savior with self-piety asking what can I do to get saved? Then they rehearse all that they have done, altogether missing the point of salvation. Do you see the message here? It is not that the wealthy cannot inherit heaven, but that each individual has a limitation that prohibits them from entering into eternal life, "For all have sinned and come short to the glory of God" (Romans 3:23). Jesus knew this man's heart was set on self-preservation, that his confidence rested in his bank account. This is why Jesus directed this particular conversation to that of money. Our limitations may vary from his, nonetheless the point stands the same, "With men this (entering into heaven) is impossible; but with God all things are possible" (Matthew 19:26).

Memory Goal:

"But Jesus beheld them, and said unto them, With men this is impossible; but with God all things are possible." Matthew 19:26

20

A LESSON SHE'LL NEVER FORGET

Matthew Twenty

"Then came to Him the mother of Zebedee's children with her sons, worshipping Him, and desiring a certain thing of Him" Matthew 20:20

"Hearken unto Me, O Jacob, and Israel, My called; I am He; I am the first, I also am the last. Mine hand also hath laid the foundation of the earth, and My right hand hath spanned the heavens; when I call unto them, they stand up together." Isaiah 48:12-13

If submission means to willingly place yourself under the obedience of another and if becoming a Christian means that we are to submit our lives to the Lord Jesus Christ, and if a situation is causing contention or confusion within, could it be that God is desiring that you remember who He is and that He is the First and the Last? The First and Last. That means He was and Is and Is to come. He has been where we already were and where we are heading. He has already been, already conquered. We need to focus our eyes on the First and know that yes, this situation is hard, but He is the Last. He is standing there with His hand extended to help you. Could it be that He is reminding you to turn your eyes from the situation and remember that He is in control. Maybe He wants you to turn your eyes off of others, for what happens to them has no bearing on what God has planned for you. Rather, turn your eyes back onto Him and submissively declare, what is that to me? I will follow thee!

I sit here with this concept of "first and last" and find my thoughts bouncing to the most random of places. I think of my eldest sister whom I have always loved and admired. She was the one I desired to be like. She was beautiful on the outside (every boy thought so too), she was beautiful on the inside, always kind and caring, and she was so spiritual. If ever I needed prayer or a verse for encouragement she was the one with the answer. But there was a day in which my desire to be all that she was came to a halted stop. It was just for that day, but a day never to be forgotten.

When we were younger, our church was hosting a teen event to raise money for summer youth camp. That particular year the fund raiser, rather than the typical car wash which always seemed to work out just fine, was a Teen Slave Sale for lack of a better term. The teen class was presented on stage before the church and was sold to church members to work for them for that given day. Sad to say, I was too young to participate, but my role model sister was 13 and therefore fair game. Some were hired to do fun things and were spoiled by friends and family all for a good cause, some were not. Enter my sister. Chatting with her now as to not exaggerate the story, she says, and I quote, "I worked my butt off and got $5. All day! Doing everything including making dinner for that person. Thanks for bringing it up!" She came home that night and cried. She was so tired and utterly grossed out. She ran through her day full of outdoor labor, indoor chores, and making dinner; 13 years old…$5.00. That day my heart broke for her. That day I was sad to admit that I did not want to be her. Of her friends that day, she was the first to be picked up, the last to be dropped off, and the least paid.

First and last. I think of John and Peter sitting with Jesus as recorded in John 21. I think of the feelings that sat in the heart of Peter and in the hearts of the other disciples as they listened to Jesus' words spoken after His resurrection and before His ascension. Jesus and His fishermen-disciples were finishing breakfast on the seashore when He addressed the infamous conversation of forgiveness toward Peter for his thrice denial of Jesus before His crucifixion, and His thrice charge for Peter to follow Him. Jesus concludes this conversation with Peter by foretelling of Peter's time and manner of a servant's death. Peter, taking this all in, turns about and sees John.

There is a brief intermission point of thought here that I cannot put aside. When Peter was walking on the water towards the Savior, he performed that task amazingly until he turned his eyes from Jesus and set them on the waves around him in fear. Here Peter, full of forgiveness and encouragement to press on for His Savior even to death (which was his desire before his denial), turns his eyes off of Jesus and looks at another for comparison. Fear and comparison, there is no place for these in our hearts. Steady your eyes upon Jesus.

When Peter looked at John his thoughts quickly shifted from his personal calling to John's. Jesus' answer is astounding. He puts it simply, "If I will that he tarry till I come, what is that to thee? Follow thou Me" (John 21:22). Peter, if I wanted you to know what I want John to do, I would tell you, but I didn't tell you. I told you, rather, to follow Me; don't focus on who will be first to accomplish great things or who will be the last man in this race. Rest in the fact that I am the First, I am the Last, and I am with you entirely through what I would have you to do, which is to follow me. Therefore, follow Me, period.

First and last. I think of my God in the Old Testament declaring to the Israelites in Isaiah 41, 44 and 48 that He alone is the first and the last. He is the starter of all things and the finisher of the same. I think of my God in the New Testament as He declares in both the first chapter and the last of Revelation, His position as the first and the last.

These verses are too great to simply skim over. Listen to the words of your Heavenly Father:

"Fear not; I am the first and the last: I am He that liveth, and was dead; and, behold, I am alive for evermore, Amen; and have the keys of hell and of death." Revelation 1:17-18

"And, behold, I come quickly; and My reward is with Me, to give every man according as his work shall be. I am Alpha and Omega, the beginning and the end, the first and the last." Revelation 22:12-13

Can you set your eyes on Him? Wherever you are, regardless of what you are facing, can you set your eyes on Him? My sister, as a 13-year-old saw pure and utter pointlessness and painful devastation. Today, a few years later, she calls it a Life Lesson, a life lesson that strengthened her, built up her confidence, and equipped her to become the woman she is today. Peter refocused his eyes on Jesus, and with the help of Christ's hand, continued on in his path on the raging waters. Peter set his eyes back on Christ, even after His ascension, and became the greatest preacher of the church age until the day of his martyred servant's death. God? Well, He remains true to character, the starter of all things, and the finisher of just the same.

Contemplate these scenarios as you think about this idea of first and last, and let Christ's words sink in deep as you read and study today's chapter, "What is that to you? Follow Me."

Matthew 20:1-16

Who plays a role in this parable?

____

____

____

What is the situation at hand?

Where are the laborers working?

When did they begin; when did they finish?

Why were some disgruntled?

What is it that you have been focusing on, a life lesson, raging waves, others in your life? I encourage you to find your words to cry out in promise to the Savior, your Father, the First and the Last, that you will strive to turn your eyes upon Jesus and will submit your walk in order to follow Him. Record your thoughts below:

____

____

____

____

____

____

____

"Grant that these my two sons may sit, the one on the right hand, and the other on the left, in thy kingdom." Matthew 20:21

Next, we find Jesus and His disciples heading up to Jerusalem to fulfill the prophecy of the Scriptures regarding His death as the Savior of mankind. Jesus attempts again to prepare the heart of His men regarding this upcoming heartache. At the end of this conversation a mother of two of these disciples, James and John, approaches Jesus with a request, "Grant that these my two sons may sit, the one on the right hand, and the other on the left, in thy kingdom" (Matthew 20:21).

Jesus' response differs greatly from any response I have heard or seen by a carnal mind. The ten other disciples heard it with indignation (vs. 24), preachers have used it as a 'what not to pray' illustration, my girlfriend and I have debated our differing opinion about it, but Jesus, what does Jesus say? Does He respond with criticism, accusation, indignation, illustration, or judgment? No, His response was sweet and understanding. He gives the opportunity for the sons to express why this question even came about. He says, "Are you able to drink of the cup that I shall drink of, and to be baptized with the baptism that I am baptized with?" (vs. 22) They answer Him with a confident, yes. Sometimes one's confidence in Christ is perceived as pride when really it is just that, confidence in Christ. Jesus knows the heart of every man; what is that to thee?

Jesus proves that He knows the heart when He quickly agrees with His men. In truth, He says, you are able to drink from my cup and be baptized with my baptism, but to sit beside Me is not Mine to give. These men showed themselves faithful in the way and in the walk of the Christian life. Jesus sees their heart through their faithfulness and heart of character. Understanding Christ is to know the innocence of the request at hand. He sweetly answers this desire with a no and a reason why. Namely, it is not His to give, but it is in the hands of the Father. This is a bright light shone on submission yet again through words of reverence toward God the Father from God the Son.

All too often it is said that this mother was in the wrong for asking this thing of Christ, and maybe the content of her desire was wrong, but the manner and boldness it took to present her desire to the Lord is a model approach we ought to take in prayer. Submission in prayer will only ever come when we ask according to His will, yet until we ask our desires of God and willingly receive His answers, we will no sooner learn what His will may be.

Do you see? Who are we to declare what is asked of God and what isn't? God is your Father; ask of Him. This is what He told us to do. If He and He alone deems it inappropriate or ill-willed in our individual life, then He and He alone will say no. We know this truth because it is instructed to us in the pages of the Bible. This mother had to learn this lesson as she laid her desire in the hands of Jesus and received of Him instruction and was given a no to her request.

If you hear of a request presented to the Lord, remind yourself who you are, and that you are not God. What is their request to you? Perhaps some of us need to become less right about spiritual truths and more reliant and open and honest before God.

I'm not condemning you; I'm referencing myself. Sometimes I talk myself out of taking my heart to God thanks to my 'knowledge of His Greatness,' all the while forgetting that it is okay to cry to God, to ask Him why, to tell Him truthfully that I don't understand why He said no to one request or the other. I have to remind myself that I can be honest and I can be me when I pray to the One who created me. When I do this, I am not demanding anything of Him; I am simply giving Him my heart.

Many times we ask questions of the Lord that are stemmed from our desires. Right or wrong we approach the throne of God and ask that He grant the needs and or wants of our hearts. In such cases we fail to remind ourselves that our hearts are desperately wicked and we neglect to follow the example of our Savior and pray, not my will, but thine be done. It is far easier to recall the verses of the psalmist that assure us that God will grant us the desires of our hearts then to remember that our hearts are wicked. That too has the same simple solution as seen above; keep your eyes on Jesus, look full in His wonderful face, and the things of this world will grow strangely dim.

"And Jesus stood still, and called them, and said, What will ye that I shall do unto you? They say unto him, Lord, that our eyes may be opened." Matthew 20:32-33

This chapter ends with another request presented to Jesus; this request, however, was in His power to answer and He answered with a yes. Some will quickly retort that of course Jesus would answer yes and heal the blind man's eyes, for that is what He came to do. I remind you of Paul's request regarding his personal health issue in which he approached Christ three times, and each time received a no. God the Father knows the hearts of man. God the Father knows the outcome, for God is the first and the last. He and He alone will answer each individual request with a yes or a no. The question for you and I is, do we believe this truth or not? If we do, then we will trust that He is in control of every situation, and regardless of the answer to our request, He is the one who knows why He answered the way He did and we need to say thank you. If we believe that God is the ultimate decider of answered prayers then we need to let God be God and not judge the prayers or the hearts of others.

Take some time to take the prayers of your heart to God. Follow after the patterns laid out in this chapter. Write them out, giving them over to the First and the Last. If you do have a question about the fruitfulness of your prayers for whatever the reason, consider this evaluation; is the content of your desire supported in the Word of God? Are your motives pure, is your heart pure, and are you open to receive the answer, whether it be a yes or a no?

I encourage you to reread the two requests that were brought to the Lord, the first requested from the mother and the last from the blind. Read through this chapter in the light of submission to His position as the Almighty. For some, there is a lot to contemplate in this idea of "rightful" prayer. Please allow yourself the time and the words to think through your thoughts and especially your prayers.

Our woman of example presents us with this suggestive approach in prayer; come directly to Jesus, boldly approach the Lord, take time to put forth worship, and ask the question on your heart.

Memory Goal:

"Let us therefore come boldly unto the throne of grace, that we may obtain mercy, and find grace to help in time of need." Hebrews 4:16

"And immediately Jesus stretched forth His hand, and caught him, and said unto him, O thou of little faith, wherefore didst thou doubt? And when they were come into the ship, the wind ceased." Matthew 14:31-32

"Jesus saith unto him, If I will that he tarry till I come, what is that to thee? Follow thou Me." John 21:22

21

I'M SO CONFUSED

Matthew Twenty One

"But what think ye? A certain man had two sons; and he came to the first, and said, Son, go work today in my vineyard. He answered and said, I will not; but afterward he repented, and went. And he came to the second, and said likewise. And he answered and said, I go, sir; and went not. Whether of them twain did the will of his father?"
Matthew 21: 28-31

Submission to the will of God can be intimidating and confusing. The will of God can mean a vast diversity of callings and opportunities. The mere concept that the will of God is distinct and intimate for each and every individual child of God, is a reality too great for a mortal soul to digest. And if the will of God is hard enough to locate, hear, and attain, then to submit to it is a far greater obstacle. Or is it?

There is quite the array of examples in this one chapter alone. Consider these characters, both likely and unlikely, a duo of disciples, a donkey, a donkey's owner, worshippers, temple salesmen, children, a fig tree, chief priests and elders, a father, two sons of opposition, a vineyard owner, employees, servants, and sons. With that list we see the fruit of each individual's labor and effort in accomplishing the will of God.

The will of God is already laid out for each of us. It is not only a big moment that may occur or something that you try to achieve over time, rather it is day by day, moment by moment. It is ever present and ever attainable if only we, yes, submit. What truly matters is not whether we go or do; for He is not looking for vain or empty words, nor is He seeking after obedience done out of obligation. What ultimately matters is whether or not we have submission to His leading. You see, Christ is searching for that one response that stems solely from the heart and spills out with the action that comes only from the depth of submission.

Look at Verses 1-11 about the Triumphal Entry of Jesus Christ in the flesh, publicly declaring Himself as the King of Kings. Every year on the Sunday before Easter many churches celebrate Palm Sunday. On this day this very passage and its parallel passages in Mark, Luke and John are presented to the body of Christ as the preacher expounds on the very heart of Jesus at this time. Here, Christ prepares for His proclamation, knowing that this is not a praise-worthy, prideful proclamation. But that, by fulfilling the prophecy of Zachariah 9:9, "Rejoice greatly, O daughter of Zion; shout, O daughter of Jerusalem: behold, thy King cometh unto thee; He is just and having salvation; lowly, and riding upon an ass, and upon a colt the foal of an ass," He is in turn accepting the praise from those who believe on Him as their coming Messiah.

Many preachers, as my brother-in-law did so many years ago, will give a four point outline on the behaviors portrayed in this passage. They often discuss how we ought to obey as the disciples did in vs. 6, and be as the multitudes as they willingly gave in vs. 8, offered praise in vs. 9, and boldly sharing their faith in vs. 11. But as I read through the words of Chapter 21 my heart is drawn to a small phrase in the beginning of the chapter. Verse 1 says, "And when they drew nigh unto Jerusalem, and were come to Bethphage, unto the Mount of Olives, then sent Jesus two disciples."

The history of the Mountain of Olives is rich throughout the Bible. King David fled for his life in 2 Samuel 15 over this very mountain, the Mount of Olives that Jesus is entering near Jerusalem. David's son, Solomon, in his evil days, built up high places to worship false idols on this mountain (1 Kings 11). These same high places were cast down under the reign of King Josiah a few years later (2 Kings 23). Furthermore, both Ezekiel (Ch. 11) and Nehemiah (Ch. 8) had experiences on this mount with and for their God. Here in Matthew 21 is the first of three occurrences in which we will see Jesus on the Mount of Olives. The other two will be in Matthew 24 and 28. Its final reference is in Acts 1 when Jesus Christ ascends into Heaven bidding His disciples, followers, and loved ones to go into the world and preach the gospel to all mankind.

If you will, join me as I look at what Jesus sees as He stands upon this momentous mountain. Consider His thoughts throughout history, His memories, and brokenhearted moments as He remembers David's sorrow, Solomon's sin, Josiah's eager obedience, Nehemiah's leading of God's people back to the peace of restoration, and Ezekiel's glorious vision of Christ's coming ascension. As He must have remembered what had happened here those many years ago, He can see what is about to happen in the approaching days to come. Such a mix of human emotions makes it a bit clearer where Jesus' passion comes from as He enters into Jerusalem and the Tabernacle, the very Tabernacle built and restored throughout the ages for His Glory. What He sees is not a sacrifice brought on by remorse and sorrow, not a sacrifice brought on by determination to get right with God, and not a sacrifice of love from one's heart of purity for the eyes of their Almighty God, but rather a sacrifice of haste and convenience.

Leviticus is a time consuming, thought provoking, detailed, and picturesque book full of the laws of sacrifice. Honestly, it is one of my favorite studies throughout the books of the Bible.

Maybe it was amazing to me because I was laid up on my couch with hours to pour into it while a soccer game of MS ran through my legs. Maybe it was amazing simply because of Who it was all about, God, the receiver of our sacrifices, and Jesus, the sacrifice. Nonetheless, this book is awe inspiring. It is in this book, that we find what Moses said initially in the book of Exodus, that each person's sacrificial lamb at the time of the Passover ought to be without blemish and without spot. The sacrifice ought to be nothing less than your very best. Cain and Abel demonstrated this importance from the beginning of time. Clean, heart-led sacrifice is the key to offering that sweet smelling savor to your God.

"And in process of time it came to pass, that Cain brought of the fruit of the ground an offering unto the Lord. And Abel, he also brought of the firstlings of his flock and of the fat thereof. And the Lord had respect unto Abel and to his offering: But unto Cain and to his offering he had not respect. And Cain was very wroth, and his countenance fell." Genesis 4:3-4

What Jesus saw in His temple is more of a Cain sacrifice than an Abel one. Salesmen were lining the inner courts of the temple with any animal sacrifice you'd need for your income level, rams, lambs, and turtledoves. People were paying others for the sacrifice they needed to offer to God. Stand with Jesus for a moment and see this scene, feel this pain. Where did Abel's example of love and devotion go? When did Cain's sacrificial obligation become the ordinary? You see, love left the temple and it was replaced with greed and obligation. This scene was not a shock for Jesus to see, but the pain of seeing was still ever present with him as he stood observing on the Mount.

With Jesus there is no time, He is the beginning and the end, He knew the final outcome of the account written in the book of Matthew. How? He was there; He sees and knows it all. More than that, He knows the final outcome of your life, of my life, of the life of Satan. He knows what is going to happen to the Church, the body of believers, and the world as a whole. He knows the value of a soul. He knew the reason why He was standing on the Mount of Olives. He knew that by His standing on this mount he was tying the laws of old and the love of the New Testament together. He was giving a reason for all mankind to live. That reason, He knew, is Salvation. Because of what He knew, He willingly stood. Stand with Jesus.

With all that being said, knowing what Jesus knows, seeing what Jesus sees, and feeling what He feels, walk with Christ as He experiences Jerusalem. In the midst of His vision over Jerusalem, Jesus sends two of the guys on a mission. Some say it is Matthew and Thomas, others James and John; the Bible says "two disciples." The mission is spelled out in Verses 2-6. Jesus tells them to find an ass and her colt, loose them, and bring them, and if any inquire of their boldness, to simply reply, "The Lord has need of them" and all will be fine. When you read this account in Mark 11 and Luke 19 you will see how detailed Christ saw the scenario. In the small details of life, He is the beginning and the end. The disciples heard Jesus' words, His will for them, and the disciples obeyed. I partly see them laughing as they walked away from the stable, donkeys in hand, marveling once again that "it actually worked."

Jesus sits upon the donkey and is led down the Mount of Olives and enters into the city of Jerusalem all the while being praised as, "Hosanna to the son of David: Blessed is he that cometh in the name of the Lord; Hosanna in the highest" (vs. 9). God's servant Zechariah prophesied this detail some 500 years prior, and here we see Jesus performing the words of the late prophet and the will of His Father.

Luke's account, in my eyes, is the most beautiful as He rehearses the continued foolishness of the Pharisees as they demand that Jesus rebuke the multitude for this 'blasphemy.' Jesus responds in Luke 19:40, "I tell you that, if these should hold their peace, the stones would immediately cry out." This truth is beautiful, yes, but it is the heart of my Savior that strikes this passage as beautiful as I read Verses 41-44 and feel the pain of a parent over their child as they see the destruction they will face all because of determined rebellion and complacency. Oh, the sorrow Jesus Christ felt for His city!

Feel that cry, feel that frustration as you enter into the Temple with Jesus and see up close the dirtiness and disgrace being sold and purchased within the House of God. It is here, in Verses 12-17, that we see the disobedient hearts towards the will of God as He says, "My house shall be called the house of prayer; but ye have turned it into a den of thieves" (Matthew 21:13; Isaiah 56:7). It is here also that we see the sweet spirit of the innocent as the children cry out to the confusion of the adults, "Hosanna to the Son of David." You can see this encouraging the heart of the Master, and annoying the very core of the Pharisees. You are there; what do you see, what do you hear…what do you do?

Jesus does what He always did; he purified his church, he healed the sick, and he proclaimed the truth. In the midst of this scene Jesus enters the temple and begins to overthrow the tables and cast out the money changers, proceeding, for the second time (John 2) to purify His temple. We see the low of the low approach Jesus to heal their vision and their broken bodies; He heals them. That's always there, isn't it? His healing. We see the children praising the Savior and we see the Pharisees approach the Messiah. Being ever true to character, they come to Christ demanding that He silence the children. Jesus retorts, "Have ye never read, out of the mouth of babes and sucklings thou hast perfected praise?" (Matthew 21:16) I love this, Jesus looks them in the eyes and says, "Have you not read the Scriptures? Do you not know the words of your father David? If not, let me quote Psalm 8 to you." Oh, can you see the expression on the faces of the Pharisees? Jesus proved yet again that Scriptural knowledge accredits nothing if you don't have faith in the One who is the Scripture.

At this point Jesus leaves Jerusalem and heads to Bethany, lodging there with His faithful friends. These friends we know and love, friends we as Christian women reference ourselves to all too often in both conviction and humor, Martha and Mary, and their brother Lazarus. Jesus' time there is recorded in John 12, however, we will study the life of Mary more in Matthew 26.

The will of God is seen in everyone and in everything. We've seen Jesus say that the rocks would cry out if we failed to praise Him. We see that when God created this world one day at a time, that He saw it all and declared that it was good. We read Psalm 19 and see the universe declares the beauty of God's handiwork. His every creature was created to bring forth praise to the Creator. Knowing this, we read Verses 18-20 and the life, if you will, of a single fig tree:

"Now in the morning as He returned into the city, He hungered. And when He saw a fig tree in the way, He came to it, and found nothing thereon, but leaves only, and said unto it, Let no fruit grow on thee henceforward forever. And presently the fig tree withered away, And when the disciples saw it, they marveled, saying, How soon is the fig tree withered away!"

Jesus was hungry. He saw a tree that He had created to produce figs, to produce fruit after its kind. Jesus drew near unto His very creation and looked upon it. What He saw is not what He created. He only saw leaves. The tree was kind of like a Pharisee. It was a tree created to produce but instead it declared boldly that it was a tree without any production of the fruit it had within itself to bring forth. Jesus condemns its appearance and declares that from here on out, since it was not producing fruit presently, it will lose its ability to bring forth fruit forever. In turn by morning, the tree, leaves and all, were withered away entirely.

Why? Jesus knowing all and being in all, knew this tree. It was His tree. It was created for Himself, so why did Jesus pick this one tree to be withered away and to be recorded twice (Matthew 21 and Mark 11) for you and me to read and to learn from? What was the significance of this tree, of this tree's lack of fruit, and of this tree's eternal outcome? What ultimately was Jesus teaching the disciples at this time?

Jesus has been trying to warn the disciples of Jerusalem's rejection of Himself and of His upcoming crucifixion. The disciples did not understand the severity and the depth of Jesus' words and warnings. He had also warned them of the rejection they would receive from others due to the fact that they were associated closely with the Savior. The final week was at hand. Jesus knew what was about to happen as each new day pressed closer to His physical death on the cross. His followers were still following, but innocently, not proactively. We know this because of their lack of faith (in the boat, in healing, in heeding to His words, in fleeing from Gethsemane, in fleeing from the cross, in hiding after His death).

Jesus has His 12 men with Him. They all stand near this tree. He sees the demonstration of tree-ness from the leaves, but He sees no depth of roots from the lack of fruit on the tree. I begin to wonder at this point if it really has nothing to do with the fig tree in and of itself. I think, more than anything, it was a lesson of importance for the disciples to see the difference in knowing who they were and who they were in Jesus Christ. Jesus then gives a powerful message on faith and believing.

Taking our eyes off the tree at this point and onto the growth of the disciples, we can see more clearly how faith can become the desired outcome. In short, He is saying, build up your faith. If you each build up your faith, then what you do with your faith can be unstoppable. If you fully grasp who you are in Me, then your fruit will never dry up as this fig tree. My power in your hands is insurmountable. Have faith. Have faith in Me and see the power you have over even such a one as this fig tree. There is power in faith.

Later, Jesus returns to the temple with His disciples and is greeted by some questions from the Pharisees. Namely, "By what authority do you do these things? And who gave you this authority?" (Matthew 21:23) Can you hear the irritation in their words? They were fuming from the actions and words of Jesus from the day before. Again, Jesus responds perfectly, not by giving an answer, but by asking a question, "The baptism of John, whence was it? From heaven, or of men?" (Matthew 21:25) The ever-proclaiming Pharisees were silenced. If they were to answer of Heaven, then that would prove their defiance toward believing in God, and if they were to answer of Men then the people would be riotous against them, for John was well loved by many. They could not answer Jesus and Jesus would not answer them. He would however teach them what His heart desired for them to know; He did this by way of two parables.

My request for you as we read through these next few verses is to place your thoughts on the Pharisees (for that is whom Jesus is speaking to) and connect to your "pharisaical" heart what it is that Jesus wants you to learn. Disclaimer, I am not calling you a Pharisee. I am simply placing you and me in the direction of Jesus' words. Sometimes it is easier to apply His message to our hearts when we place ourselves in the situation at hand.

We opened this chapter with some verses from the first parable. It is from these verses that we see the importance of noting and pursuing the will of God individually and submissively. This mere thought alone would shake any Pharisee at the root. Could it be that Jesus allowed the conversation and demise to occur at the fig tree with His followers knowing what conversation was about to occur with the rebellious? That is, all trees were created by God to produce fruit; furthermore, all men were created by God to do the will of God. Which path do we choose, the one of the follower or of the rebel?

The power of the Living Word! Study out the Scriptures and the Scriptures will open your eyes to its very truth. Remember, at this point we are sitting under Jesus' parables with our 'pharisaical' viewpoint. That is we are focused on living for God and not loving Jesus. Living for God is the religious mindset of the Pharisees; loving Jesus is the heart of His children. Knowing where we are hypothetically sitting, may we hear the words and study their meaning. Below the parables are broken up into simple questions. Read the verses listed and answer the questions. See the truth Christ is expounding on and feel the burn of a Pharisees heart. See if you can find what triggers their hatred toward the Savior.

First Parable: The Parable of the Two Sons, verses 28-32

The Father's request

____

____

____

____

The Response of Son A

____

____

____

____

The Response of Son B

____

____

____

____

Which Heart Followed; Son A or Son B?

Who are more prone to hear the will of God? Vs. 31

What was Christ's ironic reference of John? Vs. 32

Second Parable: The Parable of The Householder, Vs. 33-46

The accomplishments of the Householder, Vs. 33

The calling of the husbandmen, Vs. 33

The actions of the husbandmen, Vs. 34-39

The Pharisees answer to Christ’s question. Vs. 40-41

Christ's reference to Psalm 118:22-23, Vs. 42

____

____

____

____

Christ's reference to the fig tree Vs. 43-44

____

____

____

____

The Pharisees' perception and reaction, Vs. 45-46

____

____

____

____

"But when they sought to lay hands on him, they feared the multitude, because they took him for a prophet." Matthew 21:46

Here we sit with Jesus days before His crucifixion. We hear the final words of Christ we learn the importance of choosing to follow after the will of God versus the response of those who defy the will of God. Where are you? What is the will of God for your life today? What is your response to His will? Is your response similar to one of the sons from Parable One, or is it received with indignation as the servants in the second Parable?

____

____

____

____

____

____

____

____

What truly matters is not whether we go or do; for He is not looking for vain or empty words, nor is He looking for obedience done out of obligation. Rather, what truly matters is whether or not we have submission in repentance. You see, Christ is searching for that one response that stems solely from the heart and spills out with the action that comes only from the depth of repentance.

What is repentance? According to the Old Scofield Study Bible, repentance is a change of mind. The Strong's Concordance defines it as compunction for guilt, a reformation, a reversal of decision. At the start of our study on this book of Matthew, we took time to look at some key words: obedience, character, and submission. I encourage you to take that same time to search out one more key element, repentance. What is its definition and importance?

Repentance:

____

____

____

____

____

In this chapter, Christ lays out the heart of repentance ever so simply. Let's break it up. Two sons, two hearers, two outcomes. Watch for submission in repentance. The first son was given instruction by the father to go and work today in my vineyard. This vineyard is referenced time and again by Jesus within the lessons of His parables. By vineyard He means exactly that, a vineyard. However, this vineyard is also referenced by the Old Testament prophets Isaiah and Jeremiah. Isaiah 5:1-7 sets up the foundation of the Jehovah's vineyard, the purpose of it, and the fruit thereof. Reading this passage, it becomes very clear that the vineyard of the Lord is not that of creeping vines, but rather the household of His people, of His chosen nation. Isaiah 5:7 reads, "For the vineyard of the Lord of hosts is the house of Israel, and the men of Judah his pleasant plant: and He looked for judgment, but behold oppression; for righteousness, but behold a cry."

One hundred and sixty years later God sends His prophet Jeremiah to His "vineyard" to express to them the heartache they have caused in God. In Jeremiah 13, we find God's meticulous instructions for Jeremiah that demonstrate what the nation of Israel had succumbed to, that of a marred linen girdle that was altogether "profitable for nothing." Reading this chapter and feeling the sadness of Jeremiah 13:17 may bring to light the conflict that took place within this son's heart. At the start the son says no, but the thought of being that "pleasant plant" in the eyes of the Almighty God stirred that change of heart that led him to action.

Son number two is quite different from the first. He gives quick assurance that he will go work in the vineyard, but his actions speak so much louder. Words are a wonderful gift given to us from above to be used for His praise, but when our words flow while our heart stands defiled in pride or apathy, those words become bitter in the ears of the Father. That is exactly what is happening in the life of this son. His response is a sad commonality in our Christian society today. The epitome of this son is seen in every religious person out there. You see, a religious person is not one that puts his faith in Christ Jesus alone, rather he is the one that merely marks his religion by his words. They claim their personal standards of choice and abide by them with such great severity and self-righteousness, therefore making their own laws their religion. Jesus says, "This people draweth nigh unto Me with their mouth, and honoureth Me with their lips; but their heart is far from Me, But in vain they do worship Me, teaching for doctrines the commandments of men" (Matthew 15:8). Be cautious not to get caught up in your religion, but seek to follow Christ as your Savior.

Memory Goal:

"Jesus answered and said unto them, Verily I say unto you, If ye have faith, and doubt not, ye shall not only do this which is done to the fig tree, but also if ye shall say unto this mountain, Be thou removed, and be thou cast into the sea; it shall be done." Matthew 21:21

"And all things, whatsoever ye shall ask in prayer, believing, ye shall receive." Matthew 21:22

22

1...2...3...

Matthew Twenty Two

"And He saith unto him, Friend, how camest thou in hither not having a wedding garment? And he was speechless." Matthew 22:12

"He saith unto them...If David then call him Lord, how is he his son? And no man was able to answer him a word." Matthew 22:45-46

"Let your speech be always with grace, seasoned with salt, that ye may know how ye ought to answer every man." Colossians 4:6

In preparation for this chapter, I read over my previous notes and thoughts for this study and it bored me. This chapter is too much fun for the long and deep concept I had previously contemplated. This chapter is so full of idiocy that it proves rather comical in study. I don't want to take that from you, or more so from myself. May we brew a delicious espresso and curl up to good humor and rightfully conclude with doctrinal answers.

First, we see the Herodians. Much like the Pharisees, they were a Jewish people. They were temple visitors, but not as religious in their manners as the Pharisees. They were named as such for they were followers of King Herod. Even though King Herod was an evil and unjust king, the Herodians complied with his reign and began to support the taxation and power of the king. They were enamored by Greek culture and money. Due to their political stance they were enemies with the Pharisees, yet they were united with them through their hatred of Jesus.

Second, we meet the Sadducees. They didn't believe in the afterlife or miracles. What they saw is what existed. It was impossible for them to believe the truths of Jesus because it was past their comprehension. If they couldn't see the answer then the answer didn't exist. The wisdom of this world is foolishness to God. Thomas lived this life of the Sadducees. Much of the Sadducees' mindset lead to fear. It was a realm of constant unbelief, constant doubt.

Lastly, there are the Pharisees. Not much introduction is needed for this high-minded religious sect, for we have heard them speak many times before. In fact, at the close of Matthew 22 they are infuriated with Jesus Christ to the point of manslaughter. It is with this intent that Jesus answers their unspoken anger with yet another parable.

With each group of people we read of their intent toward our Savior, their intent to catch Jesus Christ in His words. They were teaming up together to frame Christ in order to put Him away. Therefore, one by one they approach Jesus with questions that would prove Him to fail. They knew these questions would cause Jesus to stumble, leading them to religious victory.

As I ponder this chapter full of questions, my heart keeps wandering back to the mother of James and John. Remember her? She was the mother who approached Jesus with the request, "Grant that these my two sons may sit, the one on thy right hand, and the other on your left, in thy kingdom" (Matthew 20:21). It was a request scoffed at by many; an answer unknown by the Son of God. As I smirk at the questions in Chapter 22, I recollect the emotional question in Chapter 20. The difference that reigns between these questions is in no doubt the approach of the heart. This mother, whether we declare her right or wrong, fell down and worshipped the King, she boldly spoke her request, and then she submissively received her answer.

These men are quite contrary in their approach. The concept of offering worship to this carpenter's Son was beyond their comprehension. They were boldly speaking their inquiry, but the manner in which their boldness came is quite different, and their response is the conclusion to this chapter's study. For now let's return to the questions at hand. Or shall I say, let's get to work.

Question 1 – Verses 15-22

"What thinkest thou? Is it lawful to give tribute unto Caesar, or not?" Matthew 22:17

Knowing the Herodians and their infatuation with modern society, you can see where their trap comes from. These men wanted to serve their physical king and they knew it was lawful to do so. They also heard Christ speak before. They knew that Jesus was proclaiming to be the Messiah. Therefore, they ask as if to set a trap, whom ought we to serve, Caesar, our king and our law, or you? Jesus does not respond with a 'Caesar or me' answer. He responds with a lesson of respect. Read these verses (15-22) and record Jesus' answer or lesson below. The Herodian's response was silent marveling and swift removal. Following Jesus' life lesson, take a few minutes to record your response or thoughts.

____

____

____

____

____

____

____

For further study on Jesus' teaching, read Peter's words some 30 years after this conversation took place. I can't help but wonder if Peter mentally returned to this day of interrogation when he penned his inspired words in 1 Peter 2:13-17.

Study out these short verses and apply them to the area(s) in which you see a need. Grow in wisdom and service and prayer. Give honor to whom honor is due. Record your thoughts below:

____

____

____

____

____

____

____

Question 2 – Verses 23-33

"Master, Moses said, If a man die, having no children, his brother shall marry his wife, and raise up seed unto his brother. Now there were with us seven brethren: and the first, when he had married a wife, deceased, and , having no issue, left his wife unto his brother; Likewise the second also, and the third, unto the seventh. And last of all the woman died also. Therefore in the resurrection whose wife shall she be of the seven: for they all had her."
Matthew 22: 24-28

Quite different from the short and to the point Herodians, the Sadducees took time to state their claim, lay out the scenario, and present the saga they knew would entrap Jesus in His response. Remember, the Sadducees did not believe in Heaven or Hell. They did not believe in anything that was not physically attainable. So, their very question is against their religious belief. Jesus, naturally, knew this. His answer, yet again, was not a debated response, rather a lesson of religious heresy and a lack of intellect.

Read His words in Verses 29-33, and compare them to Exodus 3:6 (the Scripture He quotes in response), then record your thoughts below:

____

____

____

____

____

____

____

Question 3 – Verses 34-40

"Master, which is the great commandment in the law?"
Matthew 22:36

These Pharisees knew and abided by the Ten Commandments recorded in Exodus 20. However, those commandments given by God were not enough to fulfill their need for self-righteousness. If you were to count the laws there were well over 600. They had good laws and bad laws, light laws and heavy laws. They even wrote books about their laws in which they added even more laws. They took God's laws and expounded on them in a way God would not have asked them to.

Jesus answers this question of self-righteousness with one word, one concept, one "law" if you will. That one word is love. Paul says in 1 Corinthians 13:13, "faith is good, hope is great, but love; love is the greatest of them all." You see, Paul is speaking the heart of Christ's response to the Pharisees, love the Lord, love others, and love the life that Christ died on the cross to give you. Neglect the personal spiritual limitations that you set upon yourself. God does not want your self-sacrifice, rather love the Lord your God with all your heart, and all your soul, and all your might. Then the life you lead out of love for the Lord will become the will of God for your life. Do you see the difference here? Stop living your pharisaical law and start loving the very love of the Savior.

Read Verses 37-40 as well as Deuteronomy 6:5 and Leviticus 19:18. These two verses were required memory verses for the Pharisees; they knew these words of God. And it was these verses that Jesus used to answer their 'spiritually wise' question. There are some of us who know our Scriptures, but need to be reminded that they are alive and powerful, not just words to be quoted. Record your thought on the Pharisees' question, their lack of Scriptural belief, and on Jesus' answer based on love.

____

____

____

____

____

____

____

To conclude this chapter of questions, I want to focus our attention on two questions that remained unanswered. These two questions are questions that each of us are accountable to know the answer. As Christ referenced the Scriptures when He answered the many questions given Him, so are we to follow in that same pursuit. If you were asked these and would find yourselves speechless or unable to answer in a word, then I encourage you to prepare yourself in prayer and get ready to dig, in hopes that Colossians 4:6 may ring true in you.

"And Jesus answered and spake unto them again by parables, and said, The kingdom of heaven is like unto a certain king, which made a marriage for his son," Matthew 22:1-2

The first question is found in a parable spoken by Christ to the Pharisees at the beginning of this chapter. Keep in mind, this conversation is a continuing between Jesus and the Pharisees from Chapter 21. This Parable is intended to open the heart of the Pharisees. Remember also, Jesus knows the hearts of each individual. He knew the hearts of these Pharisees and he used the illustration of this wedding guest to portray what their eternal positions will be if they do not soften their hearts and believe on Him as the Prophesied Messiah. You and I are not being represented as this ill-dressed wedding guest. You and I are the ones that were found on the highways and byways, bidden to come, and in awe of the invitation at the King's request, came.

This parable is a comparison between the Kingdom of Heaven and a king preparing a marriage feast for his son. This marriage feast should have been radiant as the preparations were all in place, the guests were arriving, and the party was being enjoyed by all, but that was not the case. The king sent out the invitations and was denied by all the invited (vs. 3). He then sent his servants to the invited guests and bid them to come (vs. 4) and they, in turn, offered up their excuses (vs. 5) and beat up the servants and eventually killed them (vs. 6). The distraught king took vengeance on their land and destroyed it (vs.7).

Then this king, in honoring his son's marriage feast, sent his servants outside to the highways in search of the good, the bad, and all who were free, and bid them to attend this glorious marriage feast. The house filled with guests, and the party commenced. During the celebration, the king spotted a man standing alone looking out of sorts. The appearance of this man was unbecoming for a wedding and it greatly disturbed the king. For here was a king celebrating his son with a group of free and willing guests all suitable and enjoying the great festivities.

"So those servants went out into the highways, and gathered together all as many as they found, both bad and good: and the wedding was furnished with guests." Matthew 22:10

Here's a thought to ponder, every newly invited guests was invited as they were, where they were. I would venture to say none of them were walking the highways in formal attire. However, there was a visible difference between these invited guests and the one not dressed in wedding garments. This makes me think that this king provided the proper wedding attire for each of his invited guests. When the king saw this man not in his wedding attire he knew that this man came in on his own basis.

"He that overcometh, the same shall be clothed in white raiment; and I will not blot out his name out of the book of life, but I will confess his name before my Father, and before his angels." Revelation 3:5

In frustration, after dealing with the apathy and cold-hearted behaviors of his original guest list, seeing a man take advantage of his goodness without accepting their position as a guest truly bothered this king. When the king approached the man he came not with accusation of words, but simply asked a question:

"Friend, how camest thou in hither not having a wedding garment?" Matthew 22:12

Often times the best answer for a simple question is a simple answer, 'Sir, I heard the noise of the party, and I wanted to come. Forgive my appearance, but here I am as I am asking that I may stay." A simple, truthful answer was the words the king was looking for. But, you know, the king saw what was going on. He had a feeling there wasn't a simple answer from this man, and his response proved the king to be right.

"And he was speechless." Matthew 22:12

Do you see the correlation between the Kingdom of Heaven and this parable of the marriage feast? God is the king, the Jewish nation was the invited guests, you and I are the ones bidden to come, and the man standing alone is the Pharisaical man clothed in self-righteousness. Romans 10:3 reads, "For they being ignorant of God's righteousness, and going about to establish their own righteousness, have not submitted themselves unto the righteousness of God." Jesus had a message through this parable for the Pharisees. The Pharisees heard it loud and clear. The sad truth is that they heard it with the ears of contempt and not of submission, for their reaction could have been a change of heart, but instead they were speechless.

Question One was an inquiry of effortless faith. Question Two is one of knowledge through faith. After answering all that came to Him by way of the Herodians and Sadducees, Christ found that He had come full circle back to the Pharisees. He gave them a rightful answer to their query about the greatest of commandments, then turned the tables asking them a knowledgeable, two-fold question:

"What think ye of Christ: whose son is He?" Matthew 22:42

I wonder where the Pharisees would have found themselves if they responded by saying as Peter once answered, "Thou art the Son of God." To answer as Peter, would have been to answer with belief in Jesus Christ as the Prophesied Son of God, but that would have required true faith in Him. Their response, however, was quick and spoken in agreement with their religious defense, "the son of David" (vs.42). How quickly Jesus trapped this religious sect in their piety, teaching them what they should already know as students of the Scripture. Jesus says, "How then doth David in spirit call him Lord, saying, The Lord said unto my Lord, sit thou on my right hand, till I make thine enemies thy footstool: If David then call him Lord, how is he his son?"

"And no man was able to answer him a word, neither durst any man from that day forth ask him any more questions." Matthew 22:46

With an end to this interrogative chapter, I leave you with the two questions for you to answer. The Pharisees had not a word to reply to either. Do you?

What are you "wearing" to the marriage feast? Or shall I say, how are you getting into Heaven; through your self-righteousness or His? Romans 3:19-23

____

____

____

____

____

____

____

What are your thoughts on Christ? Doctrinally speaking, who is He? Personally speaking, who He is to you?

____

____

____

____

____

____

Memory Goal:

"And thou shalt love the Lord thy God with all thine heart, and with all thy soul, and with all thy might." Deuteronomy 6:5

"Thou shalt not avenge, nor bear any grudge against the children of thy people, but thou shalt love thy neighbor as thyself: I am the Lord." Leviticus 19:18

"Let your speech be always with grace, seasoned with salt, that ye may know how ye ought to answer every man." Colossians 4:6

23

WHY DO I DO WHAT I DO?

Matthew Twenty Three

"But all their works they do for to be seen of men: Woe unto you, Scribes and Pharisees, hypocrites! For ye pay tithe of mint and anise and cumin, and have omitted the weightier matters of the law, judgment, mercy, and faith: these ought ye to have done, and not to leave the other undone." Matthew 23:5, 23

Do you recall the disclaimer in Chapter 21? You know, the one in which I encouraged you to listen as a Pharisee, but did not call you a Pharisee? Well, here we go again. This chapter is through and through the heart of our Savior toward the life of a Pharisee. His audiences in this chapter are the disciples, the multitude that faithfully followed after Christ, and the Pharisees. Jesus begins the chapter with a fair warning against becoming the hypocrites He is about to address. He then bestows eight damnations upon the Pharisees, and concludes with His final words of dissatisfaction and sorrow that He feels towards them and to His nation of Jerusalem.

Before tearing into the Pharisees, I ask you to look within and answer a question. Why do you do what you do? Is it because you are as the disciples who have sold themselves wholly for His glory, regardless as to what life has to offer? Is it because you are part of the multitude who believes in Jesus as the Messiah and desire to hear His precious words and witness His miraculous hand? Is it because you are consistent in your religious rituals as the scribes and Pharisees? This group of individuals spent their days displaying acts of holiness, a performance of righteous living, all for the eyes and the glory of man. To answer honestly will leave each of us with either a heart of humility or a feeling of irritation. In truth, I believe there are many of us who can say that at one time or another we thought or acted as a Pharisee. For some, the mentality of the Pharisee is all too common. Whatever you answer, for the sake of your personal growth with Jesus Christ, may it be one of unaltered honesty. Take a few moments to self-evaluate. Honestly, why do you, let's say, go to church? Why do you read your Bible? Why do you teach Sunday School, work in the nursery during service, or sing in the choir? Why? Write down your heart in words, and give your truth to the only One who will see your honesty as pure beauty.

Why do I do what I do?

____

____

____

____

Before pronouncing woe upon the Pharisees, Jesus takes the time to define their motives. First He says, "The scribes and the Pharisees sit in Moses' seat" (Matthew 23:2). Moses' seat was an ordained position for the leader over the Israelites. It was an honored position to be held by God's chosen leader. Through the years, however, this spiritually held position of humility became a self-attained position of pride.

He says in Verse 2, because of the Pharisees' position in Moses' seat, it would do us good to learn under their knowledge of the Scripture, however, he warns not to do what they do or live as they live for what they command and what they do are contrary to each other. When they teach the Scriptural laws of Moses, observe, but stop there. For they add on heavy burdens that are not written in the Bible, nor are they desired by God. These men issue out new rule books for all to follow when they themselves don't lift a finger to accomplish these rules.

Moreover, the appearance of righteousness is a greater achievement for the Pharisees than the simple act of obedience. They position themselves amongst themselves with the highest reputations. They adorn themselves in the apparel of righteousness, and they entreat all men to call them by a respectable name in order to receive the honor they feel they deserve. When all along what they should be doing in their seat of honor is directing all eyes and attention to God above. They should refer to God as Master and Father alone, not themselves. They should be living a life of service and humility and setting a strong foundation for a life lived for the King. Christ concludes this opening discourse with a verse intended for you and me. He says in Verses 11-12:

"But he that is greatest among you shall be your servant. And whosoever shall exalt himself shall be abased; and he that shall humble himself shall be exalted."

The Message words Matthew 23:11-12 this way, "Do you want to stand out? Then step down. Be a servant. If you puff yourself up, you'll get the wind knocked out of you. But it if you're content to simply be yourself, your life will count for plenty." Contentment brings confidence, confidence brings success. When you desire to be successful in Christ, then you must determine to find your contentment in who He is and who you are in Him. You must build that confidence in Him by simply being yourself. You are who God created. You are who He loved. You are who He sent His Son to die for. You are who Jesus prays for. You are loved.

Imagine being a Pharisee right about now. You are hearing this description being spoken for a multitude of ears. You can only imagine what people are thinking about you right now. Knowing your settled hatred for this Man, your blood begins to boil even more. You would hope that Jesus would wrap up about now. But no, He is now looking at you. Woe? Did He just say woe, to me?

Yes, as a matter of fact, He did say woe, eight times over He said woe. When I read this one time with my 5-year-old son his one response to all this dread was, "Why is there only eight, why didn't Jesus woe them 10 times?" To that, my answer was a laugh and a hug. But I know if I were the Pharisaical audience hearing these eight woes I would be relieved when Jesus ended at eight and didn't pursue all the way to ten. So, what are these woes? And how can we apply them as fair warning, eye openers in our own lives? This is our quest for this chapter. As your friend let me say, there is more writing than usual in this chapter. Take one woe at a time and proceed when your time and attention allows. Ponder them when you do not have the time to record your thoughts. We will title this homework, "How not to be a Pharisee." As you read through each woe, I encourage you to seek out these three fundamental facets:

1. The condemnation toward the Pharisee: What is it that Jesus saw in them that brought forth the woe at hand?
2. The warning sign in you and me: How can our actions or hearts reflect the mannerisms of the Pharisees?
3. The solution: Find a verse to aid in your personal battle for the particular area.

The verses I list are merely a suggestion or starting point for your study. Allow the Spirit to lead you to the verses or passages needed for your life.

Woe 1 – Matthew 23:13

> *"But woe unto you, scribes and Pharisees, hypocrites! For ye shut up the kingdom of heaven against men: for ye neither go in yourselves, neither suffer ye them that are entering to go in."*

Condemnation toward the Pharisee: (Matt 5:3 – humility vs. pride)

____

____

____

____

Warning for you and me: (Matthew 7:15-20)

____

____

____

____

The Solution: (John 14:6)

____

____

____

____

Woe 2 – Matthew 23:14

> *"Woe unto you, scribes and Pharisees, hypocrites! for ye devour widows' houses, and for a pretense make long prayer: therefore ye shall receive the greater damnation."*

Condemnation toward the Pharisee: (Matt 6:1-7, actions vs. words)

Warning for you and me: (James 1:26-27)

The Solution: (Psalm 34:13)

Woe 3 – Matthew 23:15

> *"Woe unto you, scribes and Pharisees, hypocrites: for ye compass sea and land to make one proselyte, and when he is made, ye make him twofold more the child of hell than yourselves."*

Condemnation toward the Pharisee: *(*Matt 15:8-14, blind vs. wisdom)

____

____

____

____

Warning for you and me: (Psalm 1:1-6)

____

____

____

____

The Solution: (Acts 1:8)

____

____

____

____

Woe 4-Matthew 23:16 (vs. 16-22)

> *"Woe unto you, ye blind guides, which say, Whosoever shall swear by the temple, it is nothing; but whosoever shall swear by the gold of the temple, he is a debtor!"*

Condemnation toward the Pharisee: (Matt 5:33-37, a promise is a promise)

____

____

____

____

Warning for you and me: (Ecclesiastes 5:2-4)

____

____

____

____

The Solution: (Psalm 50:14)

____

____

____

____

Woe 5 – Matthew 23:23-24

> *"Woe unto you, scribes and Pharisees, hypocrites! for ye pay tithe of mint and anise and cumin, and have omitted the weightier matters of the law, judgment, mercy, and faith: these ought ye to have done, and not to leave the other undone."*

Condemnation toward the Pharisee: (Matthew 5:7; Luke 6:33-38 – Give and Live; equally important)

Warning for you and me: (Malachi 3:8-10)

The Solution: (Micah 6:8)

Woe 6 – Matthew 23:25 (vs. 35-26)

> *"Woe unto you, scribes and Pharisees, hypocrites! For ye make clean the outside of the cup and of the platter, but within they are full of extortion and excess."*

Condemnation toward the Pharisee: (Matt 5:8; Luke 11:39-40 - purity vs. pretense)

____

____

____

____

Warning for you and me: (Psalm 51:5-13)

____

____

____

____

The Solution: (James 4:8)

____

____

____

____

Woe 7 – Matthew 23:27-28

> *"Woe unto you, scribes and Pharisees, hypocrites! For ye are like unto whited sepulchers, which indeed appear beautiful outward, but are within full of dead men's bones, and of all uncleanness."*

Condemnation toward the Pharisee: (Romans 3:10-18 – the irony of marvelous muck)

____

____

____

____

Warning for you and me: (1 John 1:5-10)

____

____

____

____

The Solution: (1 Samuel 16:7)

____

____

____

____

Woe 8 – Matthew 23:29-36

> *"Woe unto you, scribes and Pharisees, hypocrites! Because ye build the tombs of the prophets, and garnish the sepulchers of the righteous, and say, If we had been in the days of our fathers, we would not have been partakers with them in the blood of the prophets."*

Allow me to insert this thought toward the eighth woe; have you ever looked at history or someone else's actions and thought, I would never have done that? However, in truth, there were actions you have done in your past or in your present state that someone else would look down upon. This is the greater message for this particular condemnation. These Pharisees view themselves so mightily when compared to the Scriptures of old saying things as; Cain did a terrible act, an act of killing his brother (Genesis 4:8-10), we would never. Or the blood of Zechariah (2 Chronicles 24:20-22) is not on our hands, for we were not there at the time of his brutality, and if we were, we would never have killed him. Have you noticed the Pharisees claim their forefathers faith when it benefits their higher standards, but deny their actions when their stories condemn them? In the end, do not the Pharisees lead the execution of Jesus Christ? No, they would never kill their brother as Cain, or murder a prophet like Zechariah, but as they are saying this, they are spending their days plotting the capture and crucifixion of the Son of God.

For us, the greatest lesson here is, don't judge. You weren't there, and furthermore, you don't know where you will be down the road. Rather than looking down your nose at another's choice or outcome, why not listen to the full story and then determine to learn what you can from it?

Peter told Jesus he would never deny Christ, yet he did. His sorrow over his actions led to deep forgiveness from both God and from himself. In turn, he led one of the most victorious lives for us to model. The Pharisees declare, "We would not have been partakers with them in the blood of the prophets" (Matthew 23:30).

Yet, we are just chapters away from seeing them shed the blood of the greatest Prophet this world has ever known. Their sorrow differs greatly from Peter's though, for their sorrow is nonexistent and their actions have seeped through the ages and rears their head in our churches, homes, and hearts to this day.

Condemnation toward the Pharisee: (Matthew 23:34-36 - claims vs. reality)

____

____

____

____

Warning for you and me: (Matthew 7:1-6)

____

____

____

____

The Solution: (1 Corinthians 4:5)

____

____

____

____

"O Jerusalem, Jerusalem, thou that killest the prophets, and stonest them which are sent unto thee, how often would I have

gathered thy children together, even as a hen gathereth her chickens under her wings, and ye would not! Behold, your house is left unto you desolate. For I say unto you, Ye shall not see Me henceforth till ye shall say, blessed is he that cometh in the name of the Lord." Matthew 23:37-39

What a heart wrenching cry of a Father for His children. Those of us who have witnessed a loved one turn away from God or from obedience can understand a touch of the Savior's heart. Understand that His sorrow is leading Him to the cross to die for the very sin of unbelief. He knows that many will choose the life of the Pharisee and never know His love nor have eternal life in Heaven. What sorrow! What heaviness our Savior carried. Friend, Jesus understands your sorrow.

Memory Goal:

"That then the Lord thy God will turn thy captivity, and have compassion upon thee from all the nations, whither the Lord thy God hath scattered thee." Deuteronomy 30:3 (Matthew 23:39)

Of the eight woes studied in this chapter, review the one that touched your heart the most. Consider using the verse listed beside 'the solution' as your chapter memory goal.

24

GET THE COFFEE READY

Matthew Twenty Three

"And as He sat upon the Mount of Olives, the disciples came unto Him privately, saying, Tell us, when shall these things be: and what shall be the sign of thy coming, and of the end of the world?" Matthew 24:4

My dear friend, may I advise you to brew a pot of coffee, or pour a tall glass of sweet tea, and get in a comfortable seat in your house before you proceed in this chapter. When I think of Chapter 24, I tremble a little. When I think about Chapter 24, I get a huge cup of coffee. When I prepare for Chapter 24, I find myself on my knees. Jesus' words reign in this chapter. Jesus' words are detailed, pointed, and extremely purposeful. Therefore, consider my affirmation for caffeine as a friendly forewarning.

Have you ever asked a question and received a loaded answer? Welcome to Matthew Chapter 24. After Jesus' public pronouncement against the Pharisees, the disciples stood outside the temple looking upon the building with Jesus and heard Him declare, "See ye not all these things? Verily I say unto you, there shall not be left here one stone upon another, that shall not be thrown down" (vs. 2). It is at this point, the disciples asked their question, "When shall these things be: and what shall be the sign of thy coming, and of the end of the world?" (Matthew 24:4)

Submission is possible through salvation, it is part of God's plan for peace within and is needful for Godly responses. In this chapter, the caffeine-required Chapter 24, we see that the purpose of exercising submission in our hearts benefits us so much more than in our relationships with Him and with the world around us. Exercising submission now builds upon the foundation of our faith in Christ, so that when words are expressed by others that vary from the words of Christ, we catch it and denounce it and cling to the Truth. This matter of 'false teachers' is the prophecy that will occur in the end times. Wherever your knowledge stands on the end times, whether post-tribulation, pre- tribulation, or simply that Revelation 22 says He is coming again and you believe it, can I ask you to consider Jesus' words through our study of submission?

The best books to help understand the end times are 1 Thessalonians, Revelation, and Daniel. Now, think of these three books as, beginner, intermediate, and expert-level respectively. 1 Thessalonians, if you are a beginner, will point you to the most important aspect of the end times, the return of Jesus Christ to gather together all of us who believe on His Name. From there, Revelation is always an intriguing book, regardless of your level of expertise, for within its pages is our future's truth. Whether we can or cannot grasp its every detail is not the basis of knowledge. Rather, it is important to grasp that what is written in that book is the truth, and knowing that God our Father is the First and the Last and therefore He knows every detail and is in full control. That is where our understanding can rest.

If you are a master in the area of "Eschatological Discourse" (what a fabulously fancy way of saying 'study of the last days'), then put your nose in the book of Daniel and pop your head up whenever you need to catch your breath. Daniel is a very deep theological book regarding the events of the end times. Many of us know that book in regards to the Lion's Den and Shadrack, Meshach, and Abednego and the Fiery Furnace, but this book holds a lot more details than our favorite Sunday School stories.

For three years the disciples have walked and talked with Jesus Christ; they have witnessed His miraculous hand, and have learned fundamental truths from His ways. For three years they have listened to Him speak to multitudes, speak to individuals, and speak to them. For three years they have heard Him speak of His death and resurrection and of His return. For three years they have wondered at the meaning of His sayings, unable to grasp their Master dying on a cross and living again. This was a reality too grand for their minds to comprehend. This was an impossibility. They knew it to be an impossibility, yet Jesus continued speaking of it in definitive terms.

What about Jesus' prophecy spoken about the conclusion to the Pharisees, "Behold your house is left unto you desolate. For I say unto you, ye shall not see Me henceforth, till ye shall say, blessed is he that cometh in the name of the Lord" (Matthew 23:38-39)? What is the meaning of this destruction and when is Jesus going to return? It is a big question to ask and a greater answer to comprehend. It is a question pressed on our hearts even today. Lucky for us, we have the written word of God for the answer. The disciples, however, had the book of Daniel and had Jesus, the Author of the Scriptures to offer the answer. It is that very response we are going to study today. Remember, this chapter is a deep study. If you are still hungry for an even greater study after our time together, then I encourage you to read through the books listed above. Our study is going to center around the heart of our devotional study, submission. Therefore, our standing question is: What can we learn from this chapter that will lead us down our path to submission?

Our answer is threefold; apply wisdom, hold to our faith, and remain steadfast. Take your time as you study these three paths of submission. I will strive to supply your study with tools of thought and Scripture references for those of you who desire to dig more deeply into and…wait for it… Eschatological Study.

"Take heed that no man deceive you." Matthew 24:4

Our first path is wisdom. Know the Word of God so dearly as to not get tangled up in the imprudence of false preachers. If any of us lack wisdom, the Bible says, let us ask of God and He will give it. This is a promise to us in James 1:5. God gives us His wisdom through the Holy Spirit, in prayer, and through the words of the Bible. Matthew 24:4-14 is a great passage to read when desiring wisdom. Jesus begins with a serious charge, "let no man deceive you." Deception for many is a choice. When one neglects to hold fast to the truth of something, then persuasion can easily occur. This is why James follows up his prayer for wisdom with a description of a man who seeks not after wisdom:

"For he that wavereth is like a wave of the sea driven with the wind and tossed. For a double minded man is unstable in all his ways." James 1:6, 8

Jesus says, don't allow yourself to be persuaded and here's why. Many are going to preach the name of God and even the name of Jesus Christ, but they themselves have no knowledge of God nor do they have a relationship with Jesus Christ. Do not allow their words of eloquence or doctrines of peace to shake your knowledge of the Father.

You can see the disciples sitting at Jesus' feet, Matthew furiously documenting His every word as he frequently did throughout his time with the Savior, hearing the details of Jesus' future demise. They felt the emotions that tended to overtake their individual hearts, emotions like Thomas' doubt, Peter's fear, John's sorrow, James' anger and Judas' determination that living for this Man is simply not worth it. Grab your debilitating emotion and take a seat among the disciples in order to walk with them through their final week with Christ, not as a reader, but as a participant. Maybe then we will be less likely to judge our friends when we see them flee in Matthew 26.

My emotion is the fear of death. When I was a young girl, my father passed away of Hodgkin's disease. He was 33 years old. It is amazing how perception changes with time. I knew as a little girl that dad died at an old age. I know now that he died so young. I knew as a little girl that he was in Heaven watching over me. I know now that I want to be here to watch over my young child. My fear of dying leads me down a path of superstition all too often. Just the other day I left the house without my wedding rings. It was the first time in 10 years I had ever done that. We were running late and I didn't have time to turn around to get them. I needed to drop my husband off at work, get my son to his tee ball practice, and then head straight to a boot camp class. It would be a solid three hours before I would be able to put my rings on. I was quiet in the car. My heart was pounding. Then I saw my husband look at me as we headed to his location. He smiled and asked, "You're doing it again, aren't you?" I responded with extreme word vomit about how I knew one of us was going to die, how this had never happened before, how my heart was aching, and so forth. I was sinking. Jesus held out his hand and quietly whispered, "My child, why do you have such little faith?" My husband kissed me goodbye and said soundly, "Don't you think that maybe you just left your rings at home?" Three hours later I pulled up to my house, put on my rings and kissed my boys hello, all safe and alive.

If you have your emotion, would you mind writing it down? When you are finished, pull up a spot at His feet with the rest of us and listen.

____

____

____

____

____

____

Men will claim deity, leading many to follow them rather than God (vs. 5; 1 John 2:18-21). Wars will take place and will be rumored abroad (vs. 6). Natural disasters will occur throughout the lands (vs. 7). You will be physically harmed and even killed. Hatred by others will rain down on you for My Name's sake (vs. 9; Matthew 10: 17-18). Peace will slip away and will be replaced by animosity (vs. 10; Daniel 12:10). False teaching will lead many to hell (vs. 11; 2 Peter 2:1-2), and iniquity will reign while love will dissipate (vs. 12; 2 Timothy 3:1-7).

Did your emotion get triggered? Verse 9 triggered mine. I wonder how many of these men remembered Christ warning them of persecution and rejection when they were first called to follow after Him as Christ rehearsed this series of physical and emotional sorrows here on the Mount of Olives. Having wisdom in the area of what's to come, fills us with peace when those times do come. It's easy to see that our timeline of submission is to submit until the end. The answer on how to accomplish this task is in James 1:5. Pray for wisdom. Hold tight to wisdom with the power of the Holy Spirit … no matter what. I encourage you to pen those thoughts that are running through your head, the verse that startled your emotion or fear, and then rest in Christ's conclusion to this matter of wisdom.

"*But he that shall endure unto the end, that same shall be saved.*"
Matthew 24:13

____

____

____

____

____

____

"When ye therefore shall see the abomination of desolation, spoken by Daniel the prophet, stand in the holy place." Matthew 24:15

Our second path is that of faith. Believe Jesus' words when the legality of His message appears impossible in our finite minds. 1 Thessalonians 4:13-18 accounts for the hope found within those who have faith in Jesus Christ. Faith is a beautiful depiction of a pure heart; "Without faith it is impossible to please God, for he who cometh to God must believe that He is and that He is the rewarder of those who diligently seek Him." (Hebrews 11:6). Faith in Jesus Christ as the Risen Savior is the start of our personal relationship with God. Faith does not and should not end at salvation. Faith should be our daily path, our daily bread. The greatest definition of what faith is, is found in Hebrews 11:1; it is "the substance of what we hope for; it is the evidence of what we cannot see." Faith is the central part of believing with your very soul what you cannot see, grasp, or explain.

If faith is the internal action of our belief, then submission is the physical action of our faith. If there is ever a reason to determine to submit, it is for the descriptive reality we find in this passage of the 7-year tribulation (Daniel 9:27; 11:31; 12:11). Consider this, Christians are removed from the earth, which means no more demonstrative acts of Christ's love in your workplace, at the stores, at the airport, or within our community. There are no more servants like firemen, policemen, teachers, and doctors. There are no more pastors, no more followers of Jesus Christ in the home. Wars begin to rage, feuds strike a chord between the closest of friends and families; the government becomes one-sided and demanding. False preachers exhort all to believe their doctrines and their positions of power and of peace. The world as we know it today crumbles to a new level of socialism like never before, and it all happens within a three-and-a-half year period.

The Tribulation is very real. Although the views of the Tribulation timeline are sadly debated among Christian circles today, the truth of the matter exists; the Tribulation will occur and its devastation will be deafening. So what of you and me today?

There is nothing that you and I can do to rewrite the Bible. We cannot erase the book of Revelation or the book of Daniel. We cannot pretend that this passage here in Matthew does not exist nor that it teaches something other than the prophesied Tribulation period. What we can do, however, is soften the sorrows.

Jesus tells us in John 15 that the world knows us because of our love for one another and that by our fruits we are known. If the world is watching our love for one another and watching our fruit, they are seeing a difference in us from the others around them. In short, our lives become a testimony of the love of the Savior to a lost and dying world. Through our actions of submission to Jesus Christ, to our husbands, and to one another, we have full reign and responsibility with our mouth to proclaim the Good News of the Gospel, without guilt and without shame, for we are walking in the fullness of His grace.

Furthermore, once the words have been shared and the testimony has been shown, that memory resides within the heart and mind of the receiver. Two roads can be taken at this point that can soften the sorrow found within the seven years of the Tribulation. The first road is that of salvation. Many times when we boldly witness to an unsaved friend or family member, that person will grab hold of the love of Jesus and will receive Him as their Savior.

The second road lies in the memory of the unsaved. There will be many who hear of Salvation and for one reason or another deny Christ His rightful place in their hearts. This soul will remain on earth during the Tribulation. However, my belief on this matter is that salvation can and will take place during this time of tribulation. Therefore, those seeds that we plant will flourish in the hearts of some after the absence of the Holy Spirit is present. The love of God and the Blood of Jesus are without limitations. Therefore, although the Spirit will be removed from the earth for a time, once a person receives Jesus as their Savior the Holy Spirit resides within them. The Spirit will slowly form its way throughout the earth one heart at a time.

To conclude our spiritual application of submission on this passage on the Tribulation, I ask you to pray for an open door to which you can witness and shed Christ's light on behalf of this soon coming reality. Hebrews 10:27 says, "Today is the day of salvation."

Allow the Spirit to place on your heart an individual that you can witness to, and then determine a game plan as to how you can share a verse, invite them to church, or share your story with them. Finally, set a date by which you can accomplish this goal.

Who:

____

____

____

____

How:

____

____

____

____

When:

____

____

____

For further study on the occurrences of the seven-year tribulation timeline, here are some correlating passages to look up and reference. Feel free to begin a new journal to record your studies and thoughts or record them below. Enjoy this study of God's Word. Please keep in mind that this is an introductory study. There are many books written by God such as Ezekiel, Daniel, and Revelation to answer our questions regarding this subject, as well as many secular books to aid in our knowledge and greater understanding. Tim LaHaye is one such author full of wisdom with metaphors that are easy to follow.

Matthew 24:1-2 The beauty of the Temple is momentary (Mark 13:1-2, Luke 21:5-6):

____

____

____

____

____

____

Matthew 24:3-14 The first half of the Tribulation (Revelation 6: 1-17; Revelation 7; Daniel 9:24-27):

____

____

____

____

____

____

Matthew 24:15-28 The Great Tribulation or the second half (Revelation 13, 16; Daniel 9:24-27, 12:11; 2 Thessalonians 2:3-8):

Matthew 24:29-31 The Return of Jesus Christ (Joel 3:11-21; Revelation 19:11-21; 1 Thessalonians 4:13-18; 1 Corinthians 15:51-58):

"Behold, I shew you a mystery; We shall not all sleep, But we shall all be changed, In a moment, in the twinkling of an eye, at the last trump: For the trumpet shall sound, and the dead shall be raised incorruptible, And we shall be changed." 1 Corinthians 15:51-52

"Watch therefore: for ye know not what hour your Lord doth come." Matthew 24:42

Our third and final path of submission is in the area of remaining steadfast. Oftentimes in the Scripture, Jesus will reference the fig tree in correlation to the Jews. We saw this a few chapters back when Jesus was preparing the disciples for the encounter they were about to have with the unbelieving Jews, the religious Pharisees. We see it again here after He detailed the answer of destruction and of the signs of His coming, He is now approaching the final question of Verse 3; what are the signs of the end of the world? Jesus says, look at the fig tree.

I live in a city that knows its seasons based on the drinks offered at Starbucks. Yes, it may be 101 degrees outside, but when you can order a Pumpkin Spice Latte you know it is fall. Then comes the Gingerbread Latte, Eggnog Latte, and Peppermint Mocha, and it is winter. Just the thought alone makes me want to curl up to a nice warm fire and sip at my holiday delights, forgetting altogether that spring is in the air and in reality I am sipping my Iced Green Tea. With sundresses and the long summer months to come, I will reward myself with a refreshingly cold Mocha Coconut Frappuccino to get me through the sizzling days.

For many, however, seasons are evident by way of the harvest. This is so foreign to me, not because of my Starbucks analogy, but more so due to my previously mentioned aversion to grocery stores and kitchens. Even the thought of writing about the application of what produce grows in which season is causing a steady flow of heart palpitations. For those of you who understand the ways of the garden and successfully accomplish the miracles produced by way of sun, water, and soil, I first applaud you and secondly beg of you to think within yourself the application of harvest and seasons. For those of you who side with me in the way of horticultural uncertainty, I am going to let you take this time to laugh at the fact that we are not alone, then allow you to skip this application seeing that it wouldn't do anything for you anyway. You're welcome.

Now then, to the disciples Jesus says, if you want to know the season then look at the crop. If the fig tree branch is tender and bringing forth leaves, then you know summer is coming. Likewise, when you see all these sorrows then you know the end is near. Furthermore, "this generation" or the nation of Israel will not pass away until all these things have come to pass. Israel's peace and protection is an aged covenant between God and His chosen people. We see God's hand on them throughout the Old Testament and throughout modern history. During the days of the tribulation we will continue to see God's hand on this very nation. But what I love even more than God's reminder of the promise over His nation, is His reiterated focus for New Testament believers:

"Heaven and earth shall pass away, but my words shall not pass away. But of that day and hour knoweth no man, no, not the angels of heaven, but my Father only. Watch therefore: for ye know not what hour your Lord doth come. Therefore be ye also ready: for in such an hour as ye think not the Son of man cometh."
Matthew 24:35-36, 42, 44

Jesus points out the signs of the end times and of His return, and then concludes with the final piece of our submission timeline, be steadfast. You see, there will be signs that point to the end times, therefore be so focused on Jesus Christ's return that our heart remains focused on Him, so when the Lord returns, although the day and hour be unknown, the reality will not take you by surprise. Following His parable of the fig tree and the implications of knowing the signs as naturally as you know the seasons, He continues on with a lesson from the days of Noah:

"But as the days of Noah were, so shall also the coming of the Son of man be. For as in the days that were before the flood they were eating and drinking, marrying and giving in marriage, until the day that Noah entered into the ark, and knew not until the flood came, and took them all away; so shall also the coming of the Son of man be." Matthew 24:37-39

Noah lived, if you will, during a glimpse of the end times. He was told by God to prepare for a world disaster, a disaster unimaginable to him or to any from that generation. Yet Noah did what Jesus is imploring His followers and you and I to do. Be prepared. Jesus says in a parable in Luke 19 regarding steadfastness, "Occupy until I come." Noah had a specific checklist of preparations given him by God in order to prepare his family for the destruction of the world (Genesis 6:14-22), and the Bible says of Noah, "Thus did Noah; according to all that God hath commanded him, so did he" (Genesis 6:22).

Each of us has a calling for our lives and we are each commanded to walk "circumspectly" (with vigilance or watchfulness) according to that calling (Ephesians 5:15). Do so in order for it to be said of you, according to all that God hath commanded her, so did she. In the days of Noah, the people lived for the momentary good things in life rather than the eternal best offered by God. Those good things in life are given to us by God to enjoy, yes, but when they become so much our focus that our eyes drift steadily from God to the things given by God, then our reason for living changes to living for temporary pleasures and personal gains. May God be our number one so we are not taken by surprise as in the days of Noah!

Jesus' final charge will find itself as a comfort to the saints of the tribulation knowing that they are surrounded by pain and sorrow. Nonetheless, "Watch therefore: for ye know not what hour your Lord doth come"(Matthew 24:42). The days are at hand. The hour is near. Be faithful; be wise for "Blessed is that servant, whom his lord when he cometh shall find so doing" (Matthew 24:46).

Our timeline stands the same for our generation as it was for the disciples of the New Testament as it will stand for the Tribulation saints. Have wisdom then faith then steadfastness. The disciples accomplished this; we know this because their submission is recorded in the Scriptures. The question sits for our generations today as New Testament believers. Are we pursuing wisdom (James 1), portraying faith (Hebrews 11), and practicing steadfastness (1 Corinthians 15) on behalf of our Lord's return? Conclude this chapter with your own words regarding one or all of these paths. Focus your words on your personal determination to grow in the area the Holy Spirit is leading you. Read the passage(s) above; James, Hebrews and/or 1 Corinthians and record a verse and concluding thought below.

____

____

____

____

____

Memory Goal:

"Therefore, my beloved brethren, be ye steadfast, unmovable, always abounding in the work of the Lord, forasmuch as ye know that your labor is not in vain in the Lord." 1 Corinthians 15:58

"For the Lord himself shall descend from heaven with a shout, with the voice of the archangel, and with the trump of God: and the dead in Christ shall rise first:

Then we which are alive and remain shall be caught up together with them in the clouds, to meet the Lord in the air: and so shall we ever be with the Lord.

Wherefore comfort one another with these words."
1 Thessalonians 4:16-18

25

NAME YOUR RACE

Matthew Twenty Five

"And five of them were wise, and five were foolish." Matthew 25:2

"I have fought a good fight, I have finished my course, I have kept the faith." 2 Timothy 4:7

Other than a 44-minute 5k, I have never "finished the race" in a running sense, but I have found the good fight (John 3:16; 1 Timothy 6:12). I have discovered my course, and I pray daily that I will keep the faith. My race is not one of physical endurance in a well-loved pair of sneakers. Mine is one of words expressed by the leading of the Holy Spirit in a beautiful pair of … stilettos. My race is new. I have been married for 12 years, a mother for seven, a women's speaker for five, and a writer for one. Where will my race take me? That is not for me to know. My knowledge lies in my determination to endure and to enjoy it through and through until I reach that day in which my Savior will take me by the hand and lead me to the Promised Land. What a glorious day that will be. What is your race?

Jesus picks up here and rests on the message that faithfulness through actions displayed from the heart for the eyes of the Lord is the rewarded life that matters in the end. 2 Chronicles 16:9 tells us, "For the eyes of the LORD run to and fro throughout the whole earth, to shew himself strong in the behalf of them whose heart is perfect toward Him." Christ's message in Matthew is not a new concept. It is a message delivered by God throughout history. Some have clung dearly to its promise. Some have neglected the warning that walks hand in hand with the promise of blessing, "Herein thou hast done foolishly; therefore from henceforth thou shalt have wars" (2 Chronicles 16:9).

Regardless of the age, the results are altogether parallel to the words of Christ here in this passage; obedience brings protection and defiance brings tribulation. Yet, despite the countless examples given to us in the Scriptures, there remains a vast population of Believers in our society that are divided on these same two categories of old; those who cling to the innate protection of the Savior and those who neglect the love of God. In this chapter we will see three variances of this division, the wise versus the foolish, the example of the three servants, and the separation between God's sheep and the unsaved goats.

The unpardonable sin that reared its head back in Chapter 12 is spelled out ever so clearly in this chapter. This chapter is hard to study when you see your family and friends who are walking the way of the unbeliever, but it is also a testament and a reminder to those of us who have received Christ as our Savior to continue faithfully and to reach out to those who are heading down the path of eternal damnation.

Belief in God as the Almighty Creator and sustainer of life has been the tune of the Old Testament since the beginning of time. At that point, the Godhead was equal in their residence in heaven. They were not distant from the world they had created, but their presence was absent from it. Jesus had yet to be born as a babe, and the Holy Spirit had yet to reside in the hearts of the believers. There are passages that indicate God's walking with man in the cool of the Garden (Genesis 3:8) and shining His Glory to Moses atop mount Sinai (Exodus 33:18-23), but God's physical presence was halted at the birth of sin in the Garden of Eden.

The Holy Spirit plays a vital role in both the Old Testament and the New Testament, though they differ in each instance. In the New Testament and in modern society today, the Holy Spirit takes up residence within our hearts to guide us, comfort us, and convict us in order to mold us into the image of Jesus Christ. In the Old Testament His purpose and presence was quite different. The book of Leviticus depicts the Holy Spirit throughout its pages as the Oil of Olives. You see, back then, the oil of olives or olive oil was the substance required to use the lanterns that produced light in the days of old. Because of its distinct use, it was a representation for the majestic significance of the Holy Spirit. In other words, the Holy Spirit is the substance required in order to be filled with the Light of the blood of the Savior. The symbolism in Leviticus is a beautiful study altogether, one that I would encourage you, again, to study if you ignored my "encouragement" in a previous chapter. I forgive you for ignoring me earlier.

Let's study Leviticus' connection with our first passage in Matthew 25:1-13, the wise versus the foolish.

"Then shall the kingdom of heaven be likened unto ten virgins, which took their lamps, and went forth to meet the bridegroom." Matthew 25:1

Jesus is explaining the importance of the Holy Spirit by way of a marriage ceremony. Bear in mind, this passage is in regards to the Old Testament believers and is in no way condoning polygamy. The scene is set on the evening before the bridegroom comes to open his doors and receive his new bride. There are ten women grouped into two categories, "five of them were wise, and five were foolish" (Matthew 25:2).

Look at the story of the foolish ones. They that were foolish took their lamps, and took no oil with them, all the girls slumbered and slept. At midnight there came a cry, "The bridegroom comes; go out to meet him" (vs. 6). Then they all rose and trimmed their lamps. The foolish begged the wise, "Give us of your oil; for our lamps are gone out" (vs. 8). While they went away to buy oil the bridegroom came and went and the door was shut. Afterwards the foolish returned and cried, "Open the door! The bridegroom replied, "No, I do not know you" (vs. 11-12).

The wise had a similar account but an entirely different ending. They that were wise took vessels of oil with them along with their lamps. The girls slept. At midnight there came a cry, "The bridegroom comes; go out to meet him" (vs. 6). All the girls rose and trimmed their lamps. Others asked them for their oil, but they replied, "No; lest there be not enough for us and you; go to the store and buy for yourselves" (vs. 9). The bridegroom came and they entered in to the marriage and the door was shut.

Whether you studied out Leviticus or not, the truth of the matter is that in this passage the difference between the wise and the foolish lies with the oil. The foolish did not prepare, the wise did. Growing up I always pictured the girls all laying in hay in a barn wearing white, flowing, cotton dresses. Where that image came from could be a deep-rooted love I had for Little House on the Prairie. But now, in all my maturity, I picture the girlfriends in a chic bed and breakfast. I see them conversing, giggling, pampering in preparation, and finally turning in for an attempted night's sleep. Were the girls completely segregated? Did their conversations intertwine as they went through their checklist of preparation? Was the oil on the list, and if so was it not a topic of conversation?

I simply cannot see how the 'foolish' were so blinded by their absence of oil. Yet, here we are today, living in a world enamored by the many uses of the beloved EVOO (extra virgin olive oil), all the while clueless of the Holy Spirit and the importance of His presence in our lives. In the meantime, we who have "the oil in our vessels" walk among those that are without knowledge of the Holy Spirit. Are we telling them where to go in order to receive the Oil for themselves? Are we directing them to the Father?

They all slumbered and slept. How? Did you all sleep the night before your wedding? I didn't. I was at Wal-Mart very late in the evening, or very early in the morning, with a few of my bridesmaids looking at bras. I wasn't sure why we were there exactly. All I remember is laughing hysterically over nothing at all. I was too excited to be tired. Vacation time? Christmas Eve? It's the same thing, sleep is beyond me. What is Santa going to bring me? I know what he is bringing my son; Santa already gave me the 411 on him, but me? Oh, my, no sleep for me! Yet amazingly, the Bible says both the wise and the foolish slumbered and slept. To me that shows peace in the hearts of the wise, and unawareness in the hearts of the foolish. Merriam-Webster dictionary defines slumber as: "to be in a torpid, slothful, or negligent state."

It's amazing how even our slumber and rest is a matter of submission; slumber and sleep is not an act of our God, but sleep is a designed gift and promise of rest to you.

"I will lift up mine eyes unto the hills, from whence cometh my help. My help cometh from the Lord, which made heaven and earth. He will not suffer thy foot to be moved; he that keepeth thee will not slumber. Behold, he that keepeth Israel shall neither slumber nor sleep. The Lord is thy keeper; the Lord is thy shade upon thy right hand, The sun shall not smite thee by day, nor the moon by night." Psalm 121

The message of slumber and sleep is a very small aspect of this narrative, but it is a sweet concept to stop and ponder a moment. As women, many of us carry burdens, whether it's your private past, your desired future, the stress of your daily steps, the weights of your spouse, your innocent children, or of your dear friends. It is a privilege to hold each of them dear to our hearts, for they are ours to embrace, but may I say, if these alone are keeping you from the Keeper of heaven and earth, if they are hindering you from a promised night of sleep, then my dear friend you need to carry that thought to the Creator and lie down as the wise to slumber and sleep. If you lie down in peace, resting in the Father's promise, then take a moment to thank Him for this gift of slumber. If you struggle with this idea of laying your burdens at His feet in order to find a good night's sleep, then take this time to give your sleepless night to your God. Write those burdens down in form of a prayer, and truly let Him carry them for you. Such peace will be your reward.

____

____

____

____

____

____

The heart of the premise of Christ's words for these ten virgins is formulated in Verse 13, "Watch therefore, for ye know neither the day nor the hour wherein the Son of man cometh." The five wise girls had their vessels full and their lamps ready. It didn't matter what time the bridegroom opened the door, for they were ready for His arrival. Do you have the Holy Spirit? Have you received Jesus Christ as your Savior? These two elements walk hand in hand; salvation is the filling of the Holy Spirit. He is in you. The foolish had their lamps. They had the image of preparedness, but within they were empty. Which of these groups do you belong to? If you are wise, are you reaching the foolish? If you are foolish, are you reaching for the Oil of Olives? To summarize this narrative in your heart, what would be the greatest lesson garnered for your heart?

____

____

____

____

____

____

____

As we saw the Holy Spirit depicted by the filling of Olive Oil within a vessel in the Old Testament, He is described entirely differently in the New Testament. Jesus uses the image of three servants whose employer was leaving for a long trip and entrusts them with his land and fortune. To one he gives five talents, to another he gives two, and to another he gives one. Before seeing what each man does with their responsibilities, I want to look at 1 Corinthians 3:12-16. Keep these verses in mind when we return to our servants at hand.

"Now if any man build upon this foundation gold, silver, precious stones, wood, hay, stubble. Every man's work shall be made manifest: for the day shall declare it, because it shall be revealed by fire; and the fire shall try every man's work of what sort it is. If any man's work abide which he hath built thereupon, he shall receive a reward. If any man's work shall be burned he shall suffer loss; but he himself shall be saved; yet so as by fire. Know ye not that ye are the temple of God, and that the Spirit of God dwelleth in you?" 1 Corinthians 3:12-16

Follow me on this. This passage is difficult. I told my husband in preparation for this study that if I knew how challenging this chapter would be, I fear I would not have embarked on this Submission Adventure at all. But I am in too far and too deep. I for one want to jump in to see where it takes us and how it grows us in the ways of grace and knowledge. Jump in with me. Who knows, it could be life changing.

The Holy Spirit, since the life, death, and resurrection of the Lord Jesus Christ, was sent to earth to dwell within each of us as a comforter (John 14) and a guide. He is our source of strength and conviction. He is the light within us that shines to the world around us. Paul, in our 1 Corinthian passage states a thoughtful question that we need to always remember, "Do you not know that you are the temple of God, and the Spirit of God dwells in you?" Notice he says this right after talking about our works that we perform as a Christian. These works are not what leads us to Heaven, but rather they are the production of the Spirit that lives within us. Also, notice that the works we perform as a Christian are self-willed, just as salvation was a choice of the will. We were not a puppet before salvation nor are we after salvation. We are the individual that God designed us to be and that is one who has free will.

With that in mind, we return to Christ's second lesson in Matthew 25 regarding the servants of the king. The story of the ten virgins was directed towards the Jews of the Old Testament time, these three servants are a picture of the New Testament believers, the church. There is no indication or reference toward salvation. These servants are already saved and are working for the king. The king entrusts them with his personal financial funds asking them to be wise with what they were given. Two were wise, one was foolish, yet they were all saved. As Paul words it, two built their works on the foundation by way of gold, silver, and precious stones, and the other with wood, hay, and stubble.

Even though we have free will, there is always a consequence or a recompense for our decisions. Paul makes reference to the reward that is received if one's work abides in Christ, and of the loss that will be suffered if one's work is destroyed by the fire. He does not explain what that reward or the suffered loss is. He leaves that answer, I suppose, in the hands to whom it belongs, Jesus Christ's.

In Jesus' lesson, the man returns from his long journey and finds his three servants still residing in his land. The first and the second to whom he gave five portions and two portions, approached the man with humility and confidence proclaiming the abundance they brought forth through the talents they were entrusted. Each man doubled their gain. The feeling of success that comes from doubling a financial amount is reward enough. And yet, this honorable king looks upon his faithful servants and bids them a thank you, "Well done, thou good and faithful servant: thou hast been faithful over a few things, I will make thee ruler over many things: enter thou into the joy of the lord" (Matthew 25:20, 23).

Anyone's heart would melt with these words of appreciation. Jesus says in John 15:11, "These things have I spoken unto you, that my joy might remain in you, and that your joy might be full." My dear sister in Christ, you are the joy of the Lord, and His joy is in your heart. You see, the joy of the Lord is a continual cycle that flows from His heart to yours and back again. Why? Because He loves us and we love Him. Because we love Him we produce fruit with the talents He has given us in order to hand that fruit to Him and say, "See? You gave me this and with that I give you two fold." John 15:16 says, "Ye have not chosen Me, but I have chosen you, and ordained you, that ye should go and bring forth fruit, and that your fruit should remain." The joy of the Lord is a continual cycle and in that cycle fruit is produced and that fruit remains because of love.

"We love Him because He first loved us." I John 4:19

There was a third servant. The Bible says of this man that he came to his lord with open hands beholding the same single talent given him by his lord, tarnished and soiled. Shamefully he says to his lord, "Lord, I know you. I know that you are a hard man, that your accomplishments are high. You go out and reap where you have not sown, and you gather where you didn't even straw. Your reputation is too high for me to attain. And…I was afraid. So I went out to your field and I hid your money in the ground, and here it is, your money."

I pause here and think about this man's heart, his honesty, his fear, his excuse, his wood, his hay, and his stubble. Paul says a life of flammable works will suffer loss. What loss? What will he, what will we, suffer as a repercussion for this chosen way of life? Will we lose our salvation? The short answer is, no. The faith answer is, God's love and Jesus' blood is deeper than that (John 3:16). The scriptural answers are hundredfold throughout the Bible. One such answer is found in John 6:37-40, "All that the Father giveth me shall come to Me; and him that cometh to Me I will in no wise cast out….And this is the will of him that sent Me, that everyone which seeth the Son, and believeth on Him, may have everlasting life: and I will raise him up at the last day."

Again, John records Jesus' promise of eternal security, "My sheep hear My voice, and I know them, and they follow Me: And I give unto them eternal life; and they shall never perish, neither shall any man pluck them out of My hand. My Father, which gave them Me, is greater than all; and no man is able to pluck them out of My Father's hand. I and My Father are one" (John 10:27-30). We are His. Jesus holds us in His hand; God holds us in His hand. No man, the Bible says, can remove us from their hands. We are eternally sealed by the blood of the Savior.

So, if the suffered loss is not that of losing our salvation, then the question remains, what is the repercussion for choosing a life of wood, hay, and stubble? Could it be the loss that we suffer is the loss of the substance in which we were holding onto?

The lord looks at his servant's dirty hands, he beholds the unprofitable riches, and declares, "Thou wicked and slothful servant, thou knewest that I reap where I sowed not, and gather where I have not strawed: Thou oughtest therefore to have put my money to the exchangers, and then at my coming I should have received mine own with usury" (Matthew 25:26-27). In other words, you knew where I invested my money. Why didn't you just invest?

Speaking of money, one of my favorite pastimes is going to the mall. I have many girlfriends who greatly enjoy this hobby, but one in particular. When she and I go it is not just for an absorbance of time, it is an all-day rendezvous of glorious and miraculous memories, memories that we can display time and again as we walk our own personal catwalk in life as we "remember" our time together. When we can manage to go without the children, just the thought alone sends my heart into palpitations of extreme excitement!

Okay, I had to pray and regroup my thoughts (and add a few things to an online shopping cart). Shhh, I only did that to better my oncoming point. It's called an "Illustration." Focus. Focus. Girls, this is not good.

I just sent a message to my shopping guru to tell her that I was writing about her and me at the mall and she responds with, "good for you. I would rather be at the mall then write about it."

On one of our affairs at said location, Kate and I were strolling our babies through the Fashion Show Mall looking for works of art as a reward for our post baby bodies. I slipped into a new store and found a beautiful white sundress. It looked so good both on and off the hanger. It made me feel so beautiful. I wanted it. I bought it. I paid $200.00 for it. The attendant kindly wrapped up my new purchase, slid it into a glorious bag and with my head held high, I sauntered right out of the store. I was beaming the rest of our time at the mall. I smiled the whole way home. I grinned as I walked around my house looking at the new dress as it draped over the bed, as I modeled it for myself, as it hung beautifully in my closet.

My husband called from work to let me know what time he would be home for dinner. That was when it hit me. My smile fell. My dress went back into its bag. I sat on the couch. I thought and I thought hard. Justify….justify. How could I keep this dress?.

I'm no chef, so I couldn't fill his stomach until his heart was content. I probably made pancakes. But I'm cute and I can smile. So, that's what I will do. I will smile and seek his forgiveness for spending a grand price for an equally grand dress. Then I will wow him with the beauty of the purchase. Yes, sad to say, that was my game plan.

Even if you don't know my husband, you probably know the outcome. Sniff, sniff. My game plan failed. "Yes, I forgive you. Yes, I would like to see it on you. Yes, you're right, it is beautiful. No, you are not going to keep it." I had the dress for a total of a week. I put it on more than once, but never wore it on a date. It was mine for a moment, but gone forever. It was mine to care for while in my possession, but I didn't have the freedom to claim it as my own.

The hardest part of that whole situation was not the disappointment of having to return my dress, or the action of returning it. The hardest thing was the heaviness and guilt I felt before talking to Don, "If any man's work shall be burned he shall suffer loss; but he himself shall be saved; yet so as by fire" (1 Corinthians 3:15). My first instinct was to hide the dress and tell him later. Ever done that one? Yeah, me neither (sarcasm dripping from my mouth). The honest approach was to be as the unprofitable servant and to hold my dress out and say, "Here it is."

Salvation cannot be lost. Jesus' blood is too strong for that to happen. Through our salvation we are called to live as an example of His love. Christ enables us to do this by giving us our individual gifts and abilities to use for His glory. These abilities, or as referred here in this parable, works, are tried by fire as stated in 1 Corinthians 3. Though our works may fail our salvation is secure. This servant of unprofitable gain took the money of his master, and returned it just the same, with no fruit.

"And cast ye the unprofitable servant into outer darkness: there shall be weeping and gnashing of teeth." Matthew 25:30

Remember the fig tree? Remember the Pharisees? Both intended to produce fruit for the Master's use. Yet the fig tree produced not and the Pharisees produced for selfish gain. Both were designed to be servants and both denied their purpose. The fig tree offered up a barren branch; the Pharisees offered high minded sacrifices. Neither one was pleasing or acceptable in the eyes of their creator. You see, the fig tree is a picture of the Pharisees and of this final servant. These men worked for God, but had not a relationship founded through the blood of Jesus Christ.

"Abide in me, and I in you. As the branch cannot bear fruit of itself, except it abide in the vine; no more can ye, except ye abide in me. If a man abide not in me, he is cast forth as a branch, and is withered; and men gather them, and cast them into the fire, and they are burned." John 15:4, 6

The disciples and the disciples alone are sitting under Jesus' parables. I wonder what Judas was pondering as he told of the five foolish or unprepared virgins who waited too long and were denied the bridegroom. I wonder if any questions ran through his mind as he told of these three servants who chose to either use what was given them and to offer their fruits in the master's hands and the one who chose rather to continue living his life with no connection or accountability to the master. I wonder where his thoughts wandered as Jesus presented the final parable of empty works. All three of these parables have a common theme: Salvation is through a personal relationship with Jesus Christ alone, and by our fruits we are known.

There are some who spend their days working for God, but have yet to truly humble themselves and admit that they are in need of a Savior. There are some who have been so faithful to God for years serving at their church and fear that it is too late for them to step back and admit that they were never saved. Friends, by our fruit we are known. Your actions may fool some, but they will never fool God. For He and He alone knows your heart.

Salvation has been explained and offered throughout our time together in this book, but allow me if you will this last time to urge even the most religious of readers to evaluate your salvation today. Knowing God is not enough to get into Heaven. Working for God will not get you into Heaven. Praying a prayer will not save you, rather believing in God and confessing aloud your faith in Him is what will save you. Only by Jesus Christ can you enter into Heaven. May I leave you with these verses from Romans Chapter 10?

"That if thou shalt confess with thy mouth the Lord Jesus, and shalt believe in thine heart that God hath raised him from the dead, thou shalt be saved. For with the heart man believeth unto righteousness; and with the mouth confession is made unto salvation. For the scripture saith, Whosoever believeth on him shall not be ashamed. For there is no difference between the Jew and the Greek: for the same Lord over all is rich unto all that call upon him. For whosoever shall call upon the name of the Lord shall be saved." Romans 10:9-13

Submission to Salvation. Submission to the King. That is what submission is all about. That is what being a Christian is all about. The third parable in Matthew 25:31-46 is an explanation of the first two parables. There is a difference between the saved and the unsaved. The only thing that separates them is based on their faith in God's Son. The next three chapters will depict God's love for all mankind and His passion for all men to be saved. His Son will be the price paid for my sins and for my salvation. I'm sorry if this chapter was deep or difficult. I shrug, Matthew Chapter 25 is deep and difficult. For that reason, I am going to leave some space for any thoughts, questions, or results of personal study that you may have. These lines are yours to ponder Christ's message given us in this chapter. Hold onto these thoughts as we venture into the greatest example of submission, the death and resurrection of Jesus Christ.

Memory Goal:

"When the Son of man shall come in his glory, and all the holy angels with him, then shall he sit upon the throne of his glory: And before him shall be gathered all nations: and he shall separate them one from another, as a shepherd divideth his sheep from the goats: And he shall set the sheep on his right hand, but the goats on the left. And these shall go away into everlasting punishment: but the righteous into life eternal." Matthew 25:31-33, 46

26

DADDY'S GIRL

Matthew Twenty Six

"But I say unto you, I will not drink henceforth of the fruit of the vine, until that day when I drink it new with you in My Father's kingdom. Father, if it be possible, let this cup pass from Me: nevertheless not as I will, but as thou wilt. O My Father, if this cup may not pass away from Me, except I drink it, thy will be done. And he … went away again, and prayed the third time, saying the same words.
Matthew 26:29, 39, 42, and 44

We started our journey to submission by looking into the hearts of the characters found in the book of Matthew. Characters such as Mary and her heart of purity and acceptance, Joseph and his willingness to lead his wife in the way God directed him to follow, and Herod with his selfish submission to no one but himself. Through this study we have seen various men and women set examples of submission for you and me. They are examples in which we can learn a lot about ourselves. Sometimes what we saw within us was good and encouraging; other things were slightly humiliating and painful, but in the end we have seen our hearts polish and shine throughout this submission study.

As we find ourselves concluding our study in these final three chapters, we are going to be faced with the traits of key characters like Mary, the sister of Martha and Lazarus, Peter, Judas, the disciples, the Pharisees, and the government officials of the day. As we read these final three chapters, I encourage you to take each character for what they were, a living example written within the pages of the very Word of God for you and me to either follow after their individual approach of submission to God, or to learn a lesson from their decision of a selfish or ignorant life choice. Record your thoughts and conclusions about each character that touches your heart and even pursue an independent study of their life to better equip your walk with the Savior.

I have to tell you, this chapter was good. I wrote a brilliant excerpt on the heart of Mary seen in her tears and in her submissive heart as she sat at the feet of Jesus. I penned the words versus reality seen in the actions of Peter as he vowed his faithfulness to his Savior, yet fled in fear after a blissful night's sleep. I concluded a new thought on Judas regarding his love of money and the evil it rooted within him. Oh the heartache that followed is not one for us to judge, for in reality we have all behaved as Peter and as Judas. The difference lies in their reaction to their reality. One confessed his denial and walked in conviction, one deplored his betrayal and died in guilt.

But that chapter is gone. Vanished.

I pouted, yes, I pouted, shoulders slumping and head hanging. Eventually, I stopped pouting and prayed. I searched my computer. Nothing. I contacted my editor. Nothing. I pouted. In the midst of my pouting session, I was talking with my girlfriend, Michelle, about a book we are studying together called Unglued by Proverbs31.org author, Lysa Tyrkeurst. It is a book about making wise choices in the midst of raw emotion. This book is amazing. While we were talking about various situations of our childhood, I heard myself say, via text, "It's not about the other person, or about the situation, it's about Jesus."

That was when it hit me. As beautiful as I felt my previously written Chapter 26 was, in the light of submission, this chapter is not about the other people. It's not about the situations being faced. It is solely about Jesus. This, my dear friend, is where we are going to lie during the duration of Matthew. Jesus. The perfect characterization of submission, Jesus. He is the same yesterday, today, and forever. Jesus. The creator of the mountain high, the creator of our heart's cry. Jesus. Born of a virgin, lived as a man. Jesus. Feeler of pain, healer of the same. Jesus.

Girls, I'm venturing down this path with a new vision. I want to seep into these pages with the words that Christ penned on my heart, "Heaven and earth shall pass away, but my words shall not pass away" (Matthew 24:35). Just as Jesus pointed to a fig tree to remind His men to heed to the promise of His eternal words, so I look to Jesus to remember to heed to the promise of His eternal words. May we feel His heartache and His emotional pain, and may we learn to react as Jesus reacted. My pouting has ceased. Prayer has prevailed yet again.

Take time now to read each of the 75 verses recorded in this chapter. Yes, I said 75. It is a large chapter, but one that is full of depth and emotion. I encourage you to do as I did before embarking on this chapter, and pause for a moment of prayer in order to seek clearly the lesson the Spirit has for you in this particular study. What example of submission strikes your heart? What emotion rings true within you? Ponder these questions as you read Matthew's account of this emotional journey of our Savior, Jesus Christ. Feel free to use the space below to record your questions, answers, and thoughts.

____

____

____

____

____

____

____

Allow me to take this time to share with you what I found in my time of prayer and reading. Words and truth are both very important to me. However, I had to learn how to use words wisely and how to communicate truth the way the Lord would have me do so. Much of that understanding came through learned knowledge of my physical dad and wisdom from my Heavenly Father.

My father passed away when I was young. My mind doesn't have more than two distinct memories of him, neither of them letting me into his soul, into knowing what kind of man he was. In one of my memories I am sitting in the bed of his red pickup truck with my two older sisters heading to a fair of some kind. I remember giggling because he was going fast. Bear in mind this was before riding in the bed of a truck was unlawful, and fast for a five-year-old girl is different than fast in the eyes of reality. My other memory is of sitting on my father's kitchen counter and getting in trouble for not trusting him and taking a bite of a radish.

What silly little memories, yet memories I have analyzed time and again in my little heart in an attempt to draw close to my dad. All my analyzing has given me is the conclusion that my memories of my dad are those of normalcy between a parent and a child. I see that now as a mother teaching my five-year-old to trust me when it comes to simply tasting an unfamiliar food that doesn't happen to be PB&J or Macaroni and Cheese. So help me, my life has come full circle.

Although my youngest memories fail me, I have stories from people who knew my dad. I love these stories. Some are great, some are sad, but they are all real; they are all truths about my dad. I remember talking to a late uncle years ago. He had made an off-color joke as he all too often did and I corrected him in so many words informing him that I was a lady and would not tolerate such things. He took a drag of his cigarette and exhaled into a full-hearted laugh exclaiming how I sounded just like my father, "So sure of yourself, and so in love with truth and words." Although my uncle disgusted me that day, he gave me one of my best compliments to date. He continued telling me of Dad's love for writing and poetry and how good he was at all that "girly stuff."

My mind was racing; my dad loved poetry, so do I. My dad loved to write, so do I. Dad did it, so can I. I always knew my dad was a chef and loved to cook. I most certainly did not get that from him, but words, words are so much better than food could ever be.

I remember standing with my mother back in 2000 whispering about this tall handsome soldier that had smitten my heart. I remember telling her (again) how much I was falling in love with him, but more than that I remember what she said, "The truth is, you have fallen in love with your dad; his gentle mannerism and quiet confidence is a picture of everything your dad was." My mom didn't speak much about my dad, but that day I saw love in her eyes and admiration for the good in both my dad and my future husband.

Truth is a powerful thing and when expressed with the acceptable words and right timing, a heart can be touched in ways unexplained. My memories are small, but when they are combined with shared words of truth, my personal confidence in my dad's love for me, and my inherent appreciation and ability to use words for beauty abounded.

Here in this chapter we see Matthew's account of this grave day. Although Matthew is a key part to this day's emotions, he does not center his writing on himself, rather on the heart of a few friends. I appreciate that, for through his words we get deeper into these great men and women of God, namely, Mary, Judas, and Peter.

"Now when Jesus was in Bethany, in the house of Simon the leper, there came unto him a woman having an alabaster box of very

precious ointment, and poured it on his head, as he sat at meat." Matthew 26:6-7

Mary is a beautiful story through the pages of the four gospels. Her story is so very relatable to us all. Mary was the sister of Lazarus. If you remember, Lazarus was the friend of Jesus who fell terribly ill to the point of death. His story is remarkable and is recorded in John 11 and is preceded by John's account of Mary sitting at the feet of Jesus with her alabaster box. Mary also had a sister. A sister many love to hate, but a sister I have purposed to become more like in many ways. Her name is Martha; she was a hardworking, diligent woman who loved to serve her God. For this, I strive. The reason many use her as an example to learn from is because at one such morning her focus was wrong and her heart was displaying it in words and actions before Her Savior. Jesus sweetly corrected her vision and recorded this account in Luke 10:38-42 for all to remember. A book could be written on this dear family, in fact, many good ones have been. In short, I will conclude with this thought on Martha; hard work and diligence in your work is highly profitable and honorable. Proverbs 31 supports Martha's heart to its fullest. The one thing all women need to grasp whether you tend to be more like Mary or like Martha is that your priority ought always to be Jesus Christ. Sit at His feet before you work.

Mary's vision was set on Jesus. From the moment she met him, from the moment he forgave her of her sins, from the moment she felt His love, her eyes were upon Jesus. This is why she is a role model for all to follow. She listened intently to his words, she worshipped at his feet. When we read her story in John 11, it is easy to see her life centered on Jesus. What is it about Mary that you relate with? What is it about Mary that you desire more of? Do you desire to have Jesus your center and focus as she displayed in her words, her actions, her tears, and her worship? Or maybe you are the contrast sister recorded in Luke 10. As a Martha, what are your strengths? What are your weaknesses? Whether you are a Mary personality or a Martha, determine to make your life all about Jesus. How can you make that happen?

____

____

____

____

____

"Peter answered and said unto him, through all men shall be offended because of thee, yet will I never be offended." Matthew 26:33

Peter has always been one of my favorites. I love his energy and his fervency of love. Peter is often looked down on for his excessive actions and over eager mouth, but I am partial to him and many times wish to have his desire towards God. Like him, when I speak and when I take a step, I want to be overtly submissive to a fault. His eagerness in following is not to please men; it is the result of a burning flame within his soul that he cannot contain. It pours out of him with rushed abandon. Oh, to be seen in that light! Would that not be a compliment?

Peter is mentioned by name throughout this entire passage of Scripture. He is there in Verse 1 when Jesus speaks to His disciples and says, "Ye know that after two days is the feast of the Passover, and the Son of man is betrayed to be crucified." He is there in Verse 75 weeping bitterly as he recalls the feared truth of his Savior's words, "Before the cock crow, thou shalt deny Me thrice." Imagine walking this day in his shoes. I don't know how many hours are accounted for in this chapter, but the moments of emotions are almost unbearable to imagine. Judas would be the contrast to Peter. He was chosen by Jesus to be His disciple (Mark 3), his character was prophesied in Psalms.

Here they sit, Peter and Judas along with Jesus and the rest of the disciples, in the house of Simon the Leper when Mary (John 12:1-3) enters the room and bathes her Savior in tears and sweet perfume. Judas Iscariot and others of the disciples (Mark 14:3-9) voice criticism toward her and are quickly hushed by the love and admiration of Jesus upon her acts of the heart. Jesus then asks Peter and John (Luke 22:8) to enter into the city and prepare for the Passover there. When all was ready and the men were gathered, Jesus brings the matter of a disciple's betrayal to the table. The fear that gripped each of their hearts is apparent as they one by one cry out, "Lord, is it I?" Relief follows when their name is cleared. Then Jesus looks at Judas. Irritation and disbelief must have been overwhelming as these men witness Judas leave the room in order to betray Jesus Christ. Jesus settles the tension and emotions by braking bread and giving drink to His men and presents his death before them for the last time. The emotions of confusion and denial of the possibility that Jesus is truly going to be crucified was abounding. The sadness in each man's heart had to be at its greatest level.

On the way to the Mount of Olives, Jesus forewarns the disciples that they, "shall be offended because of Me this night: for it is written, I will smite the shepherd, and the sheep of the flock shall be scattered abroad" (Matthew 26:31). Peter is the one to open the forum by proclaiming that he will never be offended of Jesus but, "Jesus said unto him, Verily I say unto thee, That this night, before the cock crow, thou shalt deny Me thrice" (Matthew 26:34). In purity of heart Peter pleads his cause of devotion, and all the disciples utter their proclamation of faithfulness (vs. 31-35). It is then they enter into the garden of Gethsemane.

Evening has come and exhaustion has settled in. Jesus asks Peter, James, and John to watch with Him in prayer. Jesus walks a stone's cast away (Luke 22:41), kneels before His Father, and prays in earnest for this cup to pass from Him. Three times he does this, and each time he returns to His friends for prayer support and finds them asleep. Specifically, He asks of Peter, "What, could ye not watch with Me one hour? Watch and pray, that ye enter not into temptation: the spirit indeed is willing, but the flesh is weak" (Vs. 40-41).

I can't help but wonder if Peter knew the depth of what Jesus was saying directly to him. Yes, Peter's spirit was willing, he proclaimed it just a moment ago, but without prayer ,his flesh would be too weak to stand strong and remain faithful. Jesus knew this, but He did not force Peter to do what was so desperately required of him. Jesus rather allowed Peter to be a man and to face the fight with his own flesh and spirit in order to learn the lesson he needed to learn.

I wonder what difference the night may have brought on if Peter did stay up and pray? Frustrated with himself for his lack of self-control to "watch and pray," Peter looks up and sees Judas and a band of angry men head straight to Jesus. Peter, with great determination of the flesh to defend his Master, "Stretched out his hand, and drew his sword, and struck a servant of the high priest's, and smote off his ear" (John 18:10). Jesus rebukes Peter, and heals the wounded soldier.

"Then all the disciples forsook Him, and fled." Matthew 26:56

Jesus forewarned; the disciples fled. In the end it came to pass just as the Lord had said.

"But Peter followed Him afar off unto the high priest's palace, and went in, and sat with the servants, to see the end." Matthew 26:58

You are Peter. You are sitting at a quiet moment to journal about your day. You have not verbally denied Christ. The cock has yet to crow. But you run. As Jesus is being led away by a band of soldiers and by Judas, you run. But then you stop and turn around. What are those thoughts battling within you? Are you physically feeling that spiritual battle raging between the willing spirit and weak flesh? Are you wishing now that you stayed up and prayed that hour with your Savior? Are you finding yourself thankful for the friend you have in John, who in your shame, ran away with you in his own shame; and now together you return afar off to see your Savior?

At this moment Peter had yet to learn his lesson. He needed to learn about more than the physical fact of turning away from God. He needed to learn the shame that comes with denying

Christ. Although the act of denying Christ does not help us stand for Him stronger, the shame and conviction we feel keeps us from returning to such shameful behaviors. We have all physically turned our backs on God. When it is time to pray, we don't pray. When it is time to read the Word of God, we don't read. When it is time for church, we don't go. When it is time to give our tithes and offerings, we don't give. When it is time to love, we don't love. When it is time to forgive, we don't forgive. When it is time to stand, we don't stand. These are such simple commandments to demonstrate love to God and so often in our flesh, we don't. We would rather tell Him that we love Him with the simplicity of three little words and carry on as if our actions aren't speaking louder than those three words. Have you tried that philosophy out in your marriage? How is that working for you? Tried it with your children? What about with your friends? Again, how is that working for you?

Maybe simple words have been your philosophy, whether in your relationship with God or in a physical relationship, but I dare to challenge you to learn the importance of demonstrating your love to the person along with the words and see how that fares. Peter learned this lesson the hard way. He learned that fretful night in Gethsemane what was needed in order to accomplish love, both with his words and with his actions. Jesus had love he needed to demonstrate as well. But first He prayed. In earnest did He pray, for He knew without the power of His Father fulfilling Him, His cup would be impossible in the flesh.

Do you need to put yourself in Peter's shoes to feel the emotions of conviction and denial? Or are you feeling those same emotions in your own shoes? It makes a stiletto that much more painful, does it not? When you are battling weak flesh or struggling with physically turning on God or verbally denying His presence, may I suggest you do as the Savior did before He saved you? Pray. Pray. Pray. It is such a simple answer, but the most powerful answer for any given situation or struggle. Because when we pray the situation is no longer in our hands, it is now in the Father's hands and we are all submissive followers of His divine plan.

What is it that you need to submit to Him? What is the situation that you are called to handle, yet are putting off in weak flesh? Consider approaching it as Jesus did, on your knees in prayer declaring that it is not your will but God's that you desire to achieve.

____

____

____

____

____

____

____

____

____

Memory Goal:

"These things I have spoken unto you, that in Me ye might have peace. In the world ye shall have tribulation: but be of good cheer; I have overcome the world." John 16:33

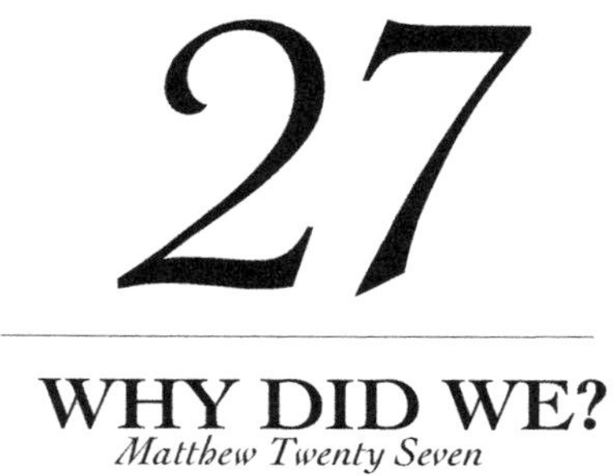

WHY DID WE?

Matthew Twenty Seven

"And Jesus stood before the governor: and the governor asked Him saying, Art thou the King of the Jews? And Jesus said unto him. Thou sayest." Matthew 27:11

I didn't sing. Ever. No one knew what my singing voice sounds like. Then one day God gave me a son. How does a mother not sing to their child? Knowing how badly I sing and knowing that God creates an innate love for a mother's voice within a child's heart, I was conflicted. Yet, I sang. I never got that rock-a-bye-baby-fall-out-a-tree song and that was the only lullaby I knew. So, I turned to the only One who knew my love for singing and asked Him to help me quietly sing my favorite praise songs to my newborn baby boy. I have many favorite songs that I sing when it is just me and my Savior, who gave me the voice I have and declared it perfectly and wonderfully made. Amazingly enough when, I sang these songs my little Gift from God would fall fast asleep (or pass out) and I would continue in the silence with my worship to my King.

One of those songs was There's Something about that Name by The Gathers. The words to this song are beautiful. They are focused solely on the sweet majestic name of Jesus. As I read Chapter 27 I hum this chorus time and again.

Jesus, Jesus, Jesus. There's just something about that name. Master, Savior, Jesus. Like a fragrance after the rain. Jesus, Jesus, Jesus, Let all Heaven and earth proclaim. Kings and kingdoms will all pass away. But there's something about that name.

I sit here and think where I want to go for our study in this chapter and the answer is simple. Jesus. Then I think about our purpose of submission and I think about Jesus. There are 66 verses in this chapter and all but 19 reference Jesus by name or pronoun. Some say this is a difficult chapter to read, some say it is beautiful. Regardless of how you feel when you read through the anguish Jesus suffered, it is entirely His reality. Jesus prayed so fervently for this cup to pass from Him. He prayed knowing the emotional price, knowing the physical price, knowing the mental price and knowing the price of spiritual separation from God the Father. Jesus knew the cup He was about to partake of was a cup too deep, too bitter for His flesh to consume. He knew the very price of submission, He prayed, and He partook.

The price of submission is a concept we ought all to understand. Submission at times is simple and natural; at times submission is trying and difficult. Regardless your road of submission, you were called to have a submissive spirit to Him, to do the work of God, to speak as salt to a dying world, to serve with your body, your mind, and your all. We are called to walk in His fullness and to fulfill His purpose and to drink the cup the Father poured for us. Why? Sometimes we won't know until later. Sometimes we will learn in Heaven. Until that day, just remember, submission is an act of simple obedience to the Father and obedience to the Father brings a blessing. Here's my story of wondering why.

My two older sisters and I could not be more different from each other. We resemble one another in appearance and smile, but from there our lives, style, mannerisms, likes and dislikes couldn't be more diverse. It is fascinating. When I go out with my friends I love to doll up in makeup, stilettos, and dresses. Sherilyn throws on her comfy pants and Uggs, while Adrienne declares her place next to her family at home on the couch with a good movie. While I listen to Josh Groban and Michael Buble, Sherilyn puts on Fergie and Adrienne does the Boot Scootin Boogie with her favorite, country artists. Seeing that we live in New York, Maryland, and Las Vegas, we don't get to play Barbies together like we used to. When we do get together, sad to say, we never talk about our days of Barbie-mania, of growing up on the perfectly named Elm St, or what life was like as teenagers. Those days are rarely mentioned. Except for this one question that we still cannot answer and we all agree that our lives are somehow better for it.

The question is, why did we submit? The answer is, we have no idea. The details all vary per story and are unnecessary to recap, but the reality is the same. Submission for us at one time was truly painful. The conclusion each time comes with a shrug, a laugh, and a promise. God is the father of the fatherless. Children are to obey their parents. Obedience brings a blessing.

One thing we each have in common is the strength of our marriages. This year we celebrated 16, 12, and 11-year marriages. We celebrated differently that's for sure. Sherilyn and her husband each bought themselves something they wanted and I think met up for lunch? Adrienne went to New York City! … And took her kids? I, courtesy of my Mother-in-Law's retirement (thanks Mom! same time, next year?), celebrated much on the wonderful island of Jamaica and we finished off with a fabulous night downtown once we got home to Vegas.

We also have wonderful children, ranging from 15 years old down to six. They are all beautifully obedient children. When they do things like skip school, gross out their sister with body noises, or lick the Sunday School wall (that would be mine) they tattle on themselves, punishing themselves with their own guilt and apology to "Never do that again I promise!" We don't know why we submitted. We know we obeyed. We know our Father promised a blessing. We know we are living a blessed life. And we shrug and laugh and continue our lives walking (in sneakers, sandals, and wedges) down our different roads, thanking the Lord for what we have; we have each other, we have our husbands, we have our kids, and we have Jesus.

The price of submission at times is simple and natural; at times submission is trying and difficult. Jesus chose to walk this same road of submission in the flesh. He was then called to have a submissive spirit to God, to do the work of God, to speak as Salt to a dying world, to serve with His body, His mind, His all. He was called to walk in the fullness of God and to fulfill His purpose and to drink the cup the Father poured for Him. Why? The answer: Me. He walked this lonely road for me.

"For God so loved the world, that He gave His only Begotten Son, that whosoever believeth on Him should not perish, but have Everlasting Life." John 3:16

The price of submission for Christ is spilled throughout the words of this beautiful yet difficult chapter. May we stop and see what His price truly entailed? Death was merely the final offering of His submission. May we return to the Man Jesus Christ as He stands beside Pilate before a thirsty crowd?

"Then Pilate entered into the judgment hall again, and called Jesus, and said unto Him, Art thou the King of the Jews? Jesus answered him, "Sayest thou this thing of thyself, or did others tell it thee of Me?" Pilate answered, "Am I a Jew? Thine own nation and the chief priests have delivered thee unto me: what hast thou done?" Jesus answered, "My kingdom is not of this world: if My kingdom were of this world, then would My servants fight, that I should not be delivered to the Jews: but now is My kingdom not from hence." Pilate therefore said unto Him, "Art thou a king then?" Jesus answered; "Thou sayest that I am a king. To this end was I born, and for this cause came I into the world, that I should bear witness unto the truth. Every one that is of the truth heareth My voice." John 19:34-37

Jesus was faithful to His character even in the worst of circumstances. I love this account recorded by John between Pilate and Jesus. Pilate asked Jesus if He was the king of the Jews. Jesus asked Pilate if he wanted to know for himself or because others have told him that He was self-pronouncing himself as such. It seems as if Pilate was getting frustrated with what he had heard, what his wife had forewarned, and what his heart was telling him. Why, Pilate seeks, are not your people fighting for you and following you if you really are a king?

But Jesus answered, "Oh, Pilate, if I were a king as you knew a king to be then, your thoughts or confusion would be validated. But I am not a king with a kingdom to reign on earthly soil. You see, I am the King with a Kingdom from Above. Those who are of my Kingdom are the reason I am standing before you today. I was born to be right here. I left Heaven Above to be right here, right now. I stand before you so I can show you what truth is. Don't ask, for words are not enough. Let me show you."

When Pilate questioned Jesus before the crowd, Jesus responded with silence. His words were for Pilate. His words were spoken for the heart questioning the truth, not for those who looked upon him with disdain. To clarify, His death was for all. But His words were chosen and spoken for the hearts that were open. We see His chosen words spilled out on the cross to His mother, to John, to the thief nailed beside Him, to His Father in Heaven. All to whom He spoke had a heart full of love and belief on Him and His cup in which He bore for them. But those who railed their tongues and wagged their heads, received not a spoken word, only an act, the greatest act of love, the very price of submission, His death for their life.

"But he (Pilate) had Jesus whipped, and then handed over for crucifixion...After they had finished nailing Him to the cross and were waiting for Him to die," Matthew 27:26, 35; The Message

Am I brave enough to identify these verses as 'simple sentences?' Verses with deep but few words. Verses in the midst of intensity. Verses that can easily be lost in the script of Jesus' pain.

Verses that depict the normalcy of the Roman law of the day. Verses that identify Him with the world of condemned sinners worthy of death. The words of these verses may be but simple sentences but the irony of them is far from simple. The fact that Christ is condemned a sinner's death on the night of the Passover is all but simple. You see, this is what the Godhead is about. This is why Jesus was born in Bethlehem, 33 years prior to this very day. He was born to bring an end to the Old Testament law. He was born to be the final Passover sacrifice. He was born to give the Gift of Heaven to you, to me, to all who hear His words and believe.

The history of the Passover feast is laid out in the book of Exodus, as the Israelites were commanded of God to prepare a sacrificial lamb offering. They were to use the lamb's blood as a testament of their belief by painting their door posts so when the Spirit came that night to fulfill the final plague upon the nation of Egypt and its Pharaoh, the Spirit would pass over the homes of those who trusted in God's providence. The Israelites that night, partook of the meat of the lamb in a standing position and in full apparel, awaiting word to leave their life of slavery and pursue a life of freedom.

Here we see Jesus condemned to die in the court of the temple near the very spot the priests' continued the annual tradition of the Passover sacrifice throughout the ages in remembrance of what God had done for their people so many years ago. Yet in all their holiness, the High Priests and elders, and the Jewish people stood there shouting, "Crucify Him." Jesus was the condemned Passover Lamb.

Here we see Jesus receive the punishment typical of the condemned, a severe whipping then crucifixion by being nailed on a cross for all to see. This was the treatment and the expected death of the guilty. Jesus was the crucified Passover Lamb. Here we see Jesus received so much more. Here we see the cup Jesus was served for you and for me. Here we see the price of submission the Christ was asked to pay; we see the price of submission He freely and lovingly paid.

Matthew 27:26 begins the physical pain and Verse 35 concludes the physical pain, but between these two verses we read what happened to Jesus was not typical. These Roman soldiers had a job. Their job was to punish and to crucify the condemned. They carried out this job and continued on in this job throughout the years. This was work. The two thieves that hung beside Christ received punishment from these soldiers. Why? Because they were condemned and the soldiers had to do their job. This was work, period.

"Then the soldiers of the governor took Jesus into the common hall, and gathered unto Jesus the whole band of soldiers. And they stripped Jesus, and put on Jesus a scarlet robe. And when they had platted a crown of thorns, they put it upon Jesus' head, and a reed in Jesus' right hand; and they bowed the knee before Jesus, and mocked Jesus, saying, "Hail, King of the Jews!" And they spit upon Jesus, and took the reed, and smote Jesus on the head. And after that they had mocked Jesus, they took the robe off from Jesus and put Jesus' own raiment on Him, and led Jesus away to crucify Him." Matthew 27:27-31

This, my friends, was not their job. This had nothing to do with their job requirements. This was vindictive, this was personal, and this was forgiven. There have been people I have hated, girls that I did not like, and people that rubbed me the wrong way. When I picture these people in my head, even in the worst level of my flesh, I cannot imagine doing one of these vindictive acts, let alone all of them. They stripped Jesus, degrading Him to embarrassment, they dressed Jesus as a mock king with a robe and thorn-laden crown, and they mockingly bowed before Jesus throwing His accusation of being "King of the Jews" in His face. They spit on Him. Spit. Who does that? Where does that level of indecency come from? They hit Jesus in the head with a staff they had given Him as a mock scepter. They greatly and thoroughly humiliated the man Jesus Christ.

Like me, do you hear, "Every knee shall bow and every tongue shall confess that Jesus is the Christ the Son of the Living God?" (Philippians 2:10) When you read of these soldiers do you feel sorrow for that day for them? These men had a disdain for this Man, and their actions, I believe, only encouraged the actions of each other and took them to the place that is unimaginable for us to comprehend. Yet, through it all, Jesus speaks not a word. Jesus was in complete control by the Holy Spirit within Him. He stood His ground in humility knowing that, "they know not what they do." Oh, the forgiveness of the Savior for our most vile of acts.

The ignorant behaviors of God's creation didn't end when they nailed Jesus upon the cross. They magnified. Words were spewed out from every angle to the Savior. Words by one of the thieves on the cross, words by people passing by, words by the Chief Priests and the scribes and elders all spilled out their thoughts of mocking doubt and hatred toward this Man on the cross. And Jesus, my Jesus, saved His words for those who would hear them. Never once did He defend, yell out, or bite back. Never once did He face His ridicule in the flesh.

"Now…" pens Matthew. Can you see him, the professional recorder that he was, hunched over his papyrus, clinching his pen in his hand, sitting at the edge of his seat ready to pen the events that followed? I can only imagine how difficult it was for Matthew and the other disciples to record the sufferings of Jesus. Merely typing out the verses above brought tears to my eyes. But these men were there. These events were their reality mingled with their own feelings of guilt for fleeing and doubt over believing. Now we see Matthew sitting, remembering, and writing:

"Now from the sixth hour there was darkness over all the land unto the ninth hour. And about the ninth hour Jesus cried with a loud voice, saying, "Eli, Eli, Lama sabachthani?" That is to say, My God, My God, why hast thou forsaken Me? Jesus when He had cried again with a loud voice, yielded up the ghost." Matthew 27:45, 46, 50

Yes, Jesus faced extreme physical pain. Yes, Jesus was humiliated and degraded to the worst degree. But none of that pain compared to the emptiness that was His final price to pay. Darkness. For three hours darkness reigned on the earth. For three hours my sin was being cast upon my Savior. For three hours Jesus thought of me. Then it happened. I was looked upon by my Heavenly Father with such love and acceptance. I was looked upon with forgiveness and purity. I was clean. I was looked upon because Jesus took my filth, my shame, my sin and covered Himself in it. I was looked upon as the daughter of God because the Son of God paid the ultimate price. The price of sin was separation from God the Father.

Christian, this is something you and I will never know. Although we may choose to walk away, God will never choose the same. He will never turn His eyes or His hands or His love from us. How? Because Jesus Christ became man, who knew no sin, but took upon himself our sin, and sacrificed the final Passover sacrifice that we may live free of sacrificial death.

The joy to know the book of Matthew and the story of Jesus Christ does not end there! The guilt we would carry to know someone died for us so we could live is unnatural and seemingly un-purposeful. For we would strive so dearly to live pleasingly for the Man who died so He wouldn't feel as if He died in vain. Oh, but He didn't die in vain, and He did die to give us purpose. I like what Oswald Chambers says in "My Utmost for His Highest" regarding sacrificial living as opposed to sacrificial dying:

Be rightly related to God, find your joy there, and out of you will flow rivers of living water. Be a center for Jesus Christ to pour living water through. Stop being self-conscious, stop being a sanctified prig, and live the life hid with Christ. The life that is rightly related to God is as natural as breathing wherever it goes.

I had to Google the word, prig. The word sounds rather harsh for the day of Mr. Chambers, but according to Wikipedia it seems quite fitting to the message he is trying to place within our hearts. Wikipedia states that the word prig, "is a person who shows an inordinately zealous approach to matters of form and propriety." We are not called to live a life of sacrificial death full of guilt and/or self-regulated restrictions. We are called to live a sacrificial life, full of the conviction of the Holy Spirit, the love of God the

Father, and the power of the Blood of the Eternal Passover Lamb.

Memory Goal:

"And be not conformed to this world: but be ye transformed by the renewing of your mind, that ye may prove what is that good, and acceptable, and perfect, will of God."
Romans 12:2

28

THE BEAUTIFUL REWARD

Matthew Twenty Eight

"And, behold, the veil of the temple was rent in twain from the top to the bottom; and the earth did quake, and the rocks rent." Matthew 27:51

"And, behold, there was a great earthquake: for the angel of the Lord descended from heaven, and came and rolled back the stone from the door, and sat upon it." Matthew 28:2

You didn't think I was going to skip over the effects of Christ's death on His mountainous creation, did you? No way. I was waiting. Chapter 27 was about Jesus, simply Jesus. Sometimes we need to quit our thoughts on our self-evaluations and remember the One whom we evaluate for, Jesus.

This chapter is about earthquakes. Earthquakes are a physical element I know very little about. I live in a city that embraces the summer weather and simply varies its heat throughout the year. Other than walking in a blow-dryer, I don't know what it feels like to survive weather disasters. This is why I turned to the professionals on this one. The Institute for Creation Research (IRC) is an amazing scientific and Biblical research center in Dallas, Texas. According to the studies of Dr. Steven A. Austin (Senior Research Geologist, Logos Research Associates, Santa Ana, CA), there are 17 recorded or prophesied earthquakes seen in the Bible (www.Irc.org).

Each of these earthquakes, according to Dr. Austin, are correlated with the Hand of God to open the eyes of His people for judgment, deliverance and/or communication. They are recorded from Genesis 1 at the creation of the land on Day 3 to the Day of Christ's prophesied return in Revelation 16:16-20. Reading this amazing scientifically proven article, I was reassured all over again that the premise of this chapter that has been pressed upon my heart stands sure.

We have walked a long journey in this study of submission. We finished the last chapter with the heart of submission and the price that was paid for you and for me for the opportunity to be able to submit to such a King as Jesus Christ. But now, as we arrive at the final chapter we hold out our hands out for our reward. Come on, I know you want a reward as much I do.

The reward for submission is freedom. It's peace that comes through freedom. It's freedom that comes through Jesus Christ. Peace that resonates presently within us simply because we believed on the name of the Son of God. Freedom. Peace. Could there be a greater reward?

"But seek ye first the kingdom and *God and His righteousness and all these things shall be added unto you." Matthew 6:33*

"Peace I leave with you, My peace I give unto you; not as the world giveth, give I unto you. Let not your heart be troubled, neither let it be afraid." John 14:27

"These things I have spoken unto you, that in Me ye might have peace. In the world ye shall have tribulation; but be of good cheer; I have overcome the world." John 16:33

So here we go. My girlfriends, Kate and Kimberly, and I are holding each other as iron sharpening iron by way of a study devotional entitled, Trusting God, a "Girlfriend's in God" publication. Other than yesterday's written account of an "Inspirational" and rather grossly detailed birthing experience of a dog (none of us have a dog), we have all greatly enjoyed this book. Every day we read the excerpt of that day, then communicate our thoughts via text messages. One day we will all gather for coffee to discuss our thoughts verbally, but until we find a way to work around the lives, illnesses, schedules, and attitudes of nine little people between the ages of two and eight, then text messages it is. The other day our reading called for us to inquire of our nearest and dearest, "Would you consider me a peaceful person?" Ha! Being that sick individual who magnetizes herself to any form of self-evaluation, I run to my husband and eagerly ask, "Honey? Would you consider me a peaceful person?" Smile. Blink. Smile.

As similar as Don and I are, we are also quite different, especially in this realm of nonsensical evaluations. I thrive on them. He thoroughly and truly despises them. Do bear in mind, the Yankees are on. Bottom of the 8th down by one, two balls, Swisher is up at bat. Ha! I smile as I see my question slapping him in the face making him inquire deep within his own soul, "Am I a peaceful person? The Yanks are on…evaluation question…Swisher…my wife…down by one...my wife..."

Enter Live TV! The individual who created a pause button on Live TV had a spouse who frequented them with self-evaluations. After re-asking my question, he looks me deeply in my eyes lovingly, and rather hesitant and slowly, says, "Yyyyeeeeeess. I would say yes. Except…" No. No. No need for that word here. Yes is good. I'll take yes. "Except for when your coffee maker breaks (happened the day before), and when you are tired, oh, and when you are hot. But, yeah. I would say overall yes." I laughed. Everything he said was too true … and the Yankees lost.

So now I am going to throw that fun one at you. Would you be considered a peaceful person? I gave you my song and dance. Be strong and ask someone. Who did you ask and what did they say?

____

____

____

____

When the price of submission is paid, the reward will be peace. Here's the best part; Christ paid our price. Christ paid our price indefinitely so He could give us His peace. When we believe on Him, His peace is in us. Did you catch that? His. Peace. Is. In. You. We do not have to pay a price to attain peace. Christ did that. We have Christ's peace. So why do we sometimes feel like our peace is missing?

Do you ever feel that? I certainly know that feeling all too well. Are you standing there in your personal struggle and wondering where that "promised peace" is because it certainly isn't there with you right now? This is hard. For one, it is hard to feel this feeling of loss and wonderment. And two, it is hard to admit that you are struggling with the feeling of the absence of peace.

May I offer an honest checklist evaluation? Hey, it's my last chapter and therefore my last opportunity to hand out homework. Bear with me.

1. Have you confessed your sin of unbelief to God the Father and asked Jesus Christ to be your Savior?

   ____

2. Have you been forgiven of your sins through His Blood?

   ____

3. Have you been freed by Jesus from sin, guilt and/or shame?

   ____

4. Do you like to curl up under your favorite familiar blanket?

____

5. Do you think that last question makes me sound as if I lost my mind?

____

If you answered Yes to all of those questions, then you are sure of your salvation through Jesus Christ. If you even answered yes to Number 5, then answer my next question.

6. What blanket do you often choose?

____

I can see it now. Some of you (my girlfriend, Michelle) are sold that I have become verifiably insane and therefore wrote not a word on the blank for that last question. Some were excited that I finally embraced the love of home economics and presently described their favorite quilt whether of old, or one recently created from an inspiring Pin they came across on Pinterest. Don't deny it. I know some of you (Dawn). Yes, your blanket is nice. Yes, I would like to have one too. No, I would not like to make one.

Meanwhile, others of you (my friend who threatened my life if I were to reference her in my book) are looking at me with that look that says, "I think I know where you are going and I already know I don't like it. I just got a pedicure and I would rather you stay off my pretty toes." If this is you, then I highly suggest you get your socks on. While you get your cozies on, I am going to list for you my go-to blankets:

- Past shame
- Past guilt
- Childhood heartache
- Death of parent
- Family rejection
- Man-made religious expectations

- Self-inflicted expectations
- Personal sin
- Selfishness
- Broken coffee maker
- Exhaustion
- Fatigue
- Financial confusion
- Medical confusion
- Miscarriages
- Self-image expectations
- Health issues
- PMS

Just to name a few.

I guess describing my baby blanket full of animal patterns on one side and a Raggedy Ann and Andy sheet on the back that is completely ripped due to excessive love and use would have been the easier route. Maybe there is something to Home Economics after all. One day I'll learn. Until then, welcome to my linen closet.

Some of my blankets have been shredded and burned. Some have been carefully folded and stored away for later. Some of them lay across the foot of my bed for nightfall. And some are clenched in my hand dragging beside me where ever I go. Regardless of where these blankets are, they each represent a picture of my life. They are stifling, they are suffocating, they are binding, and they are heavy. Yet, these blankets are comfortable, they are familiar; they are what I know. When used, they are the reason my peace is absent.

Praise be to God that this is not the end. For there was an earthquake, and in that earthquake each and every one of my blankets were cast into the crest of the earth, buried, and carried far away from the eyes of my Heavenly Father. There was an earthquake that shook the very presence of my earthly existence and replaced it with a quilt stitched together with the fabrics of the torn veil and with the robe of my Savior. This quilt doesn't cover my other blankets. It replaced each and every one so perfectly, leaving no need for any other. This blanket is called peace.

Look at my list again. Each one can be identified with one of three labels: the sins of others, the sin of self, or natural cause. Then consider this verse, "My little children, these things write I unto you, that ye sin not. And if any man sin, we have an advocate with the Father, Jesus Christ the righteous: and He is the propitiation for our sins: and not for ours only, but also for the sins of the whole world" (1 John 2:1-2).

The Message words it this way, "I write this, dear children, to guide you out of sin. But if anyone does sin, we have a Priest-Friend in the presence of the Father: Jesus Christ, righteous Jesus. When He served as a sacrifice for our sins, He solved the sin problem for good, not only ours, but the whole world's."

These earthquakes symbolize what Christ did for you and for your sins, for others and for their sins, and for the heartache that befalls us when circumstances attack. None of these situations are ours to bear. They were all conquered by Christ. The very foundation of sin was disrupted. Christ said it fully when He cried out, "It is finished" (John 19:30). My dear friend, sin is finished. Each of my blankets, each of your blankets have been shredded and burned in the earthquake of Christ's payment and His Victory over sin and death. This truth leaves only one answer to our question, "If I am saved, and Christ gave me His peace, then why can I not feel that peace?"

The answer is that it is covered with the ashen cloth recovered and stitched back together. It is the blanket you retrieved from death and brought it back to life, covering the peace of God, stifling its presence in your heart. His peace is still there. It is merely covered with remains.

Can we pause on that thought? My toes hurt. If you are feeling toe-squashed under that last statement, it is because your toes are caught under my aching toes that are being pressed heavily under the squashing of that truth. How about we agree to meet for coffee and a fresh pedicure after we make it through this one?

Condemnation comes from guilt.
Guilt comes from self.
Conviction comes from the Spirit.
The Spirit by the Lamb.

Listen, my sweet friend, I told you of my blankets. I told you of His. I don't know your personal blankets, but I know His. It does not matter how big or how heavy your blanket is. His is that much bigger. His is over you as you read this. His is ever present.

In my quest of returning my tarnished blankets to the grave I experienced something that shook me far more than any pain and fear that ever wrought within me. I felt freedom. Freedom scared me. It scared me to pieces.

As a 33-year-old girl I sat weeping on my couch feeling like I was falling. Feeling like my hands had nothing to hang on to. I felt like that small child hanging from the monkey bars only a foot above ground, but scared to death to let go. Crying, I asked my best friend, my husband, "What do I hold onto now?" "Freedom," he said. "You are free. You let go. Now stand on freedom."

As empty as my hands felt, day by day I asked the Spirit to teach me how to embrace freedom, how to make freedom my new resting place, my new normal. And day by day the Lord pressed one word on my heart. I felt like the Grinch. Jaclyn's small heart grew three sizes that day…grace. Grace. GRACE

Do you know the very definition of grace means "one receiving an unmerited divine assistance given humans for their regeneration (rebirth; salvation) or sanctification" (separation from what you once were)? Grace is unmerited. It is without price. It is promised by God. It is mine. It is yours. It is the reward for trusting Jesus. Not just trusting Jesus for our salvation, but also for our sanctification. Off with the old, on with the new, all through the Blood shed for you.

There is a final outcome to our submission. We have seen it in this study. Some of us have seen it in our own lives through our past experiences. Some are feeling it now through a present situation. Peace. The peace that passes all understanding. Grown men waver in this area of peace when facing doubt through their own strength. A few of the disciples faltered in the divine presence of the resurrected Savior because they failed to grab hold of the promise of peace. On the other hand, submissive followers, such as Mary Magdalene and the other Mary fell at the feet of their Resurrected Lord and worshipped Him. The amazing love of the Lord Jesus Christ is proven true and faithful.

Do you know peace? Is the reward of submission evident through your reactions? To submit to God is to know the peace of God. What are your final thoughts regarding freedom, God's peace, and/or His Grace?

____

____

____

____

____

____

Memory Goal:

"And they overcame him by the blood of the Lamb, and by the word of their testimony." Revelation 12:11

29

WHERE DOES THIS LEAVE US?

Final Thoughts

"And Jesus came and spake unto them, saying, All power is given unto me in heaven and in earth. Go ye therefore, and teach all nations, baptizing them in the name of the Father, and of the Son, and of the Holy Ghost: Teaching them to observe all things whatsoever I have commanded you: and, lo, I am with you always, even unto the end of the world. Amen." Matthew 28:18-20

Submission. Where does this leave us? We have studied this idea. We have believed on Jesus as our Savior and Lord. We have self-evaluated until we could no longer self-evaluate. We have seen the reason and purpose and beauty of submission. We know the rewarded peace that comes with submission. Now what?

I think the disciples were experiencing the same question. Jesus, we have left all and followed you. We have witnessed your miracles and healings. We heard you speak to the multitudes, teach us, reprimand the Pharisees and pray to the Father. We saw you get lead away by the soldiers. We know you died on the cross. We see that you are here; risen from the dead just as you told us. Now what?

All power is given unto me in heaven and in earth. Friends, believe in Me. Just as you believed on Me before my death; believe in me after my resurrection. All Power, God's power, is mine whether I am in heaven or here on earth. Believe.

Go, teach, baptize in the name of the Father, the Son, and the Holy Ghost. Now what? Look around you. There's the answer. This world is full of hungry eyes looking for the answer; the answer is Jesus. I met a gentleman named Kevin in Barnes and Noble one fall afternoon (while sipping at my pumpkin spice latte). We were standing near one another scanning the wide selection of Religious books. I was looking for Unglued while he was looking for … something. He walked back and forth. I couldn't help but notice his sad eyes, so lost. I introduced myself, shook his hand, and said, "I don't know what you are looking for, but can I tell you that the answer is Jesus. Jesus is always the answer." I handed him a tract from my church that has the plan of salvation written on the back. I placed emphasis on Jesus' death and resurrection and on His love. He looked from me to the tract and back to me. He whispered the name Jesus and slowly nodded then went back to his search. I promised him that I would pray for him, and we parted our separate ways. Sunday came and there he was in a suit sitting near the front of my church. Pastor preached, as always, a sermon centered on the love of Jesus and his free gift of salvation. Although I talked to him briefly with a smile after service I haven't seen him since. I don't know his story. But I pray.

On the plane at the age of 16 I sat beside a man name Bart. He was drinking Jack Daniels; I was reading my Bible. I didn't know Jack; he didn't know Jesus. He offered me Jack with a laugh; I offered him Jesus with nervousness. Neither one of us accepted each other's offers. Our plane landed and we went our separate ways. I don't know Bart's story. But I pray.

Wherever I go I purpose to tell someone about Jesus, whether it's Fiji or New York City, Santa Barbara or Jamaica, at school or the Chiropractor's. Why? Because one day I received Jesus as my personal Lord and Savior; one day I asked God, "What now? What's my purpose?" He answered me just as He always answers to anyone who asks, "I Am."

The question remains, where are we to go? The answer lies in the person in front of you, whether it be your spouse, your children, your neighbor, the banker, the grocer, the co-worker. Do you see how your circle of purpose grows with each step you take throughout your day. Some of us will get the opportunity, the privilege, to go to the "uttermost parts of the world" (Acts 1:8), but until we do, begin with that first step. Who is it? As you visualize your day, who do you see that needs Jesus?

____

____

____

"But ye shall receive power, after that the Holy Ghost is come upon you: and ye shall be witnesses unto me both in Jerusalem, and in all Judaea, and in Samaria, and unto the uttermost part of the earth." Acts 1:8

Teaching them to observe all things whatsoever I have commanded you. There are some of us that have a limited connection to unsaved friends or family. That does not mean we are without a purpose. Jesus has an answer for that too, "I Am." I have the opportunity to teach at a Christian school and to teach at Ladies Bible

Studies that are full of sisters in Christ. With this surrounding I have had so many beautiful conversations centered on Jesus. Why? Because He is the answer. Do you see? Jesus is always the answer. When a fellow believer (and/or your sweet children) come to you with a question of why, when, how, what am I going to do? You can open your Bible and point them to Jesus. Tell them your story of how Jesus answered your questions of uncertainty. Then conclude with a shrug and a smile and say, "I don't know how He does what He does, but He does it and I am glad He does."

Our question is answered with a full circle purpose. We asked, now what? He answered, believe on me, tell the unsaved about me, teach the saved about me, and remember … I am always with you. Matthew heard these words, then witnessed his Savior ascend into heaven. He left the Mount of Olives with his new quest. His quest, and obedience to his new purpose, provided our very study on this matter of submission. Matthew obeyed. Will we submit to our purpose and tell those around us about the Precious Name of Jesus?

Memory Goal:

"And Jesus came and spake unto them, saying, All power is given unto me in heaven and in earth. Go ye therefore, and teach all nations, baptizing them in the name of the Father, and of the Son, and of the Holy Ghost: Teaching them to observe all things whatsoever I have commanded you: and, lo, I am with you always, even unto the end of the world. Amen." Matthew 28:18-20

"But ye shall receive power, after that the Holy Ghost is come upon you: and ye shall be witnesses unto me both in Jerusalem, and in all Judaea, and in Samaria, and unto the uttermost part of the earth." Acts 1:8

For more information visit

jaclynpalmer.com

Made in the USA
Middletown, DE
09 September 2021

47929090R00169